Volume II

French All Around Us

Exploring the Legacy and Future of Francophonie
in the United States of America

Edited by
Kathleen Stein-Smith and Fabrice Jaumont

CALEC – TBR Books
New York – Paris

Copyright © 2025 by Kathleen Stein-Smith and Fabrice Jaumont

All rights reserved. No part of this publication may be reproduced, distributed, or transmitted in any form or by any means without prior written permission.

TBR Books is a program of the Center for the Advancement of Languages, Education, and Communities. We publish researchers and practitioners seeking to engage diverse communities on education, languages, cultural history, and social initiatives.

CALEC – TBR Books
750 Lexington Avenue, 9th floor
New York, NY 10022
USA
www.calec.org | contact@calec.org

Cover illustration © bgstock72 via Canva (One-design use license)
Cover design © Nathalie Charles

ISBN 978-1-63607-468-9 (Paperback)
ISBN 978-1-63607-469-6 (eBook)

Library of Congress Control Number: 2025933338

TABLE OF CONTENTS

Foreword..
Ambassador Ifigeneia Kontoleontos, Permanent Observer for the International Organization of La Francophonie to the United Nations

Introduction
Kathleen Stein-Smith and Fabrice Jaumont 1

1. Francophonie in the United States: Historical Roots, Cultural Diversity, and Future Perspectives
   Fabrice Jaumont and Marguerite Tabusse 10

2. The Alliances Françaises in the United States: A Pillar of Francophonie in America
   Hamza Djimli 26

3. Teaching, Learning, and Living in French
   Jessamine Irwin 41

4. The Economic Value of French in Louisiana: A Policy Analysis
   Jerry L. Parker 53

5. The Francophonie is Here: French Language and Francophone Identity in the Rust Belt
   Claire-Marie Brisson 67

6. French All Around Us: From Preschoolers to Senior Citizens
   Frédérique Grim 79

7. Multilingual Hospitality: African Diasporic Voices Shaping Francophone America
   Maya Angela Smith 90

8. Building a Francophone Identity in Bilingual Schools: African-Centered Reflections of a Black Educational Leader
   Bertrand Tchoumi 105

9. Weaving Haitian Roots into the U.S. Francophonie: A Personal Journey *Elcie Douce* 124

10. New Speakers of French in Louisiana: The Future of a Regional Minority Language
    Jonathan Olivier 135

11. Observing and Understanding Language Contact Among French Migrant Children in the United States
    Valérie Barrau-Ogereau 148

12. My journey within the field of Francophone studies: From Africa to America
    Emmanuel Kayembe 159

13. Collective Action to Protect our Future – Creating a Sustainable Franco-American Path Forward
    Timothy Beaulieu 175

14. Exploring the Intricacies of Franco-American Artistry
    Melody Keilig 184

15. Documenting the Francophone Contribution to American Music
    Scott Tilton 195

16. A Hard-Won Battle: The Lasting Gift of Franco-American Churches to New England's Built Environment
    Eileen M. Angelini and Rebecca P. Sewall 207

17. The Tapestry of our French-Canadian Ancestry
    Joseph Bolton 220

18. A Heritage Recaptured
    John Tousignant 226

19. Finding Franco-America in Historical Anniversaries
    Patrick Lacroix 235

20. Bridging the Francophone Archipelago: Past and Present
    Camden Martin 246

21. Le Rêve
    Jesse Martineau and Monique Martineau Cairns 255

22. The value of the French cross-cultural synergy
    Franck Mounier..267
23. The "Mindset of Possibility": The Role of External Funding in Building and Preserving College and University French Programs in the United States
    Steven J. Sacco and Megan Diercks 278
24. Just a Francophile from New Jersey
    Jennifer Schwester 288
25. La Francophonie des Amériques: Conversation and Community
    Joëlle Vitiello and Sophie Kerman............................296
26. French Education from One Generation to the Next
    Rebecca Fortgang and Jasmine Grace St. Pierre 306
Conclusion: The Ongoing Journey of French in America
    Kathleen Stein-Smith and Fabrice Jaumont...............................315
Table 1: Number of French speakers at home by state and year between 2015 and 2023..325
Table 2: Number of French speakers at home in major US cities for 2015, 2019, and 2023...327
Table 3: Number of people with a French or French-Canadian ancestry: top 10 states in 2023. 328
Table 4: People reporting French or French-Canadian ancestry for each state of the USA, 2023. 329
Table 5: Number of United States residents born in French-speaking countries, 2023..331
Table 6: List of Alliances Françaises in the United States (sorted in alphabetical order as of 03/11/2025)...................................335
References 339
About the Authors 353
About TBR Books...361
About CALEC...363

Praises

This wide-ranging volume offers a fresh and compelling lens onto the landscapes of Francophonie in America. By showcasing the resilience and creativity of communities from the Rust Belt to Louisiana, these stories highlight that French, in all its forms, is more than a language of Europe or the classroom—it is a dynamic tool of connection, identity, and growth. It is a vital read for educators, researchers, and anyone who treasures linguistic and cultural diversity.
—Prof. Teboho Moja, New York University

As someone who has spent years researching the historical arcs of French education in the United States, I find this new collection profoundly illuminating. The chapters demonstrate that, far from a relic, French remains a living thread woven through family stories, community activism, and educational innovation. This thoroughly engaging and much-needed resource will enrich the conversation around our shared linguistic heritage.
—Dr. Jane Ross, author of *Two Centuries of French Education in New York*

As a principal at École Bilingue, I have witnessed firsthand how the French language galvanizes curiosity, empathy, and creativity in students. French All Around Us reaffirms that power, delivering insightful glimpses into the communities, classrooms, and cultural spaces where French continues to thrive and inspire. This book is a testament to both the enduring legacy and the modern relevance of French in American life.
—Darcey Hale, former School Principal, École Bilingue, The International School of Boston

Acknowledgment

We want to express our deepest gratitude to all those who have supported and contributed to this project. First and foremost, we thank the chapter authors whose diverse and inspirational narratives have brought this work to life. Each chapter uniquely reflects the deep connection to the French language and Francophone culture, whether through personal stories of growing up with French in the family or through the insights of dedicated French language educators empowering students and communities.

This second edition builds upon the foundation of the first, with some familiar voices alongside new perspectives that expand our horizons. The juxtaposition of these voices—from both long-standing contributors and fresh perspectives—creates a compelling narrative that underscores the richness of the French language and culture. Reading both volumes provides a fuller immersion into the story of *French all around us*, offering a deeper understanding of the French-speaking world and its place in our lives, whether we speak French as a heritage language or as a learned skill.

As we reflect on the title of this book, we are reminded that the stories within reach those of us with French ancestry, those who speak French as a heritage language, and even those who have learned French in school. These chapters invite us to connect with personal childhood memories, family histories, and cultural perspectives while opening our minds to new understandings of ourselves and others. We must recognize that French, the mother tongue of millions of Americans and a heritage language for millions more, plays an essential global role in the United Nations and numerous other international forums.

Closer to home, French language and Francophone culture continue to thrive within families, communities, and individuals across the U.S. and North America. The continued vibrancy of the Francophone world, as reflected in online communities, social media, and educational programs, is a testament to the future of French language and culture in the U.S.

The stories in this book are rooted in the personal importance of French and represent the broader context of multilingualism in the U.S. and beyond. They remind us of the value of all languages and cultures and the importance of fostering connections through bilingualism and biculturalism.

We want to extend our heartfelt thanks to each of our contributors—Eileen M. Angelini, Valérie Barrau-Ogereau, Timothy Beaulieu, Joseph Bolton, Claire-Marie Brisson, Monique Martineau Cairns, Megan Diercks, Hamza Djimli, Elcie Douce, Rebecca Fortgang, Frédérique Grim, Jessamine Irwin, Emmanuel Kayembe, Melody Keilig, Sophie Kerman, Patrick Lacroix, Camden Martin, Jesse Martineau, Frank Mounier, Jonathan Olivier, Jerry L. Parker, Steven J. Sacco, Jennifer Schwester, Rebecca P. Sewall, Maya Angela Smith, Jasmine Grace St. Pierre, Marguerite Tabusse, Bertrand Tchoumi, Scott Tilton, John Tousignant, Joëlle Vitiello—whose expertise, passion, and collaboration have shaped this volume.

We extend our heartfelt thanks to the Organisation Internationale de la Francophonie for their support of our work and of both this volume and volume 1. In particular, we wish to acknowledge Ambassador Ifigeneia Kontoleontos, who contributed a wonderful preface to this volume, as well as Patricia Herdt, Rotane Khaled, Joseph Nkalwo Ngoula, Juliette Anne, and Nidia Buick for their invaluable contributions.

We also wish to express our appreciation for the unwavering support of the Center for the Advancement of Languages, Education, and Communities (CALEC), its board of directors, advisory council, and global supporters. The CALEC team has worked tirelessly to prepare this manuscript for publication, and we are deeply grateful for their commitment.

This collaboration between authors, editors, and the communities involved underscores the ongoing narrative of Francophonie in America, a story we hope will continue to inspire educators, advocates, and cultural stakeholders for years to come.

—*Kathleen Stein-Smith and Fabrice Jaumont*

Foreword

Ambassador Ifigeneia Kontoleontos, Permanent Observer for the International Organization of La Francophonie (OIF) to the United Nations

The Francophonie in the United States is a vibrant mosaic, weaving together a rich historical heritage with bold future aspirations. We regard this tapestry with optimism. In this second volume, French Around Us – Exploring the Legacy and Future of Francophonie in the United States of America, the exploration begun in the first volume continues and deepens, illuminating how the Francophonie on American soil has both evolved and diversified.

This book underscores an essential characteristic of the Francophonie: its diversity. In the United States, this diversity springs from multiple origins—from Quebec, Louisiana, and Acadia to the Caribbean, Africa, and beyond. Such linguistic and cultural abundance is a true asset, one the International Organization of La Francophonie is determined to promote and safeguard. Since its establishment in New York in 1995, the OIF Representation to the United Nations has been instrumental in showcasing the variety and solidarity of Francophone communities. Its work within the United Nations is extensive and is further amplified by partnerships forged across the worlds of culture and education. In 2023, under the leadership of Secretary-General of La Francophonie Louise Mushikiwabo, another milestone was achieved with the creation of an OIF Representation for the Americas, based in Quebec. This new presence deepens the Organization's roots in the Americas and strengthens connections among Francophone regions spanning from Canada to South America.

The contributions gathered in this volume are of remarkable quality. They shed fresh light on crucial aspects of French language use in the United States, from education—spanning elementary schools to university programs—to culture and the arts, the indispensable role of communities and civil society, and the importance of intergenerational language transmission. I extend my sincere gratitude to all the co-authors for sharing their experiences and perspectives. They remind us that French remains a living language in the United States—one that unites and inspires. Though this heritage is precious, it is also fragile. Its future depends on our collective dedication, including that of political institutions, civil society, and all other Francophonie stakeholders. Through close collaboration among these diverse actors, we can ensure a dynamic, enduring Francophonie in the United States. We are deeply committed to this mission and strive toward it every day.

Introduction
Kathleen Stein-Smith and Fabrice Jaumont

France. Canada. Haiti. Senegal. Louisiana. New England. The Rust Belt. American classrooms and city streets. These single words evoke a panorama of places and experiences, each contributing a unique brushstroke to the intricate portrait of American life. From the earliest colonial settlements to the diverse migrations of African, Caribbean, and other Francophone communities, the French language and its rich cultural expressions have interwoven themselves into the very fabric of the United States. *French All Around Us: Exploring the Legacy and Future of Francophonie in the United States of America* stands as a vibrant celebration of that enduring influence—a volume that brings together historical inquiry, personal narratives, community activism, and creative innovation to reveal how French continues to shape American life in myriad, transformative ways.

In a nation often presumed to be uniformly English-speaking, the persistent presence and steady growth of French speak to a resilient diversity that defies conventional assumptions. Over centuries, French has journeyed far beyond its colonial origins. It has been sustained, reimagined, and enriched by communities originating from Africa, the Caribbean, Québec, Acadia, and beyond. Robust cultural networks, bilingual schools, diaspora initiatives, and grassroots projects have all played pivotal roles in ensuring that French remains a cherished heritage and a dynamic tool for creative expression and social connection. As our global horizons expand with rapid technological advancements and local communities grapple with evolving challenges, understanding this vibrant, multifaceted Francophonie becomes not merely an academic pursuit but a pressing cultural imperative that touches every aspect of public and private life.

This dedication to French and the broader Francophone world finds resonance in two interlinked concepts: *Franco-responsabilité* and *Franco-activisme*. Together, they illuminate how American Francophone communities—and indeed, Francophones worldwide—continue to safeguard, enrich, and champion their linguistic heritage. *Franco-responsabilité* refers to the shared sense of responsibility that Francophones feel toward preserving and promoting the French language and its accompanying cultural expressions. It signifies both pride in a common heritage and a commitment to fostering linguistic and cultural vibrancy for future generations. *Franco-activisme*, in turn, transforms this sense of responsibility into proactive engagement—organizing cultural events, advancing policy initiatives, advocating for bilingual education, and forging community alliances that uphold French as a living, dynamic force. Viewed through the lens of *Franco-responsabilité* and *Franco-activisme*, the stories in this volume offer hope for the future and a broader understanding of French's local and global roles, illustrating how language is not merely preserved but actively adapted to meet contemporary needs and aspirations.

This volume unfolds as a tapestry of intertwined stories and themes, each chapter contributing a vital thread to a larger narrative that bridges the past with the present and the historical with the contemporary. Several essays invite us to revisit early French settlements, where explorers, missionaries, and settlers planted the seeds of a linguistic legacy that would grow into a distinctive cultural force. Detailed explorations of Franco-American churches in mill towns and the ancestral narratives of communities in the Rust Belt reveal how historical events have forged intergenerational memories, preserved in sacred spaces, community rituals, and festive celebrations. These contributions remind us that, even in the face of industrial migration, urban change, and shifting demographics, the legacy of French is a vital component of local identity and collective memory.

Beyond these historical foundations, the volume delves into the diasporic experiences of Francophone communities, presenting a multifaceted view of how French adapts to new environments. Narratives from Haitian, Senegalese, and other African diasporas illustrate the complex interplay of language preservation, cultural adaptation, and resilience in the face of change. These voices capture how French and its variations navigate and negotiate the intersections of race, migration policy, and social justice within diverse American neighborhoods. As community organizers and cultural practitioners recount their experiences, we are invited to see French not as a static relic of a bygone era but as a living, breathing language that evolves with every new wave of immigrants and every community initiative. In many ways, these narratives serve as a microcosm of the broader American experience—a dynamic process of cultural fusion where identities are continuously redefined.

Education emerges as a powerful and recurring theme throughout the volume. Educators and community advocates provide vivid accounts of bilingual programs—from immersive preschool projects to innovative college-level language advocacy—demonstrating how a commitment to French nurtures pride, belonging, and intellectual vitality. In these stories, every educational transition is portrayed not as a mere transfer of knowledge but as a transformative process in which cultural heritage and modern aspirations converge. The classroom, in these accounts, is not simply a space for rote learning; it is a dynamic arena where the rich legacy of Francophonie is actively reinterpreted and reinvigorated for each new generation. Whether through formal academic settings or informal community workshops, educational endeavors ensure that French remains a living language, capable of inspiring future generations to appreciate and contribute to their cultural heritage.

The creative arts further underscore the dynamic force of Francophonie in the United States. Artistic expression—manifested in forms ranging from Haitian folkloric dances and Franco-American poetry to the evolving musical landscapes of New Orleans jazz, zydeco, and creolized pop—is a powerful medium through which communities negotiate identity and celebrate their unique cultural footprints. These creative works testify to the ongoing reinvention of French traditions, transforming them into new forms that resonate with local and global audiences alike. Visual art, performance, literature, and music each tell their part of the larger story of Francophonie, highlighting the adaptability and innovative spirit that have allowed the language to remain relevant across centuries and continents.

At the same time, the volume shines a light on the critical role of bilingual advocacy and community engagement in sustaining French in

America. Across a diverse array of neighborhoods—from the historic enclaves of New England to the ever-evolving landscapes of the Rust Belt—community centers, cultural festivals, and grassroots organizing efforts are actively working to preserve language rights and promote intercultural dialogue. These initiatives illustrate that the power of French extends far beyond the confines of classrooms or performance stages; it is a catalyst for social mobilization, community building, and even public policy innovation. Whether defending language rights in schools, mobilizing around cultural heritage projects, or linking heritage tourism with economic development, the chapters demonstrate that French is a potent tool forging connections and fostering collective resilience. In many instances, the advocacy efforts described in this volume reveal how local activism can serve as a model for broader societal change, reminding us that the preservation of language is inextricably linked to the struggle for social justice and equity.

Beyond addressing present challenges, the volume also casts its gaze toward the future of Francophonie in America. Several contributions ask the critical question: How can younger generations be inspired to continue speaking French in an overwhelmingly Anglophone environment? In exploring the potential of new media and digital platforms, the authors suggest innovative ways to bridge communities, connecting age-old traditions with the demands of modern life. As the demographic landscape shifts—with increasing numbers of African-born French speakers, Haitian Creole speakers, and new immigrant communities contributing to the evolving definition of what it means to be Francophone—these reflections offer hopeful models for building a dynamic, inclusive cultural future. The discussions within these pages paint a picture of a future where French is not confined to nostalgic remembrance but is continuously reinvented through creative expression, technological innovation, and cross-cultural dialogue.

Fabrice Jaumont and Marguerite Tabusse open the narrative by laying out the breadth and depth of French-speaking communities nationwide. Drawing on historical migrations and demographic insights, they reveal the potential of French as a bridge language that connects disparate professional and social realms. Their macro-level analysis sets a broad context that naturally leads into more focused, localized explorations. Building on this foundation, Hamza Djimli delves into the vital role of the Alliances Françaises in sustaining and expanding Francophonie across the United States. By tracing their historical roots, evolving missions, and community-focused initiatives, he illustrates how these institutions function as cultural and linguistic hubs that adapt to changing demographics and societal needs. Examining their work in education, social integration, and intercultural dialogue, Djimli highlights how the Alliances Françaises not only preserve the French language but also nurture a dynamic, inclusive, and forward-looking Francophonie in America.

Meanwhile, Jessamine Irwin narrows the focus to Maine, foregrounding the importance of local history and identity. Her research reveals that the resurgence of French in the state transcends traditional language instruction and serves as a reclamation of heritage. By situating French within Maine's long-standing customs and legacies, she offers deeper insights into linguistic pride and establishes a foundation for further exploration of Francophone identity at the community level. From the cultural revival in Maine, Jerry L. Parker moves our attention to Louisiana, demonstrating that supporting French in this region is not only a matter of cultural significance but also of economic strategy. His policy analysis shows that bolstering Francophonie can drive entrepreneurship, fuel local economic growth, and foster global partnerships. This economic perspective enriches the narrative by linking cultural identity with tangible benefits.

Claire-Marie Brisson then takes us to the Rust Belt—a region marked by post-industrial challenges—where reclaimed Francophone identity serves as a powerful tool for community renewal. Her investigation shows how communities reinvent themselves by reconnecting with their linguistic roots, creating a dynamic laboratory for cross-cultural learning and social revitalization. Continuing the theme of community renewal, Frédérique Grim highlights the critical role of intergenerational teaching. Her work reminds us that language learning is a lifelong journey, one that begins in early childhood and extends well into senior years. By focusing on initiatives that serve both young learners and older citizens, Grim reinforces how cultural transmission thrives when nurtured across generations.

Expanding our view beyond local revitalization, Maya Angela Smith offers an insightful account of Senegalese immigrant experiences. Her contribution challenges conventional definitions of "Francophone" by revealing how African traditions merge with French language and culture, giving rise to new forms of expression. This broader perspective underscores the evolving nature of Francophonie in America. Building on this evolving narrative, Bertrand Tchoumi provides personal and pedagogical reflections on bilingual identity formation within African-centered educational leadership. His insights reveal the complexities of bilingualism and illustrate how culturally responsive pedagogy can empower students and strengthen community bonds, thus linking individual experience with broader educational practices. Elcie Douce then offers a deeply personal narrative that intertwines her Haitian roots with a process of cultural reclamation. Her story is both intimate and emblematic, demonstrating how individual journeys contribute to the broader tapestry of U.S. Francophonie. Douce's narrative reinforces the idea that personal heritage is inextricably linked to communal identity.

Shifting focus back to Louisiana, Jonathan Olivier examines the emergence of new speakers of French. His study on this regional minority language reveals evolving demographic trends and innovative educational initiatives that promise a vibrant future for French in the state. His work offers a hopeful counterpoint, illustrating how the language continues to adapt amid changing circumstances. Continuing with the theme of youth and language evolution, Valérie Barrau-Ogereau presents a close look at language contact among French migrant children. Her research documents the creative ways these children navigate multiple linguistic environments, highlighting the transformative nature of language learning in immigrant contexts and reinforcing the idea that language is a living, evolving practice. Emmanuel Kayembe then bridges personal migration with academic achievement through his reflective account of his journey from Africa to America. His narrative connects global Francophone networks to the evolving field of Francophone studies, emphasizing that the movement of French language and culture transcends borders and enriches our collective understanding.

Timothy Beaulieu follows by calling for collective action, underscoring the importance of harnessing cultural pride as a foundation for sustainable community building. His insights encourage proactive networking and collaborative projects aimed at revitalizing local communities, emphasizing that shared cultural identity becomes most powerful when it is celebrated collectively. Adding another dimension to our exploration, Melody Keilig investigates how visual and material culture serve as conduits for heritage transmission. Her work reveals that art, music, and performance are not only creative expressions but also living embodiments of tradition—capable of honoring the past while pointing toward the future. Scott Tilton then documents the often underrecognized musical traditions of Francophone communities. His study captures how French-speaking musicians and composers have contributed to American music, adding a vibrant thread to the overall tapestry of cultural identity in the United States.

From the realm of music, Eileen M. Angelini and Rebecca P. Sewall remind us of the enduring power of architectural heritage by examining Franco-American churches. Their study illustrates how these sacred spaces—crafted with artistic flair and practical resolve—serve as anchors for cultural identity, preserving memories and traditions even as surrounding communities evolve. Deepening our historical perspective, Joseph Bolton's genealogical explorations reconnect us with the intricate tapestry of French-Canadian ancestry. His work emphasizes the importance of oral traditions, family artifacts, and personal stories in preserving cultural memory, serving as a reminder that the legacy of French in America is both collective and deeply personal.

John Tousignant offers a stirring reflection on the reclamation of heritage, emphasizing that rediscovering one's cultural roots is an ongoing journey that resonates both personally and universally. His narrative builds upon previous discussions by reinforcing the emotional significance of cultural memory and identity. Patrick Lacroix then shifts the focus to the role of commemorative events, reminding us that historical anniversaries are not merely markers of time but opportunities to reconnect with our cultural roots. His reflections inspire renewed commitment to heritage preservation, especially among younger generations, and add momentum to the collective narrative. Expanding on the theme of interconnectedness, Camden Martin envisions the Francophone world as an archipelago—distinct yet interconnected islands of language, memory, and support. His evocative metaphor reinforces the idea that, despite their differences, diverse French-speaking communities are united by shared histories and aspirations.

 Jesse Martineau and Monique Martineau Cairns evoke the enduring "rêve" or dream of possibility, weaving personal reflection with public initiatives. Their narrative is a stirring reminder that the future of Francophonie is not predetermined but is actively shaped by the dreams and actions of those who believe in its promise. Franck Mounier then demonstrates the immense value of cross-cultural synergy in the evolution of French in America. His work shows that merging academic French with regional Creole roots fosters a dynamic environment in which diverse linguistic traditions can flourish together, setting the stage for further innovation. Turning to the intersection of education and economics, Steven J. Sacco and Megan Diercks highlight how external funding and innovative financial models can safeguard and expand French programs in colleges and universities. Their analysis illustrates that the benefits of supporting Francophonie extend far beyond cultural preservation, driving local economies and fostering global partnerships. Jennifer Schwester adds a personal touch with her reflective narrative on everyday Francophilia. Her account illustrates how a passion for French language and culture can blossom in unexpected places—even in New Jersey—contributing to a broader, more inclusive American Francophonie. Joëlle Vitiello and Sophie Kerman further explore the importance of conversation and community in sustaining the Francophone legacy. Their work underscores that language is not merely a communication tool but a living medium through which connections are forged and cultural bonds nurtured across the Americas. Rebecca Fortgang and Jasmine Grace St. Pierre share firsthand experiences of French education, detailing how generational shifts in language instruction reinforce community bonds and revitalize cultural pride. Their accounts illustrate that education is a dynamic interplay between tradition and innovation, constantly adapting to meet contemporary needs.

Ultimately, the story of French in America is one of perseverance, creativity, and hope. This story challenges us to reimagine what is possible when we embrace our cultural diversity and work together to build a more inclusive society. The legacy of Francophonie, as showcased in this volume, is a living testimony to the idea that language, far from being confined to textbooks or historical monuments, is woven into the daily lives of people who use it to express their identities, share their histories, and create new cultural futures.

Welcome to this expansive journey into the heart of Francophonie in America. May the ideas, visions, and personal stories within these pages encourage you to explore, question, and celebrate the linguistic and cultural richness that continues to flourish across our nation. French is present in every conversation, classroom, artistic performance, and community gathering—adapting, evolving, and inspiring. It is a language that connects us to our past, empowers us in the present, and leads us toward a future filled with endless creative possibilities. As you turn each page, let the stories and reflections contained within serve as a reminder that the legacy of French in the United States is not fixed in time but is an ever-changing mosaic of voices, experiences, and dreams. Embrace the journey, join the conversation, and contribute your voice to this vibrant narrative. For in the interplay between history and possibility, between memory and innovation, lies the true power of Francophonie—a power that continues to shape and redefine the American experience, generation after generation.

1. Francophonie in the United States: Historical Roots, Cultural Diversity, and Future Perspectives

Fabrice Jaumont and Marguerite Tabusse

The United States is a melting pot of cultures and languages, shaped by centuries of immigration and diversity. Among the many linguistic communities that make up the American landscape, Francophones occupy a unique and significant place. Their presence enriches the country's cultural mosaic through a deep history and vibrant traditions that carry on their linguistic and cultural heritage. From the founding of the first French colonies in the Americas to contemporary immigration trends, Francophones have played an essential role in the social, economic, and cultural development of the United States.

Historical Roots of American Francophonie

The history of American Francophonie began in the 16th century with the first French explorations of North America. Explorers such as Jacques Cartier and Samuel de Champlain paved the way for establishing colonies like New France and Louisiana, which stretched from present-day Canada down to the Gulf of Mexico. These colonies created lasting Francophone communities, often formed through complex interactions with local Indigenous peoples. Although these relationships involved significant cultural and linguistic exchange, they also occurred in contexts shaped by unequal power dynamics inherent in colonial expansion. The founding of emblematic cities such as Quebec City in 1608 and New Orleans in 1718 left an indelible mark on these territories. They contributed to the emergence of distinct linguistic and cultural traditions.

With the 1803 Louisiana Purchase, a large Francophone population was incorporated into the United States, cementing a lasting presence in strategic regions. This transfer helped sustain cultural vitality among Francophones, even as they faced growing pressures to assimilate. In the 19th and early 20th centuries, waves of immigration from Canada—particularly Acadians and Québécois—further strengthened the American Francophonie, especially in Northeastern states like Maine, Vermont, and New Hampshire. These immigrants brought their languages, customs, and values, profoundly shaping local societies. The diversity of these immigrant groups also introduced a variety of dialects and cultural practices, further enriching the social fabric of the United States.

Number of French Speakers Today

According to the 2023 American Community Survey (ACS), about 1.25 million Americans speak French at home. When including Haitian Creole speakers, that number exceeds 2 million. The U.S. Francophonie comprises various Haitian, African, French, Canadian, Franco-American, and Indigenous communities.

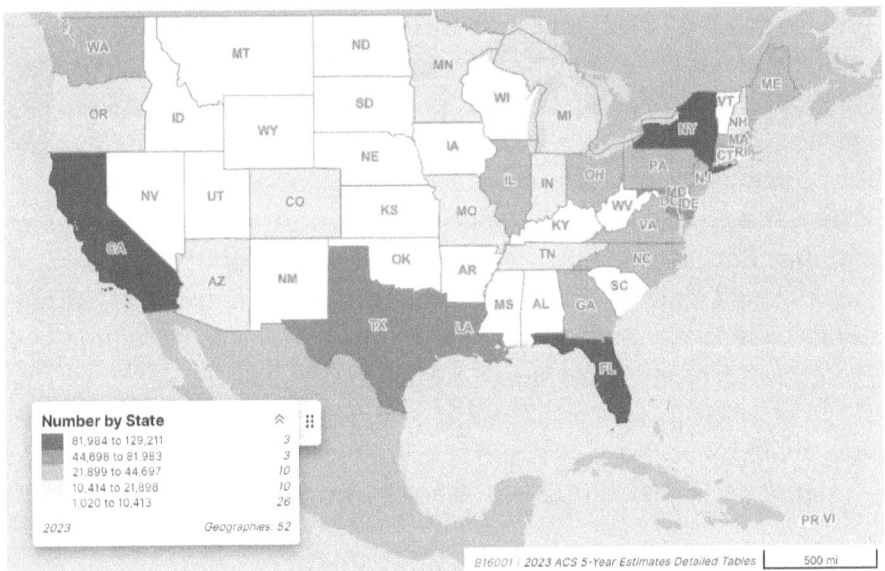

Figure 1: Number of French speakers at home – Total by State, ACS, 2023.

The largest Francophone community is of Haitian origin, with around 1,052,000 people in 2023. Among them, 925,000 speak Haitian Creole, and 175,000 speak French. Their main centers are in Florida—particularly Miami, where 46% of U.S. residents of Haitian descent live (488,000 individuals)—as well as New York, which has 18% of this community (186,000 individuals), and Massachusetts, with 7% (69,000 individuals). This community contributes a unique cultural richness, blending African, Caribbean, and French traditions, which is evident in its music, cuisine, and cultural celebrations.

Regarding Francophone Africa, more than 300,000 U.S. residents were born in countries such as Senegal (29,000 people), Togo (37,000), Côte d'Ivoire (25,000), the Democratic Republic of the Congo (63,000), the Republic of the Congo (43,000), and Cameroon (91,000).[1] These communities mainly reside in New York City, Washington, D.C., Atlanta, and Houston. They enrich the American landscape with their traditions and the use of multiple local languages—Wolof, Bambara, Lingala, Ewe, and French. Their influence is seen in creating restaurants, shops, and cultural associations that promote African cuisine and arts (dance, music, fashion). They are also active in religious and community life, founding churches, mosques, and cultural centers to support diaspora members and raise funds for humanitarian projects in their countries of origin. Additionally, they leave a mark on education and entrepreneurship: many pursue higher education at U.S. universities, while others launch startups in finance, energy, or information technology, leveraging community networks and multilingual skills to succeed. Through this dynamism, the African Francophone diaspora contributes to major U.S. cities' cultural and economic diversity while preserving ties to their homelands.

As of 2023, about 187,000 U.S. residents were born in France, mainly in California (Los Angeles, San Francisco), New York, Florida (Miami), and Massachusetts. These French-born immigrants are

---

[1] Cf. Appendix – Table 5: Number of United States residents born in French-speaking countries, 2023. American Community Survey, Place of Birth of the Foreign-Born Population in the USA in 2023, 1-year estimates, 2023

actively involved in cultural and economic activities, bringing varied influences in cuisine, fashion, art, and technology.

In 2023, there were 828,000 Canadian-born individuals residing in the United States, including 150,000 Francophones. These are primarily located in border states such as Maine, Vermont, and New Hampshire, as well as major cities like New York and Los Angeles. These French Canadians, often from longstanding communities, bring their own traditions—including Acadian festivals and winter customs—that blend seamlessly into the American context.

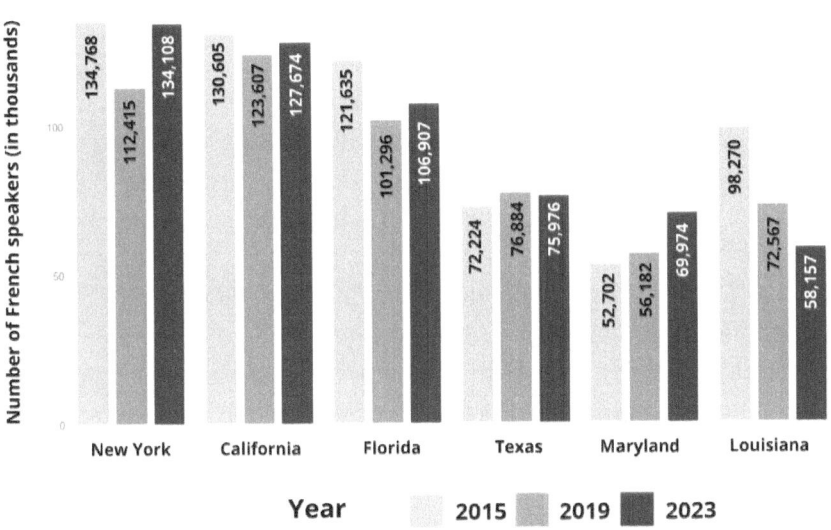

Figure 2 This display shows the American Community Survey (ACS) estimates of the number of people speaking French at home for the years 2015, 2019, and 2023 in the 10 states where this number is the highest. The states are listed in descending order of their respective number of people speaking French at home in 2023. Source: American Community Survey, Languages Spoken at Home for the Population 5 Years and Over, 1-year estimates, 2015, 2019, 2023.

Francophone Indigenous communities include three main tribes: the Houma, the Pointe-au-Chien, and the Tunica-Biloxi, representing about 19,000 people. Among the Tunica-Biloxi, approximately 30% of older generations speak French; meanwhile, the Pointe-au-Chien community, with 680 members, has a significant share of French-speaking elders, and the Houma incorporate French linguistic and cultural elements into their traditions, mainly in Louisiana and elsewhere according to their distribution. These Indigenous communities represent a unique fusion of Indigenous and French cultures, visible in their crafts, rituals, and language.

Geographic Distribution

In Louisiana, around 60,000 people speak French, Louisiana Creole, or Haitian Creole, using dialects such as Cajun French, Louisiana Creole (Kouri-Vini), Houma French, and Colonial French. Indigenous communities like the Houma and the Pointe-au-Chien also contribute to this distribution. Nevertheless, there has been a significant decline in the number of French speakers in Louisiana over the past decade, dropping from about 100,000 in 2015 to 80,000 in 2019 and 60,000 in 2023.[2] This decrease can be explained by assimilation policies that have inhibited French transmission and by the passing of older, more Francophone generations. Despite this decline, Louisiana remains historically the heart of American Francophonie, where French influence is everywhere: architecture, music, cuisine, and celebrations such as Mardi Gras—celebrated with particular intensity by Francophone communities.

Florida, home to a large Haitian community, has many people who speak languages rooted in the Francophone world. In 2023, the state had around 570,000 individuals connected to Francophonie, including 464,000 Haitian Creole speakers and 107,000 French speakers. While Florida has the largest total population tied to Francophonie, an important distinction must be made between Haitian Creole speakers and French speakers. If we focus solely on French speakers, New York State has the largest Francophone population. New York is home to approximately 315,000 people connected to Francophonie, including 181,000 Haitian Creole speakers and 134,000 French speakers, mainly

---

[2] Cf. Appendix - Table 1: Number of French speakers at home by state and year between 2015 and 2023. It is worth noting that these estimates computed in the ACS do not take into account Francophone indigenous tribes and the population under five years of age."

from France, Francophone Africa, or other regions of the Francophone world. This figure reflects the linguistic and cultural diversity within the state.

Elsewhere in the Northeast, other states also have notable populations of Francophone speakers. For instance, Massachusetts has about 125,000 people linked to Francophonie—83,000 of whom speak Haitian Creole and 41,000 speak French—representing about 2% of its total population. Maryland, meanwhile, has 86,000 Francophones, of whom 70,000 speak French—mainly from France or elsewhere in Europe—and a minority are Haitian Creole speakers. Pennsylvania and New Jersey also have significant Franco-American communities. Pennsylvania has around 51,000 French speakers, while New Jersey—closer to major migration corridors—counts 101,000 Francophone speakers, split between Haitian Creole and French speakers. Both states illustrate the continued presence of Francophonie in regions historically shaped by French or Canadian immigration.

State	2015	2016	2017	2018	2019	2021	2022	2023
New York	134,768	143,251	126,476	145,979	112,415	132,797	142,480	134,108
California	130,605	131,901	132,930	123,226	123,607	126,371	129,585	127,674
Florida	121,635	105,816	110,117	102,143	101,296	103,125	104,481	106,907
Texas	72,224	74,430	63,666	77,739	76,884	71,795	92,675	75,976
Maryland	52,702	51,994	57,705	60,237	56,182	57,606	52,848	69,974
Louisiana	98,270	87,771	87,004	77,066	72,567	60,593	64,302	58,157
Massachusetts	58,206	50,585	56,693	52,086	49,442	42,251	44,129	41,957
New Jersey	37,179	33,001	34,879	42,857	36,615	32,944	29,201	35,741
Maine	41,664	38,695	37,126	35,752	34,473	33,580	32,665	31,675
Connecticut	24,269	24,959	19,420	26,330	21,757	18,990	20,545	24,269
Colorado	16,507	19,423	16,844	19,690	18,294	17,409	24,969	18,818
Vermont	8,855	8,508	8,558	8,371	8,385	8,356	8,196	8,124

Table 2 – Number of French speakers at home by state and year for the top 10 states between 2015 and 2023. Source: American Community Survey, Languages Spoken at Home for the Population 5 years and over.

Although Vermont, Maine, and New Hampshire currently have relatively small absolute numbers of Francophone speakers (due to smaller local populations, fewer recent Francophone immigrants, and the impact of assimilation policies), they historically housed large Francophone communities. Vermont and New Hampshire each have about 16% to 17% of their populations claiming French ancestry, reflecting the legacy left by waves of French-Canadian immigration—particularly Québécois and Acadians. Last but not least, Maine has about 16% of residents identifying as having French ancestry, with 32,000 people still speaking French at home in 2023. The state remains strongly influenced by its Franco-American heritage, especially in cities like Lewiston and Augusta, where festivals, community initiatives, and bilingual schools strive to keep cultural and linguistic traditions alive. Finally, Rhode Island counts about 8,000 Francophones, or about 1% of its population. These Northeastern states remain marked by Acadian and Québécois cultural influences, manifested through festivals, cultural centers, and French-language educational programs. In this region, Boston—although located in Massachusetts—serves as a central hub for Francophones, celebrating cultural diversity through events, cultural institutions, and bilingual initiatives that keep the rich heritage of Francophonie alive.

Most cities host sizable, more recent Francophone diasporas.[3] As of 2023, New York City is home to 89,000 French and Franco-American Francophones and 108,000 Haitians. Organizations like the French-American Chamber of Commerce or the Haitian American Business Network regularly hold professional and cultural events. The greater New York metropolitan area (spanning three states: southern New York, northern New Jersey, and southern Connecticut), with 18,423,000 people in 2023, includes more than 356,000 Francophones—over 2% of the population—encompassing Haitian, African, French, and Canadian communities. Miami, which has 7,000 Francophones (3.5% of its population) and a large Haitian community, hosts annual festivals and language workshops through the Haitian Cultural Arts Alliance to highlight the Creole and Francophone heritage. Boston has about 16,000 Haitian French speakers and a notable Franco-Canadian

---

[3] Cf. Appendix - Table 2: Number of French speakers at home in major US cities for the years 2015, 2019, and 2023.

presence, with 4,000 European French speakers. Cultural institutions like the Alliance Française of Boston and Cambridge organize film clubs and literary conferences, strengthening community ties. These major metro areas are truly dynamic centers of American Francophonie, offering numerous cultural (festivals, cultural centers), professional (networks of bilingual entrepreneurs), and educational (Francophone school programs, universities) opportunities for Francophones of all origins.

Heritage Francophonie

The heritage Francophonie in the United States encompasses roughly 6.2 million people claiming French ancestry, rising to about 7.8 million if those with French-Canadian ancestry are included. This population is mainly concentrated in the Northeast—Maine, New Hampshire, Vermont, Massachusetts, Pennsylvania, and Rhode Island—each having significant proportions of French descendants. In the Midwest, states like Michigan, Illinois, Wisconsin, and Minnesota also house notable communities of French ancestry. Around 12% of Louisiana's population claims French or Acadian heritage. At the same time, states such as California, Texas, Florida, and New York also attract sizable populations of French descendants due to internal migration and economic opportunities.[4]

This geographic diversity highlights the richness of American Francophonie, where each region brings its own cultural and linguistic character. For example, Northeast Francophonie is shaped by Acadian and Québécois influences, whereas Louisiana's culture is imbued with Cajun and Creole traditions. Franco-Americans have often preserved the Midwest's rural and industrial heritage elements, contributing to the region's economic and social diversity.

Although French is no longer widely spoken as a native language within these communities, certain pockets remain where French is taught and used—particularly in some schools, churches, and cultural

---

[4] Cf. Appendix - Table 3: Number of people with a French or French-Canadian ancestry: top 10 states in 2023 and Table 4: People reporting French or French-Canadian ancestry for each state of the USA, 2023.

associations. French culture and traditions are maintained through festivals celebrating French heritage, such as the Festival International de Louisiane in Lafayette, the Festival Acadiens et Créoles, and Franco-American festivals in Maine and New Hampshire. Traditional French cuisine endures in dishes like *tourtière* (meat pie), sucre à la crème, and other regional specialties. Traditional music, including Cajun music in Louisiana and Franco-American songs in the Northeast, remains an integral part of the culture.

Organizations like the Franco-American Centre in Manchester, New Hampshire, and the Franco-American Centre at the University of Maine in Orono have long played an essential role in preserving and promoting the French language and culture. These centers offered educational programs, art workshops, and community events that fostered a sense of belonging and intergenerational transmission of traditions. Some schools and universities still provide courses on Franco-American culture, the French language, and the history of Franco-Americans, contributing to the education and awareness of younger generations. Though less common, there are publications and radio broadcasts dedicated to the Franco-American community—such as *Le Forum*, published by the University of Maine—which play a crucial role in disseminating information and promoting Francophone culture.

Diversity of Speech Varieties

French in the United States stands out for its incredible diversity, the result of historical blending involving the colonial French of the early settlers, the heritage of deported Acadians (the origin of Cajun French), the influence of Haitian immigrants, and contributions from African and Indigenous communities. In Louisiana, this linguistic richness is reflected in multiple forms: Cajun French, tied to Acadian descendants; Louisiana Creole (or Kouri-Vini), born from the contact between colonial French, African languages, and other idioms; and regional variants of French adopted by some Indigenous groups (like the Houma or the Pointe-au-Chien), often rooted in older colonial French tinged with Indigenous and Anglophone influences. Although these speech varieties are endangered today, they are still used by thousands of people in family or cultural settings. Revitalization efforts by organizations like the Council for the Development of French in Louisiana (CODOFIL) help preserve and promote these unique forms of Louisiana French, reflecting the region's diverse and complex history.

In Northeastern states—particularly Maine, Vermont, and New Hampshire—the French spoken is linked to Québécois (and, to a lesser extent, Acadian) immigration. This regional French, often called "Franco-American," retains distinct characteristics, such as vocabulary inherited from Quebec or Acadia and region-specific turns of phrase, all while adapting to a predominantly Anglophone environment. In former industrial cities like Lewiston and Biddeford (Maine) or Manchester (New Hampshire), families once passed the language down through cultural associations (Franco-American clubs, festivals) and, in particular, Catholic parishes where French was used in liturgy. However, language assimilation pressures have gradually reduced the number of active speakers, and many young people today turn to English. Even so, educational initiatives such as immersion programs and after-school French classes aim to reverse this trend, emphasizing local Franco-American culture and fostering a sense of belonging in the new generation.

Elsewhere, in urban centers, French mirrors the diversity of contemporary Francophone origins. In New York, Miami, and Boston, one finds a true linguistic mosaic: "standard" French spoken by French expatriates, Haitian Creole and French used by those raised in Haiti, as well as African varieties of French (Senegalese, Ivorian, Congolese, etc.). Creole dominates everyday neighborhood life in some New York neighborhoods (Brooklyn, Queens) or Miami (Little Haiti), while French remains the formal language for professional or academic settings. In these cosmopolitan environments, this "blended French" also absorbs influences from English and other global languages, creating a rich cultural and linguistic tapestry.

Outside the major urban hubs, the Mississippi region holds remnants of colonial French, notably in Missouri around St. Louis and the old mining districts. Here, Missouri French—sometimes called 'Paw Paw French'—traces its origins to the first French settlers in the 18th century, before other significant waves of immigration. This dialect, evolved in relative isolation in a rural setting, is now critically endangered, with its remaining speakers being elderly. Despite some documentation and revitalization initiatives, Missouri French remains one of the most threatened varieties of French in the United States.

The Haitian community, primarily concentrated in Florida, New York, and Massachusetts, is another significant pillar of American Francophonie. Here, Haitian Creole is the language of daily life, while French, often spoken by those who received a French-language education in Haiti, remains an important cultural and professional vehicle. The alternating use of French and Creole within these communities reinforces a strong sense of identity and nurtures a dynamic network of associations.

Finally, the more recent Francophone expatriates and immigrants have reshaped the linguistic map in major American cities over the last few decades. Whether these are French professionals moving for work, Africans from Francophone countries (Senegal, Côte d'Ivoire, Congo, etc.), or Canadians (Québécois, Acadians, Franco-Ontarians), their presence is felt in cosmopolitan neighborhoods, university campuses, international companies, or nonprofit organizations. This plural French is often a standard or regional variant (depending on origin), enriched with Anglicisms and intercultural contacts, mirroring the country's multicultural dynamic. In cities like Los Angeles, Chicago, or Washington, D.C., bilingual schools, media outlets (radio stations, podcasts, publications), and associations (Alliances Françaises, Franco-African clubs, etc.) help animate the local Francophone scene.

In short—whether referring to Franco-American varieties in New England, Missouri French, Haitian communities, recent Francophone arrivals, or Louisiana's many Cajun, colonial, and Creole varieties—these forms of French attest to the richness and diversity of the French language in the United States. Each community evolves within its own historical, linguistic, and sociocultural context, with differing degrees of initiative to preserve, transmit, or highlight its traditions. Together, they make up the vast tapestry of American Francophonie, whose vitality is measured by the number of speakers and the strength of associative, cultural, and educational networks that continue to sustain the French language on American soil.

Challenges of Transmission and Preservation

Francophone communities in the United States face several challenges in preserving and passing on their language and culture. However, their resilience in the face of these challenges is truly inspiring. The pressure of linguistic assimilation, which translates into a gradual reduction of French use among younger generations in an English-dominant environment, is a significant hurdle. This leads to a linguistic gap between older individuals, for whom French remains the primary language, and younger people, who are generally more comfortable speaking English. At the same time, a lack of educational resources exacerbates the problem: French immersion and bilingual schools are few, limiting access to French-language education. Without adequate programs, families struggle to teach French to their children, and local communities see a decline in competent speakers. Reduced visibility of Francophonie in the media, schools, and public discourse can lead to cultural marginalization, threatening to erase various Francophone communities' historical and ongoing contributions to American society. However, the determination of these communities to preserve their language and culture is a testament to their resilience and strength.

French language instruction in the United States reflects the multiplicity of Francophone realities: heritage French within historical communities, standard French among recent expatriates, and varieties in urban settings. Data from 2024 and previous years shed light on these challenges and guide strategic objectives for strengthening the place of French in the U.S. education system. In 2024, 3,623 bilingual programs nationwide (covering all languages), including 182 French programs with 33,000 students enrolled in French immersion schools. Additionally, American high schools offer 17,778 foreign-language programs, of which 3,738 are in French (FLE, or French as a Foreign Language). The 2017 National K-12 Foreign Language Enrollment Survey counted 1,289,004 students studying French (about 2.3% of all American students). This figure has remained relatively stable despite a slight decline, suggesting stagnant popularity for French at the high school level. However, these numbers gradually increase overall, reflecting a growing interest in multilingual skills in a globalized world.

Despite nearly doubling bilingual programs over the past 20 years, those devoted to French remain poorly represented compared to languages like Spanish. This underscores the urgent need to promote French more robustly, particularly in areas with strong cultural demand (for instance, New England, parts of the Midwest, or Louisiana). The importance of the French language in the U.S. education system cannot be overstated, and we must work to promote and preserve it.

There are 36,412 foreign-language programs at the university level, of which 1,316 are in French (FLE). Approximately 135,088 students are enrolled in French at the university level in 2024, marking a 23% decrease from 2016 (when there were around 175,000). University-level French instruction is declining significantly: 135,088 learners in 2024 is a 23% drop compared to 2016. This trend is part of an overall reduction in foreign-language learning in the United States, where total enrollment fell by 16.6% between 2016 and 2021. This reality is reflected in the elimination or downsizing of numerous language departments at universities. Beyond short-term factors, the rise of Chinese, Spanish, or other languages considered more "useful" in the job market also weakens French's position.

According to a March 2024 IPSOS study, 30% of respondents believe learning French is useful abroad, 20% consider it an asset in academic settings, 16% say it is helpful at work, and only 14% see its relevance in daily life. However, 88% of Americans have a favorable view of French, associating it with romance (85%), social status (63%), and elitism (60%). This gap between the symbolic appeal of the language and its perceived usefulness highlights the importance of leveraging its cultural and prestigious image while boosting its practical dimension (professional programs, internships in Francophone settings, etc.).

In 2024, the national shortage of foreign-language teachers in the United States could reach 100,000 unfilled positions by 2025, with a particularly acute shortage of French teachers. In 2010, the total number of French teachers was estimated at 10,000, which has scarcely changed. This lack of qualified instructors is a significant barrier to developing and sustaining French programs, as schools struggle to recruit competent teachers to meet demand (whether related to heritage French, Cajun French, or FLE programs).

Areas of Action Through 2050

According to Organisation Internationale de la Francophonie projections, the global Francophone population will reach 700 million speakers by 2050, mainly driven by African demographic growth. This trend not only positions French as an increasingly strategic language in various fields, from business and diplomacy to culture and science but also underscores its global significance. Against this backdrop, Francophone communities in the United States would benefit from strengthening their position and deepening ties with the countries and regions where the language is rapidly expanding.

First, French as a Foreign Language must be expanded and aligned with job market needs. French already ranks as the third most in-demand language after Spanish and Chinese, according to a 2018 ACTFL study, and it is poised to grow in importance with the demographic boom in Francophone African countries. New specialized French courses (business French, professional French, or technical French) could focus more on economic and diplomatic relations between the United States, Africa, and Europe. Concrete activities, such as partnerships with companies active in African markets, would provide students with tangible employment prospects and opportunities for international mobility.

At the same time, it is essential to bolster French departments at universities by offering more flexible programs suited to the realities of the 21st century. Courses in French for health care, engineering, international law, or environmental studies would better meet the needs of a globalized economy. Establishing internships and exchange programs in Francophone regions—particularly in Africa—would further broaden students' career horizons and enhance their intercultural skills.

Additionally, supporting French-language schools in historically Francophone regions—whether Louisiana, New England, or specific Haitian communities—would help preserve and highlight the French linguistic heritage. This involves promoting differentiated teaching approaches that consider the language levels of already Francophone students by offering advanced literature classes or intercultural projects that link them with fast-growing African Francophone regions. Such initiatives would protect and connect the local linguistic heritage to global developments.

Given the expected demographic growth in the Francophone world, a primary long-term focus will also be training enough French teachers to meet the forecast shortfall. To address this, collaboration with organizations such as French for All (led by Villa Albertine) and other initial or continuing education institutions should intensify. Improving teacher training and diversifying recruitment would ensure quality instruction and help sustain French programs—immersion, French as a foreign language, or heritage French.

Despite these challenges, ongoing initiatives form a foundation for future progress. For instance, bilingual schools and immersion programs already provide increased access to French instruction. In Louisiana, CODOFIL has significantly enriched the educational landscape while boosting the revitalization of Louisiana French. Culturally, associations such as the Federation of Alliances Françaises USA, the Franco-American Centre, and Franco student clubs organize festivals, workshops, and exhibitions, helping spread the language and build bridges with stakeholders across the Francophone world. French-language media—including newspapers, radio, podcasts, and TV channels—help maintain linguistic and cultural ties, while Indigenous communities such as the Houma and the Pointe-au-Chien develop specific programs to pass on the variety of French inherited from the colonial era and uphold their cultural practices. Collectively, these efforts highlight the vitality and resilience of an American Francophonie comprised of longstanding heritages (Cajun, Missouri French, Franco-American) and newer arrivals (Haitian communities, African immigrants, French and Canadian expatriates). The goal will be to strengthen the cohesion of these initiatives and adapt them to expected changes by 2050 so that global French-language growth becomes a genuine opportunity for the United States.

Conclusion

Drawing on its historical roots and cultural diversity, Francophonie in the United States is pivotal in its evolution. As the global Francophone population heads toward 700 million speakers by 2050, American Francophones hold a significant advantage: they live at the crossroads of the world's leading power and a rapidly expanding linguistic sphere. This circumstance allows them to play a decisive role diplomatically and in the economic, academic, and cultural arenas. Diplomatically, American Francophones provide valuable expertise for reinforcing partnerships between the United States and Francophone countries in Africa, Europe, and the Caribbean, thanks to their linguistic and cultural mediation skills. Economically, knowing French and a nuanced understanding of cultural norms facilitate access to emerging markets in regions experiencing significant demographic and economic growth. Moreover, international collaboration in scientific and artistic fields can be much more productive if American Francophones forge strong ties with researchers, academics, and creators from across the Francophone world, especially where it is experiencing the fastest growth.

Looking ahead, creating effective linkages between different Francophone communities and other American economic, cultural, and political stakeholders will be key to success. Investment in education, ongoing teacher training, and pedagogical innovation—combined with supportive policies for Francophone associations and media—will give national and international resonance to this revival of American Francophonie. Efforts to bolster the status of French in schools, universities, and businesses will also ensure the language's cultural and linguistic longevity while fostering recognition of the diversity that characterizes Francophonie in the United States.

Ultimately, by celebrating their regional differences and multiple heritages and engaging with countries whose Francophone populations are expanding, American Francophones will be able to contribute to building a more inclusive and interconnected world. Their role as facilitators and bridge-builders between cultures enables them to strongly influence a global Francophonie where diversity and cooperation remain the driving forces of shared prosperity.

2. The Alliances Françaises in the United States: A Pillar of Francophonie in America
Hamza Djimli

Since its founding in 1883, the Alliance Française has occupied a central position in spreading and promoting the French language worldwide. Now present in 135 countries, it provides high-quality instruction, recognized certifications, and a wide range of cultural programming to support French learning. With over 830 autonomous institutions governed by local law, the Alliance Française is currently the largest cultural NGO in the world. Its model relies on the involvement of local civil societies and fosters intercultural, apolitical dialogue. This local grounding and autonomy make it an essential pillar of the international Francophonie. Spread throughout the country, the Alliances Françaises in the United States form a unique and dynamic network, reflecting the enduring American interest in French language and culture. Since their emergence at the end of the 19th century, these institutions have adapted to societal and pedagogical changes, evolving into true cultural and linguistic centers committed to the values of inclusion and sharing. With more than 100 Alliances Françaises across 44 states—from Florida to Hawai'i, including Missouri, Utah, and Oregon—the United States hosts the largest network of Alliances in the world. Their mission is clear: promote the French language and francophone cultures while reinforcing intercultural exchanges between France and the United States.

Each Alliance Française operates independently with its own governance and local initiatives, while receiving support from two key entities responsible for network coordination, guidance, and oversight. The Federation of Alliances Françaises USA, founded in 1902, and the National Coordination Office, operating under the aegis of the Cultural Services of the French Embassy in Washington, play a vital role in fostering cohesion and development within this network. A major driver of Francophonie in the United States, the network continuously evolves with cultural and educational shifts, adapting to the ever-changing needs and interests of learners and the public.

A Century-Old Heritage and an Ever-Evolving Mission

The Alliance Française was established in Paris in 1883, driven by a group of French intellectuals, diplomats, writers, and scientists, including Louis Pasteur, Jules Verne, and Paul Cambon. Its goal is to promote the French language and francophone cultures worldwide through an independent, international associative network. In the United States, the context was particularly favorable: the legacy of French support during the War of Independence, the prestige of French writers and artists, and France's diplomatic influence all contributed to a strong enthusiasm for Francophonie. The first American Alliance Française was founded in 1889 in San Francisco (CA), quickly attracting intellectuals and artists seeking to attend lectures, discussion circles, and cultural events inspired by French literature, philosophy, and the arts. Around the turn of the 20th century, additional Alliances Françaises opened in the United States, notably in Chicago (IL) and Denver (CO) in 1897, then in Boston (MA) and New York (NY) in 1898. They found support from committed figures dedicated to advancing culture and education.

In Denver, one woman alone exemplifies this openness to the world and love for the French language. Margaret Brown, better known as "Molly Brown," is a legendary figure in Denver, notably for her role during the sinking of the Titanic in 1912. During World War I, Molly Brown was actively involved in France, supporting Allied troops by working with the Red Cross and aiding wounded soldiers and refugees. She was also renowned for her philanthropy and her passion for French culture. Enthusiastic about arts and languages, she became a founding member of the Denver Woman's Club, an organization aimed at improving women's rights through education and philanthropy. Her interest in French culture also led her to co-found a branch of the Alliance Française in Denver. Her commitment to Francophonie and her humanitarian efforts earned her the prestigious French Légion d'honneur in 1932. Thanks to figures like Molly Brown, the Alliances Françaises also became spaces for social emancipation. From then on, they served as cultural hubs, hosting lectures, exhibitions, and performances that spurred the exchange of ideas. Both World Wars reinforced their social and cultural role. During World War I, they supported intellectual exchanges and contributed to Franco-American cultural diplomacy. During World War II, in light of France's occupation, they became hubs of mobilization in support of the Resistance and Free France, organizing events and advocacy campaigns.

After World War II, approximately 50,000 European women (including around 6,500 French women) married American soldiers and immigrated to the United States.[5] Many of these women, coming from educated backgrounds or possessing a certain cultural capital, sought to maintain a connection with French culture—both for themselves and to pass it on to their children. In this context, some turned to the Alliances Françaises and even played an active role in the creation or revitalization of local chapters. There is no comprehensive study listing all the Alliances Françaises founded by War Brides, but several oral histories and local historical accounts report such cases in mid-sized cities in the Midwest or the South, and in communities without a strong prior institutional Francophone presence, but where francophiles or former military personnel maintained an emotional connection to France.

During the 1950s and 1960s, new Alliances Françaises were established in college towns and medium-sized cities—such as Orlando (FL), Saint Louis (MO), and Birmingham (AL)—making French instruction accessible to a broader audience. Starting in the 1970s, business and industrial partnerships between the United States and France increased, particularly in aeronautics, luxury goods, and the automotive industry, which led to growing demand for French. In addition, the rise of the European Union and transatlantic economic discussions prompted some professionals to learn French. In the 1980s, Alliances diversified their offerings by creating film clubs, festivals,

---

[5] Zeiger, 1996.

specialized courses, and academic partnerships with American universities. Interest in the French language extended well beyond academia, opening new professional and cultural horizons.

With the expansion of the internet and globalization in the 1990s, the American linguistic landscape changed: Spanish and Mandarin gained prominence in school curricula. To remain competitive, the Alliances Françaises equipped themselves with computer resources to reach a broader audience. They also began highlighting francophone cultures from Africa, the Caribbean, and Quebec, organizing diverse events such as wine tastings, lectures, roundtables, and music festivals. Some Alliances, like those in New Orleans, Lafayette (LA), Miami (FL), and Portland (ME), place particular emphasis on Creole and Caribbean cultures, while those in San Diego (CA), Seattle (WA), Chicago (IL), and Greenwich (CT) specialize in francophone film and entrepreneurship.

Alliances at the Heart of American Francophonies

Alliances Françaises are not merely language schools; they are places of exchange, transmission, and inclusion. They create spaces for dialogue between francophones and francophiles, bringing together people with diverse backgrounds. Ken D., who had studied French in high school, found far more than language classes at the Alliance Française of Santa Rosa (CA): "The Alliance rekindled my love for the French language. During troubled times in the U.S., my classes at the Alliance were a generous source of friendship and joy." Similarly, Laura M. from the Alliance Française of Austin (TX) says, "J'adore le yoga en français! I love the yoga class in French, both online and in person. It is a great way to practice French in a fun, new way! C'est le meilleur! It's the best of multitasking—great yoga and a great opportunity to improve my French listening and comprehension! Merci beaucoup!" Like them, many learners discover, through these institutions, a valuable social connection and a welcoming environment that goes beyond language instruction. Alliances play a key role in dialogue between communities of varied backgrounds—Haitian, African, Franco-Canadian, Louisianan, and Spanish-speaking. Their contributions are essential to sustaining Francophonie in North America, both culturally, educationally, and socioeconomically.

This francophone diversity is also reflected within the teams and volunteers who keep the Alliances Françaises in the United States vibrant. Teachers, administrators, cultural facilitators, and volunteers hail from a wide range of backgrounds: francophone Africa and Asia, the Caribbean, Canada, Switzerland, Belgium, Romania, and beyond. This human plurality makes Alliances living spaces where the spirit of global Francophonie thrives.

A Francophone Presence Shaped by History and Migration

Francophone diversity in the United States is the result of complex historical trajectories, often linked to economic migration, colonial relationships, and transatlantic cultural dynamics. Certain Alliances Françaises, due to their geographic location, economic and migratory factors, and local history, play particularly active roles in supporting and promoting these communities.

Haitians: A Dynamic Community Supported by the Alliances in Miami, Boston, and New York

Haitians represent a significant francophone diaspora in the United States, with about 1.2 million people. They are especially numerous in Florida, where Miami is home to one of the country's largest Haitian communities. Since the late 18th century and the Haitian Revolution, several waves of migration have occurred in the United States, but a stronger and more permanent Haitian diaspora presence took root in Florida beginning in the 1990s. Miami, with its Little Haiti neighborhood, became a major hub of the Haitian diaspora. The Alliance Française of Miami Metro helps highlight Haitian culture, organizing film screenings and cultural events celebrating Haitian literature, history, and music.

In the 1950s and 1960s, some Haitians—often from middle-class or elite backgrounds—emigrated to the United States, notably to New York, Boston, and Chicago, to pursue higher education or escape political instability. Though these numbers were relatively modest, they marked the emergence of the first organized Haitian communities. The Alliance Française of Boston and Cambridge is another key hub for the Haitian community, notably through partnerships with local organizations that promote access to culture and educational services in French. The Alliance Française of New York also attracts a large Haitian audience, hosting exhibitions and debates on Haiti's history and its influence in the francophone world.

Francophone Africans: A Growing Presence at the Alliances in Washington and Atlanta

Rapidly expanding francophone African diasporas are particularly visible in cities like Washington D.C. and Atlanta (GA). They include immigrants from Senegal, Côte d'Ivoire, Mali, Cameroon, and the Democratic Republic of the Congo, often involved in entrepreneurship and service sectors. Through community associations, cultural events, francophone churches, or community media, these diasporas actively keep the languages and cultures of their homelands alive while building bridges with American society. In this context, Alliances Françaises located in Washington D.C. and Atlanta serve as spaces of welcome, visibility, and dialogue for these groups. By hosting events showcasing African literature, music, and cinema, or collaborating with artists and intellectuals from these diasporas, they help include these communities in the local francophone dynamic.

Franco-Canadians and Quebecers: A Living Heritage at the Alliances in Maine and Chicago

Historically, thousands of Quebecers migrated to the United States in the late 19th century, primarily to work in textiles, lumber, and manufacturing—sectors flourishing in New England. This migration focused on industrial towns like Lewiston (Maine), Manchester (New Hampshire), and Worcester (Massachusetts). These francophone workers built neighborhoods, parishes, and schools, leaving a lasting mark on local culture. Today, that heritage endures through a strong collective memory and still-active Franco-American communities, although intergenerational transmission of French can sometimes be fragile. Here, Alliances Françaises play a crucial role in preserving, showcasing, and revitalizing Franco-American culture.

The Alliance Française of Portland (ME) fulfills this mission by reconnecting the threads of francophone history in a region still home to many descendants of Quebec workers. It collaborates with Acadian and Quebec institutions, organizes Franco-American festivals, intergenerational workshops, documentary screenings about working-class history, and bilingual cultural gatherings. In Chicago, another city shaped by incoming Quebecers and Franco-Canadians in the 20th century, the Alliance Française of Chicago promotes this francophone presence through lectures, exhibitions, concerts, and artistic exchanges. It maintains strong ties with Quebec's cultural and educational institutions and actively participates in the cross-border francophone network linking Quebec and the American Midwest. These initiatives not only maintain strong cultural ties between the United States and Quebec but also renew interest among younger generations in their francophone heritage.

Louisianans: Showcasing French with the Alliances in New Orleans and Lafayette

In Louisiana, French is not just a foreign language; it is a heritage language deeply woven into the state's history and cultural identity. Inherited from French colonists, deported Acadians (Cajuns), and Creole populations, Louisiana French has given rise to a unique linguistic variety, mixing local expressions, distinctive accents, and older forms of the language. In the face of the gradual erosion of this regional language over the generations, linguistic revitalization has become a major concern for both public institutions and grassroots organizations.

The Alliance Française of New Orleans is central to preserving and transmitting French. It offers courses tailored to heritage speakers—that is, Louisianans with a family or cultural connection to French, though not necessarily fluent—and works to strengthen ties between heritage francophones, new learners, and international French speakers. The Alliance Française of Lafayette, meanwhile, is based in the heart of Acadiana, a region strongly shaped by Acadian heritage. It showcases Cajun and Acadian culture through a rich program: francophone festivals, Louisiana French classes, traditional music workshops, lectures on local history, and meetings with francophone artists and storytellers. It also supports intergenerational transmission of this culture by collaborating with immersion schools and community centers. Both Alliances contribute actively to recognizing Louisiana's intangible cultural heritage and to restoring the value of a linguistic identity in flux, situated at the intersection of local and global.

Spanish Speakers: A Key Audience for Learning French

The United States has a large Spanish-speaking population, largely composed of immigrants from Latin America and those living close to the region, making up about 18.5% of the total U.S. population. This community has shown growing interest in learning French, motivated by professional, cultural, and educational considerations. The similarities between Spanish and French—both Romance languages—make French easier to learn for Spanish speakers. Moreover, proficiency in French offers career advantages, notably in international trade, tourism, and diplomacy. Culturally, learning French also provides access to a rich literary, artistic, and philosophical tradition.

In some states, such as California, Texas, Arizona, and Florida, several Alliances Françaises have begun designing programs specifically for Spanish speakers. These courses rely on linguistic similarities between Spanish and French, making for a smoother transition for learners. The teaching approach is tailored to the distinct needs of this community, taking into account their cultural and linguistic heritage. In states where Spanish is widely spoken, these Alliances welcome many Spanish-speaking members and organize events that highlight cultural links between France and Latin America. Such initiatives foster intercultural exchanges and offer Spanish speakers new opportunities to learn.

Alliances Françaises Serving All Francophonies

By strengthening ties between these different communities, the Alliances Françaises in the United States fulfill their core mission: making French a language of sharing, opportunity, and intercultural dialogue. By showcasing these diverse heritages, they deepen their local impact while expanding their global reach. In a country defined by diversity, the wealth of multiple francophonies is a major asset. Far from being just language schools, the Alliances Françaises are places of memory, transmission, and innovation that actively contribute to America's cultural and economic dynamism. For over 140 years, the Alliances Françaises in the United States have evolved to keep pace with societal and cultural shifts. Once perceived as elitist institutions, they have transformed themselves into cultural centers open to all, playing a key role in promoting French and strengthening ties between the two countries. Facing the challenges of the 21st century, they continue to innovate and reinvent themselves, remaining an essential player in the francophone sphere in America.

The Alliances Françaises in the United States: Social Projects Serving Communities

Alliances Françaises also act as key social and cultural drivers within their local communities. Thanks to their own revenues, private donations, and grants from the Federation of Alliances Françaises USA and the Embassy of France in the United States, many socially impactful projects emerge every year, providing educational, cultural, and infrastructural opportunities for a wide audience. This commitment is rooted in an American tradition where community initiatives and volunteerism play a fundamental role in civic life. In the United States, nonprofit organizations and cultural institutions largely depend on private donors' generosity and citizen engagement. The Alliances Françaises fit naturally into this dynamic, involving their members, volunteers, and local partners to promote the French language and francophone culture while meeting the specific needs of the communities they serve. Their social engagement is evident in educational programs accessible to diverse groups, whether children from heritage francophone families, newcomers wishing to maintain their connection to French, or adults aiming to improve their language skills for professional reasons. For instance, at the Alliance Française of Miami Metro, the Jacques Brion Scholarship provides a full year of training to help recipients achieve French language proficiency. It also funds a two-year teacher training program leading to a master's degree, creating new academic and professional opportunities. In New Orleans, the Alliance Française supports the promotion of children's literature through the annual "My French Book Fair," an event that gives students in French immersion schools priority access to francophone literature.

Diversity and inclusion are also central to their cultural mission. In a country known for its significant ethnic and linguistic plurality, Alliances Françaises organize events highlighting the rich cultures of the global francophone world. For example, the Alliance Française of Seattle hosts performances by francophone artists such as the Compagnie Pyramid, which blends dance and theater to deliver an immersive audience experience. The Alliance Française of Kansas City staged a theatrical adaptation of Amélie Nothomb's *Stupeur et Tremblements*, offering an intercultural viewpoint through literature. Their outreach extends beyond education and culture to broader social issues. Several Alliances Françaises partner with local associations to support causes such as disadvantaged youth education, cultural access for marginalized communities, and the promotion of women's and LGBTQ+ rights.

The Alliance Française of San Francisco, for example, opened the Bay Area's first museum dedicated to francophone history, spotlighting francophone communities' historical contributions to the region. In Louisville, the Alliance Française offers an after-school program in local public schools, making French language learning accessible to younger students and providing cultural exposure. As the role of cultural organizations continues to evolve, the Alliances Françaises demonstrate that they are far more than language schools: they are centers of social innovation, spaces for encounters and dialogue, and places where Francophonie is experienced as a tool for global openness. Their commitment to diversity, education, and inclusion firmly aligns them with America's tradition of civic engagement and public service.

The Alliances Françaises in Sanctuary Cities: Spaces of Welcome and Integration

In some American cities, this commitment takes on an even greater dimension in light of the local social and political context. Alliances Françaises located in sanctuary cities—municipalities that limit their cooperation with federal immigration authorities—become vital resources for assisting newly arrived francophone populations. Sanctuary cities in the United States are municipalities that have adopted policies to restrict cooperation with federal authorities enforcing immigration laws. Characterized by cultural diversity and openness toward immigrant communities, these cities emphasize social integration. This setting creates fertile ground for local Alliances Françaises, whose mission to promote the French language and francophone cultures plays an important role in welcoming and supporting immigrant communities, especially those who speak French. In these sanctuary cities, Alliances Françaises go beyond promoting French language and culture: they serve as spaces for integration, dialogue, and cultural transmission. They exemplify a form of openness that resonates with the values of these cities, offering a place where francophone diversity finds an echo in local social and political realities.

Establishing Roots and Reinventing Themselves: The Alliances Françaises between Tradition and Innovation

To ensure their longevity and strengthen their local foothold, Alliances Françaises in the United States are increasingly developing collaborations with academic institutions and cultural and economic stakeholders. Faced with shifts in the American linguistic landscape—and declining enrollment in French in higher education since 2008—they rely on strategic partnerships to expand their audience and diversify their funding.

For a long time, the Alliance Française network in the United States has maintained close ties with American universities. Many Alliances were originally founded through the efforts of university professors, such as in Houston (at Rice University) and Boston (at Harvard), a model that still prevails. As French steadily loses ground to other foreign languages, these partnerships are essential. The Alliances work with universities to organize cultural events, administer language certifications, and sometimes benefit from space on college campuses. In Charlottesville, Birmingham, and Philadelphia, these collaborations help keep them at the heart of academic communities, reaching students and enhancing their visibility within educational institutions.

Simultaneously, the Alliance Française of Seattle—operating in a technology-focused environment—began transitioning to flexible learning formats well before the pandemic, gradually introducing remote, hybrid, and "comodal" course offerings. Far from being a mere response to COVID-19 constraints, this shift was already aimed at attracting a wider audience: professionals, students living far from urban centers, and francophones wanting to maintain or improve their language skills without geographic limitations. Certain Alliances, such as those in Puerto Rico and New York, were among the first to offer fully online or hybrid classes, with à la carte modules and synchronous/asynchronous options tailored to individual needs. This approach, now widespread, enables Alliances Françaises to optimize accessibility while incorporating digital tools into a renewed pedagogical model.

Beyond traditional in-person or online classes, several Alliances Françaises in the U.S. have enriched their teaching programs by offering immersive language-learning trips. These programs allow students to strengthen their French skills in a francophone environment while discovering diverse cultures. The Alliance Française of Charlottesville partners with several Alliances Françaises in France—especially in Bordeaux, Lyon, and Montpellier—to organize customized stays combining intensive morning classes with cultural activities and interactions with local French speakers, creating a fully immersive experience. Meanwhile, the Alliance Française of Minneapolis has initiated a program of trips to France and Morocco, enabling members to improve their French while exploring various facets of the francophone world. These stays, blending language learning and cultural immersion, fulfill the core mission of the Alliances Françaises: to render the French language vibrant, dynamic, and accessible to everyone. They also underscore the Alliances' role as a bridge between cultures, forging stronger ties between American francophiles and francophone communities worldwide.

Beyond academic alliances and pedagogical innovation, the Alliances Françaises network is also adopting a new spirit of internal collaboration. Some chapters choose to pool their course offerings, an approach that ensures more efficient resource management and broader access for students. In Detroit and Grosse Pointe, for example, two Alliances have an agreement that grants students access to the same classes while letting them choose the site that best suits them. Likewise, the Alliances in North Shore and DuPage coordinate their offerings to propose complementary training. Such initiatives illustrate a drive to adapt to economic realities by encouraging cooperation rather than competition. In the same vein, several Alliances are aiming to diversify their financing by strengthening partnerships with local cultural and economic players. Patronage and donations from private individuals are critical for the survival and development of the Alliances Françaises in the United States. By connecting with companies, foundations, and cultural institutions, these organizations can secure financial support that fuels innovation and broader programming. Through fundraising events, collaborations with art galleries, festivals, and joint ventures with businesses that embrace French culture, they reinforce their place in the American cultural landscape. Whether through academic partnerships, new learning approaches, resource sharing, or enhanced economic alliances, the Alliances Françaises in the United States demonstrate their capacity to adapt. These efforts reflect a commitment to modernization and openness—critical for meeting contemporary challenges and continuing to champion the French language and culture in a constantly evolving world.

Toward a Francophonie in Motion

As the world changes at breakneck speed, the Alliances Françaises in the United States are called upon to rethink their role so they can continue attracting new audiences by 2050. Far more than a mere French-language learning network, they form a living mosaic—an archipelago of Francophonie—where each center plays a distinctive role while contributing to a larger global dynamic. They are not simply classrooms but crossroads where languages, cultures, and individual journeys intersect, weaving connections across generations, continents, and shared imaginaries. To meet tomorrow's challenges, the Alliances will need to strengthen their partnerships with businesses, local institutions, and other language associations in order to develop educational and cultural pathways aligned with evolving job markets and the aspirations of younger generations. Beyond being a literary and diplomatic language, French can offer many opportunities, particularly in technology, international commerce, and the green economy. Partnerships with economic actors and academic institutions will enable them to tailor learning to the professional world's needs, through specialized modules in business French, artificial intelligence, diplomacy and international relations, and sustainable tourism. In a context of increasingly fluid international mobility and cultural blending, Alliances will also have to open themselves up to other languages and linguistic communities, building bridges with Spanish-speaking, Creole-speaking, Arabic-speaking, or Chinese-speaking institutions. Linguistic diversity is not a threat but a strength—one that can further establish the French language in major American cities. Francophonie in the United States is diverse, carried by African, Caribbean, Quebecois, and European diasporas, and it is by celebrating this diversity that the Alliances Françaises will remain relevant and appealing. Digital technology will also be central. The expansion of online learning, virtual reality, and immersive methods opens up unprecedented opportunities to reach a wider audience beyond the physical confines of the Alliances. Why not imagine virtual francophone campuses where learners worldwide could gather to interact, study, and build collaborative projects? Augmented reality could enable interactive cultural encounters, with Alliances serving as gateways to immersive linguistic experiences.

Finally, the future of the Alliances Françaises will hinge on reimagining their social and cultural roles. By further engaging with societal issues—diversity, inclusion, sustainable development—they will remain places of community, dialogue, and empowerment. In a world searching for meaning and connection, they can serve as laboratories of ideas, incubators for intercultural projects, and havens for those seeking to reconnect with their linguistic and cultural heritage. By 2050, the Alliances Françaises will no longer be just language schools but spaces for shaping the Francophonie of the future: inclusive, open, and in dialogue with the world. An archipelago in constant transformation, where the French language continues to resonate, inspire, and unite.

Acknowledgment

I am especially grateful to Melissa Saura, National Program Manager at the Fédération of Alliances Françaises USA, for her insightful collaboration and deep knowledge of the network, both of which greatly contributed to the success of our joint efforts in supporting the Alliance Française network. I would also like to extend my heartfelt thanks to Upi Struzak, Isabelle Leroux, and Linda Witt—three exceptional presidents with whom I had the privilege of working during my mandate as National Coordinator. Each of them, in her own way, made a lasting impact through her dedication and clear vision, strengthening the outreach and effectiveness of our collective initiatives.

3. Teaching, Learning, and Living in French
Jessamine Irwin

The state of Maine is experiencing a renaissance of the French language and cultures within local communities. Although the presence of French speakers in the state is longstanding, the number of French speakers was dwindling until recent years. This resurgence is largely thanks to New Mainers arriving from countries such as the Democratic Republic of Congo, Burundi, Rwanda, Djibouti, and others, bringing new energy to Maine's Francophone landscape.[6]

This chapter will explore the history of French in Maine, trace the role of the language in both my personal and professional journey, and highlight the ways in which language intersects with identity and inclusion. It will also examine the transformative potential of community-based educational initiatives, drawing from my experiences implementing community-based pedagogy inside and outside the classroom over the past eight years (2017–2025) as a French professor at New York University and a documentary filmmaker. While much of the evidence presented is anecdotal, some statistical insights have been gathered through participant surveys to further illustrate the impact of the Maine Schools Initiative (2022) and the Intersection Schools Initiative (2024).[7]

A Brief History of French in Maine

The presence of French language and cultures in Maine dates back to 1604, when a group of 79 French colonists, including cartographer Samuel de Champlain, settled on the coastal island of Muttoneguis—known today as Saint Croix Island or Dochet Island.[8] After enduring a

---

[6] Craig, 2016; Fawthrop, 2023.
[7] Irwin, 2024.
[8] National Park Service, n.d.

harsh winter, the surviving settlers moved across the Bay of Fundy to Port-Royal, establishing what would become the capital of Acadia. Although their settlement in Maine lasted only a year, they were far from the last group of French speakers to call Maine home.

The massive deportation of Acadians from Acadia under British rule, known as *Le Grand Dérangement* (1755–1764), marked the first major wave of French presence in Maine.[9] There were two primary phases of expulsion: the first forced Acadians to the 13 British colonies, and the second sent them to France. Many Acadians migrated to Louisiana—where they became known as Cajuns—or escaped to the Saint John Valley of northern Maine and adjacent areas of present-day New Brunswick. Of the approximately 11,500 Acadians expelled from the region, nearly 5,000 perished due to disease, starvation, or shipwreck.

In homage to the Acadian story, Maine poet Henry Wadsworth Longfellow wrote in *Evangeline:*

A Tale of Acadie:
"*Many a weary year had passed since the burning of Grand-Pré,*
When on the falling tide the freighted vessels departed,
Bearing a nation, with all its household gods, into exile,
Exile without an end, and without an example in story."
(Longfellow, 1847).

Originally an important meeting and food-gathering site for the Maliseet people, the Madawaska region became home to Acadian refugees in the mid-18th century.[10] Driven by overcrowded farmland in their home province and the growing timber industry in Maine, a new wave of French-speaking settlers arrived from Quebec in the mid-19th century. The blending of Maliseet, Acadian, and Québécois influences gave rise to the distinct Brayon identity that continues to define the region today.

---

[9] National Park Service, n.d.
[10] University of Maine, n.d.

Longfellow's *Evangeline* was published in 1847, just before the onset of the Industrial Revolution in the United States. Maine's abundant waterways made it an ideal location for water-powered mills, giving rise to mill towns such as Saco, Biddeford, Lewiston, Auburn, and others along the state's major rivers.[11] The growing demand for labor in these mills sparked a wave of French-speaking migration to Maine. This movement mirrored the French-speaking migration to Madawaska, with French Catholic families arriving to work in Maine's booming textile industry.

According to statistics from the Gendron Franco Center, Maine's French-Canadian population grew from 7,490 residents in 1860 to 77,000 by 1900, with 13,300 French-Canadians living in Lewiston alone at the turn of the century.[12] In Lewiston today, Franco-American locals still recall growing up French. French was spoken both inside and outside the home—on the radio, in *Le Messager* (the local French newspaper), at mass, in stores, in the mills, and in parochial schools. However, years of linguistic and cultural discrimination faced by Franco-Americans, combined with the closure of the mills in the 1970s, contributed to the unraveling of this French-speaking world.

The year 2010 marked the beginning of the most recent and farthest-reaching wave of French-speaking migration to Maine. According to Catholic Charities Refugee & Immigration Services, 437 people from the Democratic Republic of Congo, Burundi, and Rwanda arrived that year alone, many fleeing political instability, conflict, and economic hardship in search of safety, stability, and new opportunities for their families.[13] Since then, newcomers from Cameroon, Djibouti, Angola, the Republic of Congo, and other Francophone nations have continued to settle in Maine, primarily in Portland and Lewiston.[14] This influx has not only diversified Maine's cultural landscape but also revitalized its longstanding French heritage.

---

[11] Maine Memory Network, n.d.
[12] Franco Center, n.d.
[13] Craig, 2016.
[14] Fawthrop, 2023.

The Franco-African, French-Canadian, Franco-American, Acadian, and Brayon experiences in Maine are complex and shaped by a variety of historical and social factors. Age, socio-economic status, and geographic location, for example, often play an important role in how individuals perceive their heritage and language. Educators and advocates across Maine— particularly within the University of Maine system and at the Alliance Française— continue to work to preserve, celebrate, and promote the state's rich Francophone history.

French: A Constant Connection

I learned my first words of French from my mother, who learned her first words of French—Valley French, to be exact—on the playground of her Madawaskan preschool in 1970. At that time, Maine's total population was just under one million, with approximately 141,000 individuals claiming French as their mother tongue or home language.[15] This meant that nearly one in seven Mainers spoke French. Although Aroostook County—where Madawaska is located—has experienced a greater decline in population than any other county in Maine since 1970, the region's French language heritage has withstood the test of time, with 83% of Madawaska's inhabitants continuing to speak French as a first language today.[16]

Given the local history and longstanding ties to Canada, it is only natural that my mother found herself surrounded by French as a kindergartener. Her experience underscores the profound linguistic and cultural imprint left by French speaking communities across the Saint John Valley. Woven into the fabric of her identity from a young age, my mother has always maintained some kind of connection to French in Maine. She sought it out as an undergraduate living in the French wing of Oxford Hall at the University of Maine, Orono, in the mid-1980s and again as a graduate student working to bring French business to Maine alongside Yvonne Labbé at the University's Franco-American Center.

---

[15] USAFacts, n.d.
[16] University of Maine, n.d.

Today, as a nurse practitioner in northern Maine, French also allows her to provide care to local Francophones in their native tongue.

My mother opened the door to the world of French for me. I didn't realize at the time that what began as singing *Alouette* from the back seat of our family's Dodge minivan would evolve into such a defining part of my adult life. French lingered in the backdrop of so many childhood memories—befriending French Canadian children on the swing set at Hadley Point Campground in the mid-1990s and early 2000s, and later, when I was old enough for my first job at Bagel Central, becoming the go-to employee for French-speaking tourists. Giving directions to Stephen King's house in French was just another part of the summer grind.

My first experiences with French outside of Maine were in the not-so-distant Quebec. Growing up south of the Canadian border, I didn't quite grasp kilometers and Celsius, but the forests, snow, and maple syrup felt as much like home as the sounds of French. Following in my mother's footsteps, I too pursued French as an undergrad at the University of Maine in Orono: one of the rare schools in the country offering a degree in Franco-American studies.

In my junior year of college, with the help of a generous scholarship that covered my airfare—and lots of overtime at Bagel Central—I found myself at l'Université d'Angers. In the France of Sarkozy and strikes against the rising retirement age, my memories of 2010 are forever filled with images of train travel, Erasmus parties worthy of history books, and the French children I babysat to stretch my budget beyond wine and Nutella from the local Super U.

Babysitting for French families had its highs and lows, but it made the intrinsic link between language and culture unmistakable. *"Language is the road map of a culture. It tells you where its people come from and where they are going,"* wrote Rita Mae Brown. Despite my fluency in French, I had been navigating a different cultural map before studying abroad—one without raclette, *Mille Bornes*, or *sirops à l'eau*. I am grateful to the French families of Angers for unintentionally teaching me so much.

My first year away from home was pivotal in shaping my academic pursuits and career. After graduating from the University of Maine, I returned to France as a graduate student, gaining invaluable insight into how the rest of the world perceived Maine—and the U.S. more broadly. The more distance I had from home, the more I realized just how rare and significant it was to have grown up with access to Maine French. No one in my entourage seemed to know that Maine French even existed, let alone that it is still spoken today.

Largely due to the lack of representation, the stories of Maine's French speakers have remained relatively unknown outside of the French-speaking communities within New England and certain academic circles. What's more, even within community conversations —especially prior to the arrival of Francophone Africans—the overarching narrative about French was framed in the past tense, further undermining its status as a living language in the state. Beyond the sphere of Maine French, everyone was under the impression that English was the only language spoken in Maine—which totally contradicted my firsthand experiences. The French speakers of Maine were my first teachers and I wanted to honor that and give back in some way.

In 2017, I was hired as a Clinical Associate Professor of French at New York University. I have since had the immense privilege and opportunity of pushing back on the narrative of monolingualism through my course *Living in French in North America*. This course explores both the historical roots and contemporary presence of French in Maine, deepening students' understanding of the linguistic and cultural dynamics within the U.S. Designed to bridge academic study with real-world experiences, it integrates key principles of community-based pedagogy.

The Power of Community-Based Pedagogy

Community-based learning connects classroom instruction to the surrounding community, incorporating local institutions, history, literature, cultural heritage, and natural environments into education.[17] This approach is driven by the belief that all communities hold intrinsic educational assets that can enrich learning experiences.

---

[17] Sabbott, 2014.

Bridging the gap between academic study and real-world experience is not only a logical approach to language learning but also a sustainable one. Well-designed community-based learning enhances educational engagement, empowers community members, and strengthens connections between individuals and institutions. These interactions reinforce the relevance of language beyond the classroom, demonstrating that French is not just something students study—it is something people live.

The following sections will provide a brief overview of community-based pedagogy, as well as concrete examples from my own experience as an educator.

Approaches to Community-Based Pedagogy

Community-based pedagogy can take many forms, but The Glossary of Education Reform outlines four general approaches that serve as a foundation: instructional connections, community integration, community participation, and citizen action.[18] These categories provide a flexible framework that can be adapted to fit the needs of individual classrooms.

Instructional connections involve the intentional integration of local issues, contexts, and concepts into language instruction. Examples may include:

- Using local archives, oral histories, and visual materials as authentic documents.
- Discussing current events related to French-speaking communities nearby.

Community integration entails inviting community members into the classroom in order to provide students with a local resource. Examples may include:

- Inviting community members for storytelling, presentations, and workshops.

---

[18] Sabbott, 2014.

- Introducing students to local experts in history, arts, and cultural preservation.
- Encouraging interaction through interviews, performances, and collaborative projects.

Community participation would involve venturing outside the classroom walls to actively engage with the local community. This firsthand exposure allows students to apply what they are learning in a real-world context. Examples include:

- Taking students outside the classroom to interview local community members and report their findings.
- Attending community events.
- Engaging in local heritage projects such as documenting oral histories.

Citizen action involves students drawing upon what they have learned to influence, change, or give back to the community in a meaningful way. This could take shape as:

- Producing a short film featuring locals.
- Organizing a community event to celebrate local heritage.
- Collaborating with museums, cultural centers, or community organizations on projects that benefit the local community.

Living in French in North America

This unique course pairs in-classroom instruction with a week-long road trip through New England and Quebec, during which students visit Lowell, Massachusetts, Biddeford, Portland, Lewiston, and Orono, Maine, and finally Quebec City and Montreal, Quebec. Here is a detailed breakdown of how community-based learning is implemented in this course:

- Instructional Connections: Before traveling, students study Franco-American history through literature, film, and research on local language policies.

- Community Integration: Students interview French speakers in Biddeford, Lewiston and Orono, Maine, gaining first hand insight into linguistic identity and cultural preservation.
- Community Participation & Citizen Action: Through oral history documentation, students contribute to the preservation of French in Maine, producing work that extends beyond the classroom.

Upon returning, students create final projects that reflect their experiences. These projects have included poetry collections, recipe books, documentary shorts, plays, and musical compositions—many of which are shared with the communities that welcomed them. This exchange reinforces the power of language to connect people across generations and geographies.

Through these encounters, my students come to recognize that French is not a distant, foreign language—it is a significant part of North American history and central to the cultural mosaic of the United States. In amplifying the stories of Maine's French-speaking communities, past and present, we shine a light on what it means to live in French.

Language is more than a means of expression; it is a key marker of identity and belonging. In my work as professor of French, I have witnessed how the French language serves as a powerful tool for inclusion. Teaching French extends beyond grammar and vocabulary; it involves fostering an environment where students feel seen, heard, and valued.

In the United States, where English often dominates public and educational spaces, second language education plays a crucial role in promoting linguistic diversity. My experiences at NYU and in community-based programs have highlighted the transformative power of language education. For instance, in *Living in French in North America*, students engage directly with Franco-American and Franco-African communities in New England, documenting oral histories and exploring the rich tapestry of French-speaking cultures.

These interactions challenge students' preconceived notions about language and identity. They learn that French is not a relic of the past but a living, evolving language that continues to shape communities across the U.S. This realization fosters a sense of connection and belonging, not only for students of French heritage but for all learners who discover new facets of their own identities through language study.

Le Carrefour / The Intersection

At the end of the first semester of teaching Living in French in North America in 2018, I was incredibly moved by my students' final projects. It was clear that these community-based methods had had a profound impact on my students, local communities, and myself. Motivated to continue to amplify francophone voices and increase visibility both in and outside the classroom, I began working on documentary films. In 2021, my first film, *Le Carrefour / The Intersection* premiered at the Camden International Film Festival where it won the audience award for the Best Short Documentary. I co-directed this film with Maine-based filmmaker, Daniel Quintanilla.

In *Le Carrefour / The Intersection*, Cecile Thornton reconnects with the French of her childhood thanks to recently arrived Franco-African immigrants, like Trésor Muteba Mukendi, seeking asylum in Cecile's hometown of Lewiston, Maine. Cecile's Franco roots tie her to the thousands of French-Canadians who came before her to power the local mills, and who suffered from decades of discrimination and oppression. As history repeats itself, Cecile and Trésor develop a close friendship that helps Cecile finally find her pride in being Franco-America

Careful planning and community involvement were crucial to ensuring the accuracy of this film. We turned to community members and local experts to support us in this project. The advisory team consisted of three scholars and one documentary film consultant:

- Georges Budagu Makoko, publisher of the multilingual and widely read *Amjambo Africa*, offers his experience having settled in Maine after fleeing violence in Rwanda and the DRC.
- Dr. Chelsea D. Ray, Associate Professor of French Language and Literature at the University of Maine at Augusta, is one of the leading scholars of the French language in Maine.
- Dr. Emmanuel Kayembe, Fellow for Franco-American Studies and French Instructor at the University of Southern Maine,

provides expertise in both the Franco-African and Franco-American experience.
- Ben Levine, early video pioneer and documentary filmmaker, who made two previous films on the Franco-Americans, *Si je comprends bien* (1980) and *Réveil - Waking Up French* (2003).

Le Carrefour/ The Intersection received the first ever Maine Heritage Film Grant from TV5Monde and the Points North Institute, as well as a grant from the Maine Humanities Council in 2020. It made it into the Official Selection at the International Film Festival Boston in 2022, and was awarded the Maine Tourmaline Award at Maine International Film Festival in the same year. In 2024, it won the Spirit of Action Award at Vacationland Film Festival.

The Intersection Initiatives

Since the beginnings of my documentary film work, giving back to fellow teachers has been high on my list of priorities. In order to honor this goal, I have since launched the Maine Schools Initiative (2022) and the Intersection Schools Initiative (2024). The 2022 iteration of this initiative made Le Carrefour/ The Intersection available to all Maine educators for free during a two week period in November. The most recent initiative extended this offer to all of New England and New York.

According to data collected in 2024, approximately 3,184 students viewed the film, with around 420 of these students speaking French as a home language. Nearly 60% of viewers were high school students and nearly 25% were adult learners (18+). Out of 105 educators, 98 used the provided teaching guide, and 77 educators are considering purchasing the film through Documentary Educational Resources. The Intersection/ Le Carrefour was largely accessed by French teachers but also included Spanish, Arabic, and History teachers.

These initiatives have been instrumental in making space for discussions on French in the U.S., bridging academic study with lived experiences, and ensuring Franco-American and Franco-African voices are heard in classrooms.

The Future of French in Maine: A Holistic Approach

By placing real-world engagement at the heart of language education, community-based pedagogy challenges outdated narratives about French in the U.S. and demonstrates that linguistic diversity is both relevant and alive. Initiatives like *The Intersection Schools Initiative* show students that language learning is not just an academic exercise—it is an act of connection, inclusion, and empowerment.

In today's polarized political climate, language instruction holds a unique power to counteract narratives rooted in fear, exclusion, and economic reductionism. We often hear justifications for rejecting certain groups framed in economic terms, perpetuating the idea that diversity is a threat to stability. This reductive reasoning narrows our understanding of community and belonging. As language educators, we have both the privilege and the responsibility to challenge these narratives.

Through language, we cultivate empathy, critical thinking, and cultural awareness. We open windows into histories, literatures, and lived experiences that humanize "the other" and reveal the richness found in diverse perspectives. Language education can disrupt monolithic narratives and serve as a counterforce to fear-mongering. By offering students authentic encounters with local francophone communities, we help them see that difference is not a deficit but an asset.

The future of French in the U.S. lies in embracing its role as a language of diversity, inclusion, and connection. To ensure its continued relevance, we must create opportunities for meaningful engagement beyond the classroom. This means encouraging creative expression, fostering community connections, and advocating for educational policies that value multilingualism.

The French language has been a constant thread in my personal and professional life, weaving connections across time, place, and identity. Through education, community engagement, and cultural exchange, I have witnessed the power of language in fostering inclusion and creating community. I am proud to play a part in this ongoing endeavor.

4. The Economic Value of French in Louisiana: A Policy Analysis
Jerry L. Parker

Many Francophone advocates view French as the one thing that can save Louisiana from its economic issues.[19] However, among many policy makers French is seen as an economic tool useful only in the tourism sector to attract visitors to the state. Beyond tourism, there has been little to no intentional large-scale investment in French in Louisiana. This chapter aims to advance the conversation on Louisiana French and the potential economic benefits of allocating funding and developing intentional policies aimed at the proliferation of a Franco-Louisiana economy. In taking an economic approach to policy reform, this analysis aims to forgo the question of "Why are people not speaking French in Louisiana?" and instead focus on "How can more support and resources be strategically invested in French in Louisiana as an approach to growing its economy?"

The Louisiana Economy

Louisiana's primary economic drivers are general sales taxes, vehicle sales taxes, individual income taxes, corporate income and franchise taxes, gaming revenue, severance and royalties, premium taxes, and tobacco settlements.[20] Yet, natural disasters, mainly hurricanes, hinder the state's economic prospects.[21] Parts of Louisiana are still recovering from damage from Ida, Laura, Delta, Zeta, and, famously, Katrina. Companies are consequently hesitant to invest because of the continuous adversities, the need to possibly relocate, or the low returns on investment due to having to rebuild consistently.

---

[19] Hurt, 2023; Dunn, 2023.
[20] Boxberger & Brasseaux, 2023.
[21] Hurt, 2023.

Louisiana Economic Policy

While Louisiana has many assets, such as natural gas sectors, oil refineries, affordable land, control of the mouth of the Mississippi River, and unique food and culture, it has a long history of population loss due to poor public policy.[22] Louisiana ranks third out of the states most dependent on federal funds.[23] To fix the economy, it has been suggested that there needs to be a decrease in tax rates and government spending along with a significant tax reform focused on making the state more competitive and broadening the base for the state sales taxes along with creating a more uniform and centralized system for state and local sales tax collections. The rationale is tax policy shapes business ecosystems. Entrepreneurship, innovation, and private sector growth can be achieved with a strong business ecosystem.

Strong economic policies and economic freedom go together, so a less burdensome tax system is needed to attract businesses, investments, and skilled labor. Other recommendations to fix the budget include controlled spending, increasing revenue, reviewing state contracts, and reviewing constitutional dedications for possible consolidations, renegotiations, or elimination.[24] However, none of these approaches have been effective, resulting in continued budget problems and the possibility of a fiscal cliff.

Overall, there is a need to restructure spending in Louisiana and change the tax system.[25] Likewise, Louisiana's economy is strongest when all citizens are provided the resources they need to fulfill their potential. This includes access to great schools, safe neighborhoods, affordable housing, health care, and reliable safety nets during economic trouble.[26] French should be viewed as a natural, untapped resource that has yet to be cultivated and developed.[27]

---

[22] Ginn & Tairov, 2024.
[23] The Pelican Institute, 2023; The Public Affairs Research Council, 2017b.
[24] Task force on structural change, 2017.
[25] The Public Affairs Research Council, 2017a.
[26] Louisiana Budget Project, 2023.
[27] Dunn, 2023.

The History of French in Louisiana

To thoroughly understand the economic value of French to Louisiana, one must first understand the historical development of French in Louisiana and the distinctive French culture that had developed throughout North America since the language arrived in 1604 when French citizens came to Canada.[28] Living in this territory was rough because they were unprepared for the harsh winters. They also did not know how to grow and hunt their food; thus, they eventually returned to France. A second wave of French settlers arrived in 1632 in Acadia in an attempt to build a settlement. Unfortunately for them, the British had taken control of the territory by 1755 after the Twelve Years' War. Anyone who identified as Acadian and would not convert to Protestantism was arrested and later deported. Some individuals returned to France, while others resettled in New England or went to Louisiana for religious freedom under Spanish rule. This group, later known as the Cajuns, settled in southern Louisiana and built communities while adjusting to growing food, trapping, and hunting as they did in Canada.

Francophone culture in Louisiana flourished throughout the 19th century. Because of its proximity to the Caribbean, Louisiana also began to assimilate linguistic and cultural aspects of the Antilles, which resulted from immigration caused by the Haitian Revolution.[29] Over the years, southern Louisiana developed a unique culture consisting of a mix of Colonial, Creole, and Cajun French dialects that are still spoken today. The title "Louisiana Regional French" has been developed by academics to describe the French dialect that developed in southern Louisiana.[30] However, others argue that Cajun French and Louisiana Creole (also called Kouri Vini) are separate languages. With Americanization and the growth of industrialization, English became commonly spoken in Louisiana except among Black Creole societies and the poorer Cajun communities in the southern part of the state.[31]

---

[28] Ancelet, 1988; 2007; Brasseaux, 2005; Klingler, 2003.
[29] Ancelet, 2007; Brasseaux, 2005.
[30] Lindner, 2008; 2013.
[31] Ancelet, 2007; 1988; Brasseaux, 2005; Klingler, 2003.

Post-Civil War Louisiana saw a greater increase of native Louisiana French speakers assimilating into the English-speaking mainstream society.

French in Contemporary Louisiana

In contemporary southern Louisiana, there is a steady shift in the value, transmission, and usage of Louisiana Regional French among families.[32] Previously, it was the dialect of daily life in Louisiana, used in newspapers, commerce, and quotidian conversation.[33] Even though Louisiana is the only bilingual state in the union, English has become the primary language, leaving French as a sort of vernacular.

Many things, including policy, have also shaped the historical development of French in Louisiana. While initially, the language was an economic tool for natives, today, a minority speaks it. The following section aims to provide more context on what policies have been drafted in Louisiana related to French and further investigate how the language lost prominence in the region over the years.

French Language and Cultural in Louisiana Policy

Table 1 shows 28 Revised Statutes (R.S.) currently exist in the Louisiana constitution that directly mention the French language or the study of French. Likewise, there are several other R.S. that refer to French in translation. For example, there are multiple places where there was an error in translation. As suggested by the data, policymakers have used three main approaches related to French language policy: Governmental Affairs, Education, and Revenue, where there is much more potential to increase value. The remainder of this section will analyze each of the three areas.

---

[32] Lindner, 2008; 2013; Schmidt, 2001.
[33] Sexton, 2000.

Table 1: French in the Louisiana Constitution

Code	Summary	Theme
R.S. 17: 1977.1	Creates École Pointe-au-Chien, a public French immersion school.	Education
R.S. 17: 1977.2	BESE shall develop and implement a process to certify foreign language immersion education programs	Education
R.S. 17:1977.3	After 2026, students can take either computer science or foreign language including Advanced Placement French Language and Culture.	Education
R.S. 17:1977.4	The French language, culture, and history in Louisiana shall be taught in public elementary and high schools. Repealed by Acts 1971, No. 13, §3.	Education
R.S. 17:1977.5	"Immersion School Choice Law" - Allows any local public school board to establish foreign language immersion programs in any school under its jurisdiction.	Education
R.S. 17:1977.6	The LSU board and SU are required to direct their institutions which offer teacher certification programs in high school French, to also offer them in elementary school French.	Education
R.S. 17:1977.7	To be eligible for an Opportunity, Performance, or Honors TOPS award, one must take two foreign languages. One can be Advanced Placement French Language and Culture, among other things, from 2022-2026.	Education
R.S. 17:1977.8	To be eligible for an Opportunity, Performance, or Honors Award, students can take either computer science or a foreign language. Two units of the foreign language are required, and one can be Advanced Placement French Language and Culture, among other things.	Education
R.S. 17:1977.9	Any act or contract made or executed in French is as legal and binding as if it had been made or executed in English.	Government Affairs
R.S.17:1977.10	Created the Louisiana Educational Television Authority with the mission to preserve and utilize the French language and the promotion and development of Louisiana's French culture and heritage.	Government Affairs

R.S. 17:1977.11	Creates the Louisiana Educational Television Authority and allows members of CODOFIL to sit on the board.	Government Affairs
R.S. 17:1977.12	Designates the composition of the council.	Government Affairs
R.S. 17:1977.13	Department of Culture, Recreation, and Tourism, in conjunction with the Council for the Development of French in Louisiana, shall develop, provide, and implement a program that will provide state government services in French.	Government Affairs
R.S. 17:1977.14	Department of Culture, Recreation, and Tourism shall make recommendations for improving the provision of French language services to state departments.	Government Affairs
R.S. 17:1977.15	The Council for the Development of French in Louisiana is created to preserve, promote, and develop Louisiana's French and Creole culture, heritage, and language; the official working language of the council and its employees shall be French; the council shall be domiciled in Lafayette, Louisiana.	Government Affairs
R.S. 17:1977.16	Designates a council to serve as a representative of Louisiana in relation to any country that is a member or observer of L'OIF. All members must be proficient in French.	Government Affairs
R.S. 17:1977.17	Establishes Louisiana French Language Services Program to provide state government services to French-speaking citizens and visitors in the French language, among other things.	Government Affairs
R.S. 17:1977.18	The Department of Transportation, Federal Highway administration shall develop a supplement to the manual with all symbol-based or bilingual signs that display terms in both English and Louisiana French, subject to approval by the United States.	Government Affairs
R.S. 17:1977.19	Advertisement related to a judicial process, the sale of property for unpaid taxes, or any kind of other legal process shall happen in English and can also happen in French. State and local offices can publish documents in French as well as English.	Government Affairs

R.S. 17:1977.20	The clerk of court shall employ a full-time professional archivist to assist with the responsibilities of the office; the archivist shall possess a baccalaureate degree in French, Spanish, among other things.	Government Affairs
R.S. 17:1977.21	French Acadian descendants are included in a study related to discrimination against blacks and women.	Government Affairs
R.S. 17:1977.22	CODOFIL may accept donations and grants from any source to accomplish its organizational goals.	Revenue
R.S. 17:1977.23	The department shall collect an annual fee of five dollars for inclusion of the designation "I'm a Cajun" on any class of driver's license. The monies received shall be disbursed quarterly by the department to the Council for the Development of French in Louisiana. The monies received from the additional five-dollar fee shall be disbursed solely to fund scholarships for the "La Fondation Louisiane" for the "Escadrille Louisiane" scholarship program of the Council for the Development of French in Louisiana.	Revenue
R.S. 17:1977.24	The department shall collect an annual fee of five dollars for inclusion of the designation "I'm a Cajun" on the special identification card. The monies shall be disbursed quarterly to the Council for the Development of French in Louisiana. The monies received from the additional five-dollar fee shall be disbursed solely to fund scholarships for the "La Fondation Louisiane for the "Escadrille Louisiane" scholarship program of the Council for the Development of French in Louisiana.	Revenue
R.S. 17:1977.25	The secretary of the Department of Public Safety and Corrections shall establish a special prestige motor vehicle license plate to be known as the "I'm Cajun" plate provided there is a minimum of one thousand applicants for such plate. The plate shall be of a color and design selected by the Council for the Development of French in Louisiana. The department shall collect an annual royalty fee of fifteen dollars for this special prestige license plate. The monies received from the additional fifteen-dollar fee shall be disbursed solely to fund scholarships to "La Fondation Louisiane" for the "Escadrille Louisiane" scholarship program of the Council for the Development of French in Louisiana.	Revenue

R.S. 17:1977.26	The secretary of the Department of Public Safety and Corrections shall establish a specialty license plate known as "En français S.V.P" pending there are 1000 applicants to be used on certain vehicles. The secretary shall work with the Saint LUC French Immersion Cultural Campus Board of Directors to select the color and design. There shall be a special phrase and logo. The department shall collect an annual royalty fee of $25.	Revenue
R.S. 17:1977.27	The secretary of the Department of Public Safety and Corrections shall establish a special prestige motor vehicle license plate to be known as the "Chez nous autres" plate, provided there is a minimum of one thousand applicants for such plate. The department shall collect an annual fee of twenty-five dollars for this special prestige license plate. The monies received from the additional twenty-five dollar fee shall be disbursed to the Council for the Development of French in Louisiana.	Revenue
R.S. 17:1977.28	The secretary of the Department of Public Safety and Corrections shall establish a special prestige motor vehicle license plate to be known as the "I'm Creole" plate, provided there is a minimum of one thousand applicants for such plate. The department shall collect an annual royalty fee of fifteen dollars for this special prestige license plate.	Revenue

Governmental Affairs

Francophone Louisiana has always had a hostile relationship with English speakers.[34] The cultural division was so strong during the Louisiana Purchase that Thomas Jefferson thought the state was not capable of immediate statehood. Between 1803 and 1812, Louisiana was in a trial period during which its citizens were assimilated into the Union. Legislatures eventually pushed for official statehood so they could control their government.

Over the years, Louisiana has enacted 11 constitutions, each mentioning the status of the French language.[35] The original constitution of Louisiana was in French and was translated into English for those in Washington D.C. Laws and public records in Louisiana were only in English at this time because part of the Enabling Act which established the rule of maintaining English documents as a prerequisite for statehood and required that they follow suit linguistically with what the United States federal government was doing. However, all state and local governments continued functioning in French in Louisiana.[36] English was only used to preserve laws for a long time. The original 1812 constitution aimed to keep political power with the French-speaking citizens. It preserved the civil law system and blocked common law. French was not mentioned in the 1812 constitution.

By 1845, French had diminished in status because of the increase of Americans and the growth in English speakers.[37] Article 6, Section 15 of the 1812 constitution was amended in 1845 to give status to both French and English as the language that can be used for writing laws. This was protected in the 1852 constitution as well. The 1864 constitution removed the bilingual clause and stated that all acts must follow the language of the constitution of the United States. Thus, French was used as a language of political power and control throughout the 19th century. Even as it relates to how politicians were trained, there

---

[34] Ward, 1997.
[35] Ibid.
[36] Ibid.
[37] Ibid.

is a historical relationship between French and Louisiana law.[38] Still today, many law students, and usually most future politicians, come into contact with French as part of their studies. However, they do not and are not required to study the language.

Education

French has a very long and detailed history in education in Louisiana. Since before its founding, many Louisiana natives spoke French as a first language and thus educated children on core subjects using the French language. It was not until the constitution of 1864 that instruction in common schools was ordered to also be in English.[39] This was the first time that education in Louisiana was affected by the use of French.

The 1868 constitution stripped all French protections because of the lack of representation of Francophones in the legislature who could protect them. This constitution also retained the English-only policies in public schools and required all laws, public records, and judicial and legislative proceedings to be published only in English. The hardest hit to French in Louisiana was thus the constitutions of 1864 and 1868. As education is a direct link to poverty, there was no choice but for the children to learn English or for the future families to be in poverty.

The constitution of 1879 reversed the English-only education rule and re-introduced French instruction in primary schools where French predominated only if no additional expense had been incurred. This later became a standard for all grades in the Acadiana region. The constitution of 1921 later reversed the laws again, eliminated all references to French in the constitution, and stated that all general teaching in schools be done in English. It was not until the 1960s and 70s that French heritage pride grew, and French in Louisiana was reintroduced.

In 1916, English became the mandatory language of education, which further pushed the assimilation of French and Creole-speaking children (both black and white) into mainstream English-speaking

---

[38] Ward, 1997.
[39] Ward, 1997.

culture or excluded them as participants in only Francophone Louisiana society. Post-World War II, Louisiana experienced a linguistic and cultural revitalization with the young soldiers returning from France.[40] The "Cajun Renaissance" had started.

By 1968, Act 409 authorized the Council on the Development of French in Louisiana (CODOFIL). CODOFIL was created to cultivate French in Louisiana so that it would be widely spoken again and preserve Louisiana's French heritage.[41] CODOFIL's primary efforts can be seen through its teacher programs. Teachers are empowered to do all things necessary to accomplish the development, utilization, and preservation of the French language as found in the State of Louisiana for the state's cultural, economic, and tourist benefit. Later, in the constitution of 1974, "any group was given the right to preserve, foster, and promote their respective heritage, linguistic, and cultural origins." This includes Francophones from Louisiana.

- K-12 & Immersion

CODOFIL still works to nourish and increase efforts in teaching French in the K-12 system by importing teachers and establishing immersion programs throughout the state.[42] The result of CODOFIL's work is that students taking French courses in Louisiana view French not just as a means of communication with those living abroad. This is why French is one of the many languages and aspects of culture engrained in Louisianian life.

- Higher Education

As Dr. Margaret Marshall argues, higher education is essential to promoting and retaining the French language and heritage in Louisiana.[43] 2010 and 2011 were detrimental periods for Louisiana's

---

[40] Ancelet, 1988; 2007.
[41] Ancelet, 2007; Lindner, 2008.
[42] Ward, 1997.
[43] Westerman, 2012.

French language and cultural study. The University of Louisiana System alone experienced the closure of seventeen bachelor's degree programs in French and French education. The study of French at the university level has steadily declined.

The Economic Value of French

Along with governmental affairs and education, there has also been a focus on policy looking to generate revenue. Unlike education and governmental affairs, revenue is the key area that will make a difference in comprehensive support for French. To advance Louisiana's French language and culture, clear economic goals and quantifiable outcomes must align with the political aspirations. French is a key aspect of the Louisiana tourism industry; however, there is room to advance.[44] Thus far, the only policy related to revenue generation has been related to license plates that yield funding for scholarship programs. To see fundamental policy changes related to French, there must be a clear return on investments in French. As long as there is money to be made in tourism, French will continue to be a key aspect of this sector. However, there is more money to be made in other sectors of the state economy with French.

Recommendations for French Language Policy in Louisiana

Economists and researchers have provided many alternatives to understanding that there is an economic crisis within Louisiana. Louisiana has strong potential for economic growth through a strategic focus and economic investment in Louisiana's French language and culture. There must be a strategic alignment between education, governmental affairs, and revenue generation. The following policy recommendations serve as strategies and/or policy approaches to capitalizing on the economic value of French in Louisiana:

---

[44] Ward, 1997.

- Education

- Increase financial support, grant programs, and/or realign resources to increase French and immersion education across the state.
- Work with school districts to provide French immersion options in every parish.
- Connect language programs to college readiness, school performance scores, and/or MFP funding.
- Build a K-12 to college pipeline program.
- Work with recruitment offices at colleges and universities to target recruitment efforts towards French-speaking countries; provide incentives for increased enrollments of French-speaking students.
- Work with colleges and universities to create low-resource, bilingual degree programs and undergraduate certificates.
- Work with colleges and universities to drive curriculum change, focusing on increasing interdisciplinary programs in French, Political Science, STEM, and Business/management to increase job opportunities in governmental affairs and business.

- Governmental Affairs

- Review constitutional dedications for possible consolidations, renegotiations, or elimination, and strategic re-alignment with local and international French businesses and immersion schools.
- Review state contracts and make recommendations on how key areas can be re-aligned with the priorities of French-speaking countries.
- Create a governor cabinet position specifically for dealing with international diplomacy, relations, and affairs between Louisiana and other countries.
- Increasing governmental relations and diplomacy with French-speaking countries.
- Re-build trade agreements with Haiti.

- Increase state-backed business and industry partnerships in French-speaking countries.

  - Revenue

- Examine constitutional dedications to determine if they are still a priority.
- Aligned budget priorities to allow for increased revenue from gaming.
- Increase funding and/or other forms of support for cultural revenue generators that target French-speaking tourists and/or showcase Louisiana French culture.
- Provide corporate income tax and/or franchise tax relief to local and international companies that conduct 60% of business deals and/or overall documented company affairs in French or with French-speaking companies.
- Provide tax incentives for French-speaking individuals living in Louisiana and/or tourists coming to Louisiana. This also includes a general sales tax reduction on products bought from French-speaking vendors, a reduction on vehicle sales taxes when transactions are conducted in French, including all documents, decreasing individual income taxes for individuals who can prove proficiency in French, earned a degree in French, and/or who have a child in French immersion.

By enacting some and/or all of the proposed policies, Louisiana should expect long-term economic growth. All three areas are recommended to receive policy endorsements as these three work in tandem to support and advance Louisiana French. It is also recommended that technology and interdependence be at the forefront of the policy planning implementation.

5. The Francophonie is Here: French Language and Francophone Identity in the Rust Belt
Claire-Marie Brisson

The Rust Belt is known for its resilience, rawness, and revival. Innovation springs forth in the cathedrals of engineering and manufacturing in my hometown, Dearborn, Michigan, ten miles northwest of the international border with Canada. Metro Detroit has varying depictions in the collective imagination. Two of its best-known artistic representations portray the rise and fall of man and machine: first in *The Detroit Industry Murals* (1932-1933) by Mexican painter Diego Rivera and then in the austere photography of Yves Marchand and Romain Meffre, two French photographers who spent five years (2005-2010) capturing a series of photographic portraits of the crumbling, abandoned spaces within the Motor City. While employing distinct mediums, Rivera, Marchand, and Meffre share a common objective: to deconstruct the Midwest as a monolithic region defined solely by manufacturing, innovation, and a history of erasure. In this paper, the picture I paint is different still: one of a region rich with linguistic diversity, cultural dynamism, and a hidden potential for global connection, particularly a newly envisioned connection to the Francophonie.

Rivera's murals depict the Ford River Rouge Plant, a factory where my great-grandfather was employed, then laid off due to the Great Depression at the time the murals were commissioned. Rivera's artwork speaks to the anonymity of the workers amidst the machines, whose forms stretch into an almost infinitesimal grouping of bodies that fade away into the depths of the assembly line. Like these murals, Midwesterners face the same anonymity and abandonment today, existing on the periphery of linguistic and cultural representation in North America and beyond. This is particularly true in French Studies, where the term "Franco-Michigander," which I have begun to use to describe myself, is met with enthusiasm as often as it is challenged with a sense of confusion. As Farzan Sharifian acknowledges, the challenge in identifying, articulating, or even studying language and culture stems from the fact that they both have "been viewed differently by different schools of thought."[45] The relationship between peripheral culture, local communities, and transnational cultural learning - particularly language learning - can offer new perspectives for a Francophone approach that includes speakers and learners from outside the traditionally recognized borders, geographies, and sociocultural contexts of the French-speaking world.

Viewing the paint-cracked decay in Marchand and Meffre's photography is a reminder of what Detroit once looked like as I finished middle school, graduated high school, and entered college; interestingly, the view of Metro Detroit from the outside stagnates in the narratives of its ruin and decay. Today, many of the once-grand symbols of the city's prosperity have been revitalized with fresh coats of paint, new occupants, and correspondingly higher rental costs. Only one thing continues to elude Metro Detroiters: deeper recognition of the global interconnectedness that is possible when opening areas like the Midwest and the Rust Belt to multilateral cooperation with diverse linguistic and cultural entities, such as the Francophonie, to enrich the pathways forward for a community where French, Arabic, Spanish, Romanian, Tamil, Bengali, Polish, and numerous other languages thrive, ebb, and flow at the international border between Canada and the United States.

Drawing on my experiences growing up in Metro Detroit, this chapter argues that the Rust Belt, often portrayed in narratives of decline, holds untapped potential for global linguistic communities such as the Francophonie. The Rust Belt, currently undergoing a transformative period, should be central to multilateral cooperation, economic growth, and education discussions. As a cultural crossroads, the Midwest's linguistic and cultural diversity offers untapped potential for global networks. As Massie and colleagues recognize, "The ambitious engagement of the Francophonie in favor of democracy, human rights, and peace is far from being contrary to Anglo-American

---

[45] Sharifian , 2015, p.3.

interests."[46] Indeed, new opportunities for collaboration and mutual benefit can emerge by fostering connections between the Francophonie, higher education, and the multilingual Midwest. This approach values diverse perspectives, challenges traditional geographic and cultural hierarchies, and promotes a more inclusive, equitable global community that reimagines language boundaries and eliminates the perceived *foreignness* of language learning.

Life as a Franco-Michigander: Entanglements, Experience, Existence

Few would think that great discoveries of the self ever happen in rooms with thick cinder block walls, beaming fluorescent lights, and no windows. Yet, this was my experience while sitting in a classroom in Manoogian Hall on the campus of Wayne State University in the heart of Detroit. Michael Giordano, Ph.D., a specialist in the French Renaissance and Baroque Literature, offered a course entirely dedicated to Michel de Montaigne. This was the first day of the first semester of my master's degree program in French Studies, and despite being a Francophone and having grown up with deep familial ties to the Francophonie, I had never heard of this author. Something had compelled me to enroll in the course, anyway, and Montaigne led me to understand myself in a new way and, ultimately, transcended the walls of that classroom to foster new ways of thinking, living, and being in the world, particularly as a Midwesterner with a multilingual background. The first class blended into the second, then the third, as we analyzed Montaigne's short, yet poignant, introductory note "Au Lecteur" – to the reader, penned in 1588. He articulates his intention for writing as a humanistic endeavor:

> S'il s'était agi de rechercher la faveur du monde, je me serais paré de beautés empruntées. Je veux, au contraire, que l'on m'y voie dans toute ma simplicité, mon naturel et mon comportement ordinaire, sans recherche ni artifice, car c'est moi que je peins. Mes défauts s'y verront sur le vif, mes imperfections et ma façon

---

[46] Massie et al. , 2013, p. 479.

> d'être naturellement, autant que le respect du public me l'a permis. [47]
>
> Had I intended to seek the world's favor, I should indeed have adorned myself with borrowed beauties: I desire therein to be viewed as I appear in mine own genuine, simple, and ordinary manner, without study and artifice, for it is myself I paint. My defects are therein to be read to the life, and any imperfections and my natural form, so far as public reverence hath permitted me.[48]

The Montaigneian view of the self in the world - imperfect, mutable, and authentic - reminded me of how my peers, neighbors, and friends grappled with their own identities in the twenty-first century, mainly linked to their cultural attachments and multilingual upbringings. It was the reading of Montaigne that prompted my academic and personal trajectory. Initially focused on the Renaissance's emblematic literature, I delved into Enlightenment thought. My path then led me to explore the intersections of semiotics and visual imagery in the early twentieth century. Ultimately, my research converged with Montaigne's original inquiry: the self and the importance of understanding the multiple versions of that self within community entanglements, where we are in a constant state of growth. Marie-Clarté Lagrée affirms that for Montaigne, "the self is a reality always moving, vanishing, and elusive, and therefore self-knowledge is a constant work in progress."[49] French speakers transform how we share our experiences and our existence within and outside the boundaries of the Francophone world as we navigate this ever-changing notion of *the self*.

The Francophonie has always held a certain elusiveness for French speakers born outside the officially recognized boundaries of the French-speaking world. Until recently, the United States has had no official language, and this quest for the self - and particularly the linguistic self - is often challenging to disentangle from the diverse mosaic of languages, cultures, and geographic regions that co-exist here. This quest for the self

---

[47] de Montaigne, p. 2.
[48] de Montaigne, translated by Frame, D., p. 18.
[49] Lagrée , 2016 , p. 470.

- or at least, the quest to disentangle the Frenchness from my upbringing in Metro Detroit - motivated me to pursue my Master of Arts in French Studies at Wayne State University (Detroit, MI) and dedicate five years to my doctoral studies at the University of Virginia (Charlottesville, VA). The more I have learned, the more I have discovered that I am not alone in the pursuit of understanding this sense of self. Instead, I feel compelled to extend a hand and inspire change pathways for those who still feel they are searching for where they truly belong.

At a July 2024 interdisciplinary faculty gathering on the campus of Harvard University, where I have been continuously employed since defending my dissertation in July 2021, I encountered familiar reactions when sharing my background and research. Using terms like "Francophone," "Francophonie," and "Franco-Michigander" elicited raised eyebrows and interested facial expressions as I conversed with faculty, staff, and administrators alike. One attendee admitted that it was the first time she had heard either "Francophone" or "Michigander" and reacted positively to the connections I had hoped to foster between the miles that now separated me from my hometown.

From an academic standpoint, the definition of being a *Franco-Michigander* and understanding Francophones outside of the traditional limits of the French-speaking world intersects several areas of thought: sociology, anthropology, history, and quite possibly even philosophy, yet I feel limited if I choose only one method to begin to disentangle my identity from the very fabric that has so tightly bound it to my family and to friends whose cultural lives diverge significantly from my own. The main problem with defining identity as a Franco-Michigander - or as a modern individual - is that our lives transcend the very categorizations we have created to help make meaning of our world. As Bruno Latour recognizes, we do not live in the "social collective imagined by classical sociology, which immediately imagines a form of superstructure in which all social relations would [be held] together."[50] Instead, we live in the interspaces and overlaps of culture, language, community, history, and our aspirations for the future, where we negotiate the sense of belonging and self as we interact with the world.

---

[50] Latour , 2024, p. 82.

I am a Franco-Michigander. This means I am a French speaker, but I grew up in a city where signs were written in Arabic, English, and Spanish. I am not exclusively a Francophone, either; I am a multilingual individual who has spoken English and German since childhood, adding other languages along the way. While my parents were at work, my grandfather would speak to me in French and taught me to count in a language he had mastered in his lifetime: Japanese. The blurring of linguistic lines extended beyond my own home, hearing my neighbors speak Arabic, Polish, and Russian, going to school with students whose parents were enrolled in night school, taking ESL courses in the same building where I left my paint brushes and pencil case in my kindergarten cubby. As a child, I absorbed the Lebanese dialect of my classmates, who would weave sentences in Arabic and English as we ran across the soggy wood chips of Henry Ford Elementary School during recess. I sat with my friends watching their Polish-American grandparents wrapping Gołąbki - stuffed cabbage rolls - who never thought to translate their terms of endearment and kindness into English. I have never been isolated from these linguistic experiences. In turn, I have become a modern realization of my ancestors' dreams - people who spoke French, German, Gaelic, Italian, and likely many other languages through the centuries.

The chance enrollment in a course on Montaigne shaped my understanding of my community and the role of the self within it. "This idea – writing about oneself to create a mirror in which other people recognize their humanity – has not existed forever," but it was Montaigne whose authentic reflections resonated with my upbringing in a way that enabled and encouraged me to think about what I knew anyway about myself or about others, who like me, tuned in to the Windsor, Ontario French language radio and television programming that made its way across the border to our homes.[51]

The complexities of multilingualism did not seem complicated at all in Dearborn. When I began to learn about "Francophone Studies," it perfectly converged with the invisible boundaries I saw between myself and the French-speaking world, simplifying the cultural

---

[51] Bakewell, 2010, p. 10.

entanglements that have defined my life since childhood. In an ongoing quest for knowledge, I met myself through the journeys I have made and continue to make with the tangible and intangible cultural heritage of my family, my community, and the multivocality of the Francophonie. As I continue to navigate and redefine my place within the Francophone world, I am reminded that the search for identity is a dynamic and evolving process, much like Montaigne's portrayal of the self—a reality always in flux, always becoming.

The Rust Belt Renaissance

Building on Montaigne's concept of the self as interconnected with the world, contemporary educational and linguistic environments, especially those outside the traditional Francophonie, should foster stronger ties with French-speaking communities in educational and community settings. As the title of this book suggests, French - both as a language and a network of possibilities - is indeed all around us here within the United States and working to broaden the reach of the inclusion and support provided by the Francophonie and its diverse communities will only continue to revitalize areas that have faced the challenges of deindustrialization. I envision a "Rust Belt Renaissance," highlighting the potential for this region and other peripheral areas outside of the traditional Francophonie to become points of connection with the Francophone world. This Rust Belt Renaissance represents a convergence between the cultural revival in cities like Detroit, Cleveland, Indianapolis, and Pittsburgh and a fertile ground for cross-cultural learning, growth, and increasing points of connection to other key players in the Francophonie.

This approach aligns with the insights of Garza and Herringer, who emphasize the interplay of external, sociocultural exchange and internal identity formation, where the self is innately distinctive from homogenous cultural norms.[52] Whereas I was a Franco-Michigander in Dearborn, Michigan, many of my classmates, neighbors, teachers, priests, and friends were not. The same can be said about my neighbors,

---

[52] Garza and Herringer , 1987.

whose backgrounds hailed from different geographies, languages, and religious affiliations. A unifying factor for many members of my community was the connection to the social identity of bridging these diverse backgrounds to a common purpose: constructing linguistic and identity bridges between our cultural identities to form a new sense of community. As Lave and Wenger suggest,

> In contrast with learning as internalization, learning as increasing participation in communities of practice concerns the whole person acting in the world. Conceiving of learning in terms of participation focuses on how it is an evolving, continuously renewed set of relations.[53]

This perspective underscores the potential for the French language and culture to catalyze community building and social transformation in the Rust Belt and beyond. By fostering a sense of belonging and shared identity, Francophone initiatives can contribute to the ongoing revitalization of the French-speaking world.

Too often, the term "Francophone" has been used as a divider rather than a unifier in the context of North America, where those who speak some level of French are faced with linguistic insecurity and doubts about whether they belong to the Francophone world if they are either:

1. non-native speakers of French, or
2. are native or heritage speakers of French who have little or no opportunity to speak the language within community or official settings.

This means that while the Rust Belt is not uniformly Francophone, seeing the potential for Francophone-ness within the Rust Belt will empower learners and native speakers to connect with other French speakers across the globe. Schecter further recognizes a need to "reconcile dialectical tensions between localized, ethnographic accounts of linguistically mediated identity construction with broader, more inclusive approaches that seek to account for how language functions to

---

[53] Lave & Wenger, 1991, p. 49.

move individuals out of local cultural identities."[54] By embracing this interconnectedness and interplay between languages and other non-Francophone identities, we can cultivate a more inclusive and vibrant Francophonie that transcends geographical boundaries, welcomes more people curious about the French language, and celebrates the diversity of its members.

Evidence of the Rust Belt's Multilingualism

Including Patois, Cajun, and Haitian Creole in its French-language data, the U.S. Census Bureau reports that French and French-based languages had more than two million speakers in 2019, a 35.2% increase from 1980 to 2019.[55] This significant growth underscores the new vitality of French and French-based languages across the United States. As Vogel and García recognize, recent immigrants to the United States use their multilingualism in the process of translanguaging, where "bilinguals, multilinguals, and indeed, all users of language, select and deploy particular features from a unitary linguistic repertoire to make meaning and to negotiate particular communicative contexts."[56] In essence, these individuals skillfully blend different languages to communicate effectively in various situations, contributing unique linguistic resources to interactions with monolingual and multilingual peers. As an example of my upbringing in Dearborn, Michigan, presented in the previous section, I translanguaged my English, French, and German linguistic backgrounds with those of my multilingual peers in settings as diverse as classrooms, bakeries, and auto repair shops. This "flexible and fluid use of language is recognized as going beyond the socially constructed boundaries of named languages"[57] and allows for a multimodal approach to the Francophonie, where non-French speakers can be invited to translanguage, exchange, and learn from French-speaking members of their community.

---

[54] Schecter , 2015., , p. 203.
[55] Dietrich & Hernandez, 2022, p. 3.
[56] Vogel & García , 2017., p. 1.
[57] Vogel & Garcia, 2017, p. 6

According to U.S. Census Bureau data, the Combined Statistical Area (CSA) of Detroit-Warren-Ann Arbor reports that its residents speak at least 126 languages at home, where 12% of the population over five years old speaks a language other than English.[58] This linguistic diversity is similar to other large Rust Belt communities, such as the Chicago-Naperville CSA, which reports at least 153 languages spoken at home and 29% of residents over five speaking a language other than English. Both CSAs rank among the top 15 U.S. cities for linguistic diversity. This evidence of linguistic diversity paints the contemporary portrait of the Rust Belt, challenging the monolithic perception of the region and emphasizing how its dynamic, multicultural communities should be prioritized for their potential for further intercultural exchange and innovation.

Innovating the Rust Belt Francophonie

By embracing the richness of its multilingual landscape, the Rust Belt should position itself as a leader in cross-cultural learning and collaboration. Likewise, members of the Francophonie should make educational, economic, and diplomatic investments in this American cultural corridor. Through an approach that prioritizes what I call the "Rust Belt Renaissance," we can foster a dynamic exchange of ideas, knowledge, and best practices. By fostering creative and business opportunities for collaboration between the Francophone and Rust Belt communities, we can develop and translanguage innovative educational programs, cultural initiatives, and economic partnerships that benefit all involved.

Such a revitalization would not only enhance the region's cultural vibrancy but also contribute to its agency on the educational and economic stage. Detroit, for example, has faced multiple rounds of economic crisis and eventual insolvency from the 1990s to the 2000s. As Pottie-Sherman affirms, the recession of 2008 "underscored a 'deepening' rift between the Rust Belt and the U.S. 'knowledge-based'

---

[58] U.S. Census Bureau data, 2015.

urban economies."[59] Whereas material memory of the Motor City holds strong - including music recorded with Motown Records, cars produced by The Big Three, and architectural feats by Albert Kahn - knowledge-based economic opportunities, including those facilitated by linguistic and cultural exchange, can catalyze the region's resurgence. Investing in the Rust Belt's linguistic and cultural capital can create a sustainable and equitable future for the region and its residents.

A revitalized Francophonie in the Rust Belt Renaissance could manifest in several key areas of knowledge-based development, including education, research initiatives, business partnerships, and diplomacy. Education is paramount, focusing on language immersion programs, K-12 French language resource development and support, and working groups between French language programs in higher education. Creating immersive language learning environments, such as French-language summer camps or exchange programs with Francophone regions - including ones with geographic proximity in Canada - could significantly enhance language proficiency and cultural understanding.

Research initiatives should be a cornerstone of this collaboration. Joint research projects between universities in the Rust Belt and Francophone regions could focus on various areas, including sustainable development, urban planning, cultural studies, and language studies. As trends in higher education have seen language learning deprioritized, recasting the use of languages and connections to linguistic communities such as the Francophonie would generate new knowledge and create opportunities for student and faculty exchange. Moreover, establishing research centers dedicated to Franco-American studies in both regions would foster long-term collaboration and expertise that would benefit America's heartland as much as it would expand the possibilities of the Francophonie.

Business partnerships that are already strong between the Rust Belt and global partners drive economic growth and create jobs. Expanding the collaborative Rust Belt-Francophone ventures in sectors such as technology, renewable energy, and manufacturing would ultimately

---

[59] Pottie-Sherman, 2018, p. 442.

leverage the strengths of both partners, fostering transcultural and translingual innovation and entrepreneurship. By facilitating cross-border investments and trade, we can create a thriving economic ecosystem that brings more innovation to the Rust Belt and, by extension, brings members of these communities - including my own - to the global stage in tangible ways.

Finally, diplomacy is essential for strengthening ties between the Rust Belt and the Francophonie. Regular high-level visits, cultural exchanges, and joint initiatives can enhance political, social, and economic cooperation. Through people-to-people exchanges facilitated by translanguaging between French, English, and other languages, we can foster mutual understanding and build a strong foundation for future collaboration. Ultimately, a revitalized Francophonie in the Rust Belt is not only about language and culture; it is about creating a shared vision for a prosperous and sustainable future where a Franco-Michigander like me can envision a future where their linguistic and cultural heritage is celebrated and valued as a catalyst for innovation and global engagement within the Francophonie.

6. French All Around Us: From Preschoolers to Senior Citizens
Frédérique Grim

If you walk the streets of northern Colorado or stop at the grocery store, you will mostly hear English around you, albeit with a significant presence of Spanish. This is not surprising considering that Hispanic and Latino Coloradans comprise 22.7% of the state.[60] This offers many bilingual opportunities, personally, professionally, or academically, and an increasing interest in training our young adults to navigate these linguistic needs shows an openness for a bilingual society. A quick job search reveals a significant portion requesting Spanish as a preferred or required skill on job applications in various fields, such as education, health, business, restaurants, manual labor jobs, etc. However, this is not the language I teach, and I want to make sure my students know that French has a significant place here in Colorado, in the west of the United States, or anywhere in the United States. Since I cannot easily rely on the natural opportunities our local community offers, I need to think outside the box and create situations that are as natural and organic as possible to showcase the value of French. I cannot ignore the French-speaking residents of northern Colorado, natives of France, Canada, or many French-speaking African countries. Our presence is there, so much that a few years ago, a Pre-K through 6th grade bilingual school offered French as one of the language options. The school's goals were to meet a growing need for children of French, Mandarin, and Spanish natives and a growing interest in the general community to equip young generations with global awareness and bilingual skills.

As a professor of French at a local mid-size university, I have been striving to find opportunities to make French an asset that goes beyond classes and takes students out into the community to bring meaning to

---

[60] U.S. Census Bureau, 2023.

their study of French. This chapter is meant to share activities developed to make French a purposeful language for college students, to ensure their engagement with the language outside the campus, and to give them experiences to enrich their professional outcomes. Several programs will be described to hopefully inspire other French educators at the high school or university levels to find what can be done in their locality. I know that not all communities will find it as easy to implement such activities, but I hope to help you think outside the box to create one or two of your own and engage your students to use their French authentically. I must add that this chapter is written in a more journal-like style, which I hope some will appreciate. I want to share my experiences and hopefully transmit my enthusiasm to spread French across our country.

Why Get Students Engaged in Their Community?

Research has been transparent regarding the value of engaging our students, regardless of content, out in their community. We see that community-based teaching, or service-learning, has a direct positive impact on learning a second language as learners make use of authentic language and therefore increase their motivation to use it, receive quasi-professional experiences, are made aware of community needs, and can be part of a solution.[61] I have seen many benefits to incorporating community-based teaching in my classes.[62] This has motivated me to incorporate community projects in every class (French or teaching methodology) I teach. As mentioned, many benefits ensue from being involved in the community; however, I find the authentic use of French more appealing. Students use what they have learned with people who communicate in French without the pressure of a grade. The needs to use the language as clearly as possible is normal; however, the interlocutors or audience will not grade them. In addition, some of these opportunities give students an idea of what some professions might be

---

[61] Caldwell, 2007, Clifford & Reisinger, 2019, Gascoigne, 2001, Grim, 2010, 2011a, 2011b, 2017, 2022.
[62] Grim, 2017, 2022.

like. In the middle of what the media calls a "teacher shortage," some of these opportunities allow students to see what teaching is about or how to communicate with different age groups. They serve as short internships or volunteering experiences that can inspire some to explore a field they were not exposed to before their community engagement.

As French instructors, part of our job is training ourselves to be experts in marketing, or so it seems! Since day 1, we not only have to prepare lesson plans and deliver them to ensure our students are learning the French language and cultures while being engaged, but we quickly realize we must constantly reach out to others around us to bring students to our classes. The 2023 MLA report is rather gloomy for most language instructors, revealing that the number of students signing up to learn a language in the United States is falling (down 16.6% from 2016 to 2021). French is one of the languages hit hardest by this decline during this same 5-year period, with a loss of 23.1% in enrollment. This can be demoralizing, but it can also make us more aware that our passion needs to translate not only within our classroom walls but outside as well to:

1. show our students how powerful their language skills can be,
2. share their skills with others who don't have them,
3. meet the needs of groups they were unaware of, and
4. attract more students to see the value of French.

For years, I have wondered what I could do to make this happen in my classes and my language section at my university, and this is what happened. These past several years, we have had the opportunity to develop three major programs that engage our students outside of the classroom.

Specifics of Current Programs

Let me share some examples that were initiated within our French language program. All these programs target intermediate-low to advanced proficiencies, depending on their needs. Novice students are not yet invited to participate; however, they hear about them as future activities they can engage in once they reach certain classes. The hope is to motivate them to keep learning French, as they can use it one day in an authentic situation.

- Library and bilingual school story times

Several years ago, with my French pronunciation/phonetics class, I was allowed to bring my students to the public library to read stories to our community's French-speaking children and internationally minded families. The library coordinator, who had been reading stories in Spanish, thought it would bring diversity to our community if we broadened the language offering. I jumped at that request. It took weeks to organize, prepare, and rehearse. The library expectations were that it should be entertaining and engaging; mine, as an instructor, was that it was intelligible for the audience and motivating for my students. For the final performance, students produced three stories in costumes or with puppets and sang songs related to the stories. The children and the students had a blast, and I was so proud of the work and outcomes of their hard work. A true success! We brought the French-speaking (but not only) community together; they read stories we could understand, put away their timidity, and gave all they had.[63]

After several semesters of doing this program, the public library shifted its practices, and we had to find a new site. I could not abandon it. My goal was to find another logical venue. The next step was just offered to us very organically. A bilingual school, AXIS International Academy, opened in our town, and one of the languages of choice was French! Immediately, I wanted to be involved in supporting the development of the school. Being in touch with their French teachers, I asked if my students could come and read stories to their children. A new tradition started, and every semester since then, my classes have been heading to that bilingual school to meet their children and share stories, songs, and fun! I wish I could share pictures because the events have been memorable. My students have been impacted much more profoundly than I had anticipated. The children enjoy seeing older students learning French and sharing such a performance with them.

---

[63] Details of that work can be found in Grim, 2011b.

The bilingual schoolteachers love the break and the opportunity to show that French is spoken by others, including "fun" college students. Still today, as part of their coursework, my classes choose stories, prepare their delivery, practice numerous times, and present at the bilingual school. College students work hard, and their pronunciation is not always stellar, but their engagement is. I haven't had one student complain about this "assignment" in the final class evaluations, so I take that as a thumbs up on their part! Every one of my classes (French composition, French conversation, Advanced French communication (grammar), French Linguistic classes, Senior seminar) has a portion of course assessment given towards storytime.

- Bilingual school volunteers and interns

Our local bilingual school, AXIS International Academy, has been a gold mine of opportunities for French, Mandarin, and Spanish students. To give a short background, in 2019, AXIS International Academy opened its doors right before COVID-19 hit. Their mission states, "By advancing academic excellence, cross-cultural competence, multilingualism, and social-emotional and cognitive development, AXIS Colorado and AXIS International Academy and Preschool empowers children to lead choice-filled lives and be thriving citizens of character in their local and global community."[64] To reach its mission, the school offers three languages (French, Mandarin, and Spanish). Concerning French, as long as the students have passed the 3rd-semester course and have written support from their instructors, they can ask to be an "assistant" (also called a "volunteer") to a French teacher at that school. They give 2 or 3 hours per week and follow the instructions given by the schoolteacher to whom they are assigned. The hours they give are based on the availability of their schedule, fitting a typical school day since the bilingual school is open from 8:00 am to 3:00 pm. The tasks vary based on their proficiency and the needs of the teachers. Still, some have been to help a child who is struggling with reading or math, manage a game, guide a craft activity, assist in the preparation of a

---

[64] axiscolorado.org, retrieved July 22, 2024.

school show, prepare materials for the teachers (cutting, gluing, photocopying, etc.), read a story to the class, etc.

Some students have been allowed to be interns at the school to achieve a higher degree of involvement based on intermediate-mid to advanced proficiency. All three languages are options. The students can choose to take 1 to 3 credits of internship that can count towards their major (possibly minor if they hold a higher proficiency), translating to 45 hours per credit (therefore between 45 to 135 hours spent at the school). In those cases, the responsibilities have ranged from assisting one or several language teachers with similar tasks as the assistants, helping English learners (in some cases, some who only speak French and therefore appreciate the intern's language proficiency in French to receive instructions in their language), helping with cafeteria or recess duties, setting up school performances, carrying administrative support work, and translating to parents who might not be comfortable in English. I oversee the interns on the university side, preparing the contracts and reading weekly journals. Students also know I play the liaison role if they are in a delicate situation.

These two types of commitment have been greatly appreciated and successful, with several students returning semester after semester. The school carefully trains them, and within a week or two, the additional help is genuinely appreciated by the teachers, the administrators, and the children, who love seeing the college students every week.

-Senior center and French students

During the spring of 2023, I was approached by the Higher Education and French Language Attaché from the French Consulate of Los Angeles, who shared an idea he and his colleagues had envisioned with me. To support the *French for All* initiative, French President Macron announced to "support diversity in access to French language education in the United States" and to develop the interest of college students to become teachers of French. The Attaché thought that maybe French could be offered to senior citizen centers while providing a teaching experience to our college students, as well as reach a population that seldom has a chance to be exposed to French and interact with 18–22-

year-old adults. We decided that an internship could be a solution for our students who would teach weekly classes for the local community senior center programs. This idea ended up being a true success! First, three intermediate proficiency students showed interest and received a 4-hour training from the Consulate before the start of the French lessons. The plan was to form a teaching team of three college students who would teach four two-hour sessions four weeks in a row and then repeat the same four lessons, making it an 8-week commitment for the students. The course was described as a beginning initiation to French:

> French Language & Culture - NEW! Explore French and Francophone cultures while learning some basics of the French language. Taught by CSU students of French. This class is presented in partnership with the CSU Languages Department and the French Consulate of Los Angeles. Space is limited. Nous avons hâte de vous rencontrer![65]

The first session ended up being full, and we had to request that the senior center add a few additional spots. There were 12 students, with three student instructors. This ratio was adequate since the student instructors were new to teaching and had busy schedules. In addition, we wanted to be sure there would always be a minimum of two instructors in case of absence. The student instructors prepared all lesson plans, presentations (PowerPoints), and materials with an outline they chose to follow every week: language content introduction with many practice activities, reviews, games, and cultural presentations (in English, on different Francophone countries, on food, on historical facts, on architecture, etc.). I supervised their work and reviewed the slides to correct possible mistakes (in particular, focusing on gender and agreements). We brainstormed activities that might work better for their learner group (i.e., seniors). Over the weeks, the student instructors learned more about their students and were able to adapt their activities and needs. For instance, they discovered that the senior students had traveled extensively and had much cultural content to share with the class. Consequently, some cultural presentations were left to the

---

[65] Frenchculture.org, 2022.

students who wanted to share their travels. The first session (first four weeks) concluded so positively that two-thirds of the senior students signed up for the second session, even though the content was supposed to be identical and be an actual beginning class. Because of this two-level session, our student instructors differentiated and taught the French language in two groups to meet the levels. They reunited for cultural presentations and some games. The success of this first semester was so strong that two of the student instructors continued in the following spring semester, with a third student joining them. For the fall of 2024, three student instructors from the two previous semesters will be in charge of the French classes (again described as beginning classes). Besides writing lesson plans and materials, the student instructors had to sign a contract with the senior center and our department. They had to write weekly reflective journals that I read. Student instructors receive one internship credit in exchange for their work. I am hopeful we will find more students in the future, as it is an excellent connection and synergy between college students and senior citizens who genuinely appreciate the commitment these students give them. Our students have committed to this program because they either wanted to serve their community while still using French meaningfully or to have experience interacting with senior citizens for their future employment (medicine for two students). This has been a positive program, and we are grateful for the support of the French Consulate.

Other Opportunities

The programs described above have occurred for the past four to six years. However, we organized other programs that stopped for various reasons, such as location, lack of on-site supervision, or change of school or school district policies. I want to share them to make sure French instructors can imagine them in their own circumstances, as one program might not fit their needs, while another might be easier to implement.

- After-school language clubs

Early in my tenure at my university, the only available option to send students into the community using their French skills was to reach out to after-school programs offered at several local elementary schools. I suggested adding a French club to their programming, which they quickly accepted as we offered free services. Every week, students would pair up and teach elementary school children basic French language and cultural facts. Some volunteered, while others received one credit for their commitment in exchange for writing lesson plans, teaching, and reflective journals. The experiences were primarily positive, and our students had to learn several classroom management strategies. A handful of those students decided to become teachers based on their experience or enrich their teaching experience as they prepared to become teachers.

- Tutoring at the bilingual school

When schools chose to go online during the spring of 2020, we had some volunteers who had been at AXIS International Academy, the local bilingual school, volunteering their time. To keep them involved and support the children who were required to go entirely online, those college students became online tutors for the families who needed additional support (which were many at the time). In the following fall, although the school eventually returned to being on-site, outside visitors were limited. Hence, the school asked if more online tutors could be part of the support system that some children needed. The school secured funding and paid those tutors, which was exceptional. The college students helped with French (as well as Mandarin and Spanish, for some), language arts, and math. The bilingual school was grateful to have this extra support until the school was fully back to normal.

- High school assistants or tutors

Another idea I haven't experimented with that could be easily feasible is to reach out to middle or high school French teachers and ask if they would like a college student assistant. Secondary school teachers are overwhelmed by the number of students they teach daily, and the additional help might be well appreciated. College students could help with homework, material preparation, negligible group supervision, and short activities. It could be based on a volunteer basis, or students could sign up for one internship credit. Secondary school teachers can share their schedules beforehand, and students can see what will work for them. This is an incredible experience for those interested in teaching, and it positively impacts teenagers who get to interact with college students and see that French can be studied at the university.

College students could volunteer to tutor middle or high school students taking French. Clear expectations need to be set up, such as supporting students' learning, not correcting or doing homework, providing additional explanations, or providing conversational opportunities. This can be done either on the college campus, after school hours, or online during a standard time.

- Refugee groups

Our college town does not explicitly have a refugee center. However, about 40 minutes away (Greeley, CO) and near Denver, a few refugee organizations support people worldwide. Among those, a significant portion of people come from French-speaking African countries. For students looking for a summer occupation, an internship, or volunteer work, this is an excellent opportunity to use their French-speaking skills for a positive change. One of our pre-med students did an internship and added a component to understand the health needs of the refugees better. After conducting a needs analysis, she developed a pamphlet to share with the refugees so that they could better navigate the medical field in case of health issues.

Conclusion

The rewards of taking students outside their traditional classes are abundant. I hope the enthusiasm and motivation of students of such programs transpired in this chapter. From using French in authentic situations to getting experiences in the world of education to impacting young learners by being role models, our students acquire skills that will sincerely benefit them and their future. Our particular community has been particularly generous in opening doors to these opportunities; however, many other communities will react similarly, as it is a benefit to them as well. Mixing generations and languages can only enrich a community when the aspirations are meant to be positive and enriching.

7. Multilingual Hospitality: African Diasporic Voices Shaping Francophone America
Maya Angela Smith

At some point in the mid-2000s, when I was in grad school, I attended a party. Another grad student asked me what I was studying, and I mentioned being in the French department studying Romance linguistics. Instead of the usual lame joke about studying romance, the grad student began telling me about his mother in New York City, who had spent time volunteering by teaching French in Harlem. I perked up, thinking we could have an interesting conversation about the importance of French in the United States or the vibrant multilingualism of New York City. Instead, he quipped, "What do children in Harlem need with French? My mom can be so ridiculous at times."

I sighed. He was just like so many other people I had encountered in my life. People who questioned the value of learning foreign languages. Doesn't everyone speak English? Or people who assumed only white people spoke French, because let's be real, the guy's response was actually a racist and classist view of who could claim the French language. As often the only Black person in my college French classes and as someone who had learned from French textbooks that only presented images of white people in its pages, unless, of course, the white protagonists were traveling to some far-off exotic land, I was well versed in narrow-minded expectations about the French-speaking world.

As I began to enthusiastically talk about New York City's thriving West African population and the languages they spoke, including French, and how their cultural home was Little Senegal in the heart of Harlem, I saw the look of annoyance flash on his face. He was not interested in learning from me. He was content with his myopic worldview and was not going to have it challenged by some fellow grad student at a random house party.

Instead of leaving the party angry that evening, I left it with a research project—exploring multilingualism, mobility, and Blackness in the Francophone world—that would guide the next 15 years of my life. In 2017, I wrote an article on Francophone students from West Africa and the Caribbean, capitalizing on the French Heritage Language Program in New York City to show the importance of French and various other languages in their repertoire.[66] Then, in 2019, I published my first academic book, *Senegal Abroad: Linguistic Borders, Racial Formations, and Diasporic Imaginaries*, the culmination of years of interviews with Senegalese communities in Paris, Rome, and New York City.[67] Considering the important place of Little Senegal and Harlem in my research, these publications were my answer to that random guy's ignorance and an homage to all the people out there from the African diaspora, people such as myself, using languages in creative and complex ways.

Autobiographical entrée

Years before that graduate student party, I had grappled with my own linguistic identity. I was from a monolingual family in Houston, TX, and had struggled in my Spanish classes. I had convinced myself that languages didn't come naturally to me. It was part of a larger problem of not knowing how to find my voice.[68] But I also knew how much I loved exploring the world and experiencing places and cultures that were different from my own. Learning languages would help me achieve this goal, and so as a junior in high school I set off to Zaragoza, Spain.

The stay was transformative. My year in Spain taught me that I could indeed learn another language if I was in the right environment. It also made me question what it meant to be Black in a country that at the time was very white and theorized race very differently from the United States. As a student at New York University, I would go back to Spain, this time to study in Madrid, and then to Paris, where, once again, my understanding of race and language would be challenged both

---

[66] Smith, 2017.
[67] Smith, 2019.
[68] See Smith, 2021.

at an individual and societal level. Paris was much Blacker than I had been led to believe, which was exhilarating and eye-opening. But Paris also drummed up insecurities with speaking French that were starker than I had experienced with Spanish. Meanwhile, when I headed to Dakar the following semester, I encountered a multilingual environment, unlike anything I could have imagined.[69] The abundance of languages completely changed how I thought about communication. Just as important, Senegal was the first majority-Black country I had ever lived in, and my time there revolutionized how I thought about race and my own Blackness.

When I returned to New York for my senior year of college, I was drawn to Little Senegal, which would become the site of my senior honors thesis. I had spent the last few years being incredibly mobile as I moved from city to city. I recognized how my mobility operated differently than that of the many people I encountered in Harlem's Senegalese community. As an American, I could pretty much travel the world unimpeded, but as a Black woman, I sometimes felt that I didn't belong. I wanted to know what it was like for Senegalese—as Francophone speakers, as Black Africans, and as immigrants—to be living in New York. How did it compare to my own experiences both at home and abroad? The knowledge I gained from that research project allowed me to take that random grad student's remarks in stride. The interaction revived my desire to learn more about a community that helped me make sense of my own lived experiences.

---

[69] Senegal, a predominantly Muslim country of almost 18 million people, is a former French colony where French is the official language even though less than a third of the population speaks it (ODSEF, 2024). There are also over 25 nationally recognized indigenous languages in Senegal, with Wolof, which is spoken by over 80% of the population, as the vehicular language used by different ethnic groups to communicate (see Smith, 2019; Cissé, 2005).

African Diasporic Voices Shaping Francophone America: A New York City Case Study

Senegal Abroad

New York City's diversity is unparalleled. A third of its 8.5 million inhabitants are foreign-born, and with around eight hundred languages, it is the most linguistically diverse city in the world.[70] Almost half of New Yorkers speak something other than English at home, while in the United States fewer than a quarter speak another language. Although French is not the most widely spoken language in New York City, its presence is definitely felt. That grad student would probably only acknowledge the 60,000 or so predominantly white expats from mainland France. Still, there are thousands of French speakers from French overseas departments, such as Martinique and Guadeloupe, and from other countries, such as Senegal, Mali, and Haiti, most of whom hail from the African Diaspora.[71]

In 2014, I returned to New York City as part of a project comparing the experiences of Senegalese in Paris, Rome, and New York to understand how migration influences language ideologies–beliefs people have about languages and speakers. In my sociolinguistic interviews with this New York Senegalese community, I witnessed what I coined "global Senegality"—a phenomenon that highlights a desire by Senegalese to cross geographic, linguistic, and racial boundaries. In particular, they extol the virtues of mobility, multilingualism, and hospitality (especially of the linguistic variety).

As members of the global Francophone world, Senegalese view French as an important aspect of their linguistic repertoire, but French is just one language at their disposal. What became evident in my discussions was the centrality of multilingualism in their linguistic experiences. This multilingual focus was put in full relief during a thrilling conversation I had with Ousseynou, a 37-year-old taxi driver, at a Senegalese-French restaurant in Harlem, and our Senegalese waiter,

---

[70] Semple, 2013.
[71] See Smith, 2019; U.S. Census Bureau, 2015 American Community Survey 1-Year Estimates; and Coucou coucoufrenchclasses.com/littleparisnyc

who entered the discussion when he overheard us speaking. While the interview started in French, at any given moment in the conversation, it was anyone's guess what languages we would use:

> M: *Quelle est votre langue préférée?*
> O: Italiano.
> M: Italiano? *Vous parlez* italiano?
> O: Io parlo bene italiano.
> M: Sì? Perché?
> O: Perché sono andato in Italia e ho fatto tre anni in Italia.
> M: Dove in Italia?
> O: Io stavo a Roma—
> W: [*waiter interrupts*] Parlano italiano?
> O: **Yes**. Este li è italiano, **too**. [*points to waiter*]
> M: Sì?
> O: **Yeah**.
> M: ... L'italiano è la tua lingua preferita?
> O: Preferita, sì.
> M: Perché?
> O: Per me, l'italiano è una lingua romantica. Quando la gente parla italiano, io, quando sento un italiano parlare... mi sento bene...
> M: Sì. Come hai imparato l'italiano?
> W: Sei italiana?
> M: No. Ho vissuto a Roma.
> W: Sì?
> M: Sì. Lì ho imparato l'italiano.
> W: ... io ho studiato anche l'italiano in Italia.
> M: Dove esattamente?
> W: Vicino a Pisa. E tu?
> O: Roma.
> W: Roma? OK.
> O: ... Ma *ça fait huit ans* **ma ngi fii leegi**.
> W: Ora io sono qui da cinque mesi.
> O: Cinco mesi? Ah.
> W: Cinque mesi che sono qui.

M: Ah, OK.
W: Però io sono laureato in lingue.
M: Anch'io.
W: Perciò ho studiato lingue. Inglese, francese, spagnolo, portoghese.
M: Anch'io!
W: Sì! ...
O: Un perfetto uomo che parla tutto.
[*waiter smiles and continues working*]
O: *Ah, oui.*
[*I laugh*]
O: *Tu as vu hein? Ça c'est les Sénégalais.*
M: *Oui oui. C'est incroyable.*
O: *Les Sénégalais aiment voyager, aiment apprendre des langues. Tu vois?*

[M: *What is your favorite language?*
O: Italian.
M: Italian? *You speak* Italian?
O: I speak Italian well.
M: Yes? Why?
O: Because I lived in Italy. I spent three years in Italy.
M: Where in Italy?
O: I was in Rome—
W: [*waiter interrupts*] You are speaking Italian?
O: **Yes**. This one there is Italian, **too**. [*points to waiter*]
M: Yes?
O: **Yeah**.
M: This is interesting. Because I did the same research in Rome. Paris and Rome... Italian is your favorite language?
O: Favorite, yes.
M: Why?
O: For me, Italian is a romantic language. When people speak Italian, I, when I hear an Italian speak ... I feel good...
M: Yes. How did you learn Italian?

W: You are Italian?
M: No. I lived in Rome.
W: Yes?
M: Yes. I learned Italian there.
W: ... I also studied Italian in Italy.
M: Where exactly?
W: Near Pisa. And you?
O: Rome.
W: Rome? OK.
O: ... But *it's been eight years **I am here now**.*
W: I've been here for five months.
O: Five months? Ah.
W: Five months I'm here.
M: Ah, OK.
W: But I graduated with a degree in languages.
M: Me too.
W: For that reason, I studied languages. English, French, Spanish, Portuguese.
M: Me too!
W: Yes!...
O: A perfect man who speaks everything.
[*waiter smiles and continues working*]
O: *Oh yes.*
[*I laugh*]
O: *You see, eh? That is how the Senegalese are.*
M: *Yes yes, It's incredible.*
O: *The Senegalese love to travel, love to learn languages. You see?*]

From Ousseynou's proclamation that the Senegalese love traveling and learning languages to his and the waiter's demonstration of this societal perception through their robust multilingualism (French, Italian, Wolof, English, and Spanish), this excerpt succinctly conveys global Senegality. The perfect man speaks everything, and Senegalese people strive to embody this ability. In effect, they accumulate what Pierre Bourdieu describes as symbolic capital–"the acquisition of a reputation for competence and an image of respectability and honorability."[72] In other words, multilingual mobility garners respect.

As one can see from the dynamism of the above exchange, creativity and play take centerstage. Claire Kramsch and Anne Whiteside argue that multilingual people display symbolic competence or the "acute ability to play with various linguistic codes and with the various spatial and temporal resonances of these codes."[73] This competence bestows a certain power where people, in this case migrants, can claim languages and identities that are not often easily acknowledged by host societies. For instance, Senegalese I talked to in Paris often lamented that, because of racial and linguistic prejudice, white French people saw their French language as inferior. French people of Senegalese descent were assumed not to be French even if they spoke standard French perfectly. By switching back to French to argue how and who the Senegalese are, Ousseynou embodies Frenchness, thereby challenging these assumptions. Meanwhile, the exclamation that "Este li è italiano, **too**," [This one there is Italian, too] lays claim to being Italian by speaking Italian. Furthermore, by effortlessly switching between Spanish, Italian, and English, they demonstrate that any language and any identity is theirs, and the inclusion of the word "too" suggests that this is a communal experience. In sum, they represent a mobile and multilingual Senegality.

But Ousseynou and others make clear that claiming multiple linguistic identities is only one aspect of global Senegality. They must also practice linguistic hospitality so that others can take advantage of multilingual settings. In a different part of our interview, Ousseynou talks about the role of language in his profession as a taxi driver. "Por me, è muy interesante de hablar muchos *different languages...* si le client entre dans ma voiture, je dis, '¿Cómo estás? ¿Muy bien?' *They say 'Ah OK,* ¡tu hablas español!' Tu vois?" [For **me, it is** very interesting to speak many *different language...* if the client gets in my car, I say, "How are you? Very good?" *They say, "Ah OK,* you speak Spanish!" You see?]. Ousseynou aims to make his clients feel at home by meeting them on

---

[72] Bourdieu 1984: 291.
[73] Kramsch and Whiteside, 2008: 664.

their linguistic terms. He highlights this multilingual identity by the way he dynamically switches between multiple languages in a single sentence and the larger conversation. Both multilingual identity and linguistic hospitality are attributes that I also witnessed in the French Heritage Language Program.

French Heritage Language Program

After years of hanging out in Senegalese communities throughout the world, I no longer think twice about the inherent multilingualism in these spaces or the linguistic hospitality I encounter each time I speak with someone. The same could not be said for my initial experiences in official French spaces. In my time studying abroad in Paris in the early 2000s, my classmates and I would discuss how brutal many Parisians could be when we failed to speak perfect French and how dismissive they would be if we used English. Many people have written extensively about how the French language is depicted as a national treasure that needs to be protected, how institutions such as the Académie Française have taken up the challenge, and how societal discourse has often viewed other languages, especially English, as a threat.[74]

However, in the past few years, I have begun to notice an embrace of other languages, particularly European languages such as English, which may be a sign of how global our world has become. I hear English regularly on the streets of Paris these days, and there even seems to be more patience given to Americans' attempts at speaking French. But even now, African languages such as Wolof and Pulaar don't appear to be held in the same esteem. This seeming lack of reverence for African languages is why encountering the French Heritage Language Program (FHLP) in New York City has been eye-opening. Contrary to my expectations, the FHLP has been embracing a Francophone identity where French stands alongside the many languages found across the global Francophone world.

---

[74] See Smith, 2015; Coppel, 2007; Posner 1997; Hagège, 1996.

Founded in 2005 by Jane Ross, the FHLP is a program of the non-profit Albertine Foundation.[75] It originated in New York City after Ross visited Manhattan International High School, part of the Internationals Network of Public Schools (INPS). She was struck by how over 50 languages were spoken by 400 students, many of whom were from Francophone countries. While Manhattan International's mandate was to help recently arrived high school-age immigrants acquire English, many of the families who attended the school also worried about losing their French language skills.

Ross reached out to Fabrice Jaumont, the Education Attaché for the French Embassy in the United States, to inquire about their *nouveau public* (new public) initiative. Jaumont reflected on a meeting with Ross, noting how impressed he was by her arguments: "Why don't we make the INPS the *nouveau public*? Since they have so many kids from Africa and the Caribbean, why don't we work together? I'll bring some of my funds, and you bring yours, and we'll see if this can become a worthy, valuable initiative."[76]

Becoming a worthy initiative is an understatement. In the first three months, they opened programs in six different schools in New York. Then, they expanded to Massachusetts, Maine, and Florida because of the enthusiastic response from these Francophone communities, who wanted a way to preserve the French language education they had received in their home countries.[77] FHLP has now supported over 2,500 students in various parts of the United States.

When I visited a few of the programs in New York City schools in spring 2016, I interviewed students from various Francophone

---

[75] At its conception, FHLP was part of the French-American Cultural Exchange FACE Foundation, which became the Albertine Foundation. FHLP currently has a presence in New York, Washington, Louisiana, Georgia, Illinois and Minnesota. See villa-albertine.org for more information on FHLP.
[76] Interview, May 26, 2016.
[77] According to the 2015 FHLP New York survey data, over 87% of respondents answered on the survey that it is important to their families that they continue to speak and learn French.

countries, such as Haiti, Senegal, and Guinea.[78] As students talked candidly about what motivated them to participate, a common theme emerged: French allowed them to communicate with and be a part of a bustling Francophone community, both locally and globally. For instance, James, a 17-year-old Haitian student, remarked on French speaking opportunities in New York: "Je veux apprendre plus parler ça pour améliorer parce que partout à New York je trouve que plusieurs gens parlent français. Ils viennent des pays francophones…Tu ne vas pas avoir des problèmes de trouver un travail parce que tu parles français." ["I want to learn to speak it to improve because everywhere in New York, I find that many people speak French. They come from Francophone countries…You will not have problems finding work because you speak French."][79]

While James sees French as the key to human interaction and to finding work, others focus on cultural aspects, particularly an attraction to Paris. As 15-year-old Haitian student Gregory noted: "Tout le monde parle de la Tour Eiffel donc j'aimerais bien visiter la tour" [Everyone talks of the Eiffel Tower, so I'd like to visit the tower].[80] French cultural production ensures that Paris stays at the forefront of people's minds, as 15-year-old Madeleine from Haiti demonstrated in her interview, which she chose to do in English: "I watch movies. When people are doing movies in Paris, it looks interesting."[81]

France, and more specifically Paris, is often the first place we think of when talking about French because of its prominent place in our cultural imaginary and in the way it shows up in French textbooks. Still, many students also pointed to the possibilities that Africa held for them. Fatima, a 19-year-old Guinean student, explained: "En Afrique c'est le français qui marche. On a grandi avec ça. C'est bon parce qu'avec le français tu peux passer n'importe quel pays en Afrique. Même pas en

---

[78] According to the 2015 FHLP New York survey data, 22% of students were from Haiti, and almost all the rest were from Francophone Africa: Senegal at 18%, Togo and Guinea each at 14%, Ivory Coast at 11%, and Burkina Faso, Mali and Congo each at less than 10%.
[79] Interview, April 7, 2016.
[80] Interview, April 6, 2016.
[81] Interview, April 6, 2016.

Afrique, aussi. Tu peux passer beaucoup de pays avec cette langue-là" [In Africa, it's French that works. We grew up with it. This is good because with French you can pass through any country in Africa. Even outside Africa, too. You can pass through a lot of countries with that language].[82] French here serves as a transnational bridge where speakers can move and communicate across borders.

The students' responses about the importance of French align with what one would expect from a program that specializes in French heritage language learning, especially one sponsored by the French government. However, early in my interview with Jaumont, I quickly learned about his desire for a world that champions multilingualism:

> Some of the kids speak four or five languages in different contexts and situations. That was fascinating for me. I guess it's always tricky as a representative of a French government institution to talk about French heritage, which is a colonial heritage. Because I'm a linguist and researcher I think we have to move on and not worry so much about French Heritage Language Education but focus a lot more on Heritage Language Education in general, all sorts of heritage languages. I'm happy to contribute to the promotion of the French language, but that's not the ultimate goal. The ultimate goal is supporting heritage language education in general and making sure that the kids make good use of their linguistic and cultural heritage and turn it into an asset. And I think that that goes beyond the original mission and beyond the interest of the French government.[83]

I believe that one reason the FHLP is so effective is because it values the whole student and the multiple knowledge they bring. Much of what the students shared with me during our interviews and focus groups echoed the values that Senegalese in *Senegal Abroad* espoused, mainly linguistic hospitality and mobility. With regards to linguistic hospitality, Gregory beamed with pride: "Il y a un seul Africain à cette école. Quand

---

[82] Interview, April 7, 2016.
[83] Interview, May 26, 2016.

il est venu, je pouvais lui parler en français. Mais les autres ne pouvaient pas lui parler parce qu'il ne parlait pas anglais" [There is only one African in this school. When he arrived, I could speak to him in French. But others could not talk to him because he did not speak English].[84] He was able to soften the transition of this new student by creating a welcoming multilingual environment.

This linguistic hospitality extended beyond heritage languages. James, whose experience surrounded by Spanish-speakers in New York allowed him to gain another language, used his newly acquired Spanish to put his classmates at ease: "Parce que dans la classe il y a beaucoup de nouveaux élèves qui parlent espagnol. Moi, j'utilise mon espagnol pour aider les gens qui ne parlent pas anglais. Par exemple, si le professeur explique quelque chose dans la classe et il ne comprend pas, je traduis pour lui en espagnol" [Because in the class there are many new students who speak Spanish. I use my Spanish to help people who do not speak English. For example, if the teacher says something in class and he does not understand, I translate for him in Spanish].[85] Much like Ousseynou, whose career as a taxi driver influenced him to add new languages to his repertoire out of duty to support his clientele, James's similar desire to offer linguistic hospitality motivated him to learn the languages of the surrounding community.

This drive for inclusion is more than an altruistic worldview. It is also part of a carefully crafted identity formation steeped in multilingualism and mobility. As I argue in *Senegal Abroad*, "Senegalese in the diaspora or those who aspire to travel build symbolic capital by crossing borders and languages because they position themselves in a long-standing narrative of Senegalese mobility and multilingualism."[86] The focus group, which included primarily West African students in the French Heritage Language Program, highlighted this symbolic competence. I heard about all the ways that students moved between languages and cultures and the importance of this power within their communities. When everyone around you (parents, relatives, friends)

---

[84] Interview, April 6, 2016.
[85] Interview, April 7, 2016.
[86] Smith, 2019: 26.

moves between multiple languages, you understand this multilingualism as the norm.

This expectation of and facility with multilingualism is particularly apparent when interviewing Fatima, who excitedly told me about how she brought to New York the multilingual environment she was accustomed to in Guinea:

> C'est bon de parler beaucoup de langues. Par exemple, moi, je parle six langues. Je parle maraka, français, maninka, bambara, anglais. Maraka, je parle souvent--je n'ai pas d'amis marakas mais parfois sur Facebook je vois les gens qui parlent maraka. Je parle avec eux parce que je ne veux pas oublier la langue *so* je me force de parler. *Yes*, c'est très important pour moi parce que dans ce pays c'est anglais seulement. Quand je rentre en Afrique je ne veux pas oublier ma langue.
>
> [It's good to speak many languages. For example, I speak six languages. I speak Maraka, French, Malinke, Bambara, English. Maraka I often speak - I have no Maraka friends, but sometimes on Facebook I see people speaking Maraka. I talk with them because I do not want to forget the language *so* I force myself to speak. *Yes*, it is very important to me because in this country it's English only. When I return to Africa I do not want to forget my language.][87]

Fatima underscored the importance of her multilingualism by comparing it to the relative monolingualism of the United States. She felt compelled to speak in multiple languages, both in person and in virtual spaces, so that she wouldn't lose the multilingual gift that she had acquired in her home country. She demonstrated linguistic hospitality by including Maraka, a non-heritage language that she nurtured because of her interest in communities in Mali across the Guinean border. As I argued, "Fatima's linguistic repertoire points to the multiple heritages that many of these students bring and the complex nature of their

---

[87] Interview, April 7, 2016. Smith, 2017: 30.

multilingual identities, where each language connects them to a different linguistic world. By showing students that they can indeed keep working on all the languages at their disposal and that all languages are valuable, the program is achieving Jaumont's goal of 'supporting heritage language education in general and making sure that the kids make good use of their linguistic and cultural heritage and turn it into an asset.'"[88] Indeed, as evidenced by the FHLP students' success in 2016 when they beat better-resourced French programs to win the majority of the awards at a citywide theatre competition, their ability to bring their whole selves to their education has created empowered and thriving learners.[89]

Conclusion

The insights gleaned from my research in *Senegal Abroad* and in "French Heritage Language Learning" point to vibrant Francophone communities in the United States whose dynamic linguistic practices impact our understandings of language use and identity formation. The general population in the United States often views immigrant communities, especially those from the African diaspora, unfavorably. Furthermore, these communities are often absent in discussions about French in the Americas. That random guy's quip about French in Harlem is indicative of larger societal perceptions about who is a French speaker and what French speakers can do with language. The interviewees in my various research projects, however, are not limited by these misconceptions. They use language on their own terms, move across boundaries and borders in creative ways, and formulate complex understandings of who they are and what is important to them.

---

[88] Interview, May 26, 2016. Smith, 2017: 30.
[89] See Smith, 2017.

8. Building a Francophone Identity in Bilingual Schools: African-Centered Reflections of a Black Educational Leader
Bertrand Tchoumi

> The single story creates stereotypes, and the problem with stereotypes is not that they aren't true but that they are incomplete. They make one story become the only story. *Chimamanda Ngozi Adichie*

> Education is conceived broadly to mean the varied options, strategies, and ways through which people come to know themselves and the world and act within that world. This conceptualization of education draws on the intersections of indigenous knowledge, spirituality, culture, and identity in the learning process. *George J. Sefa Dei*

Constructing a Francophone identity within bilingual schools is a mission that transcends the mere mastery of the French language by shaping worldviews, enriching cultural understanding, and fostering global citizens who can navigate complex international spaces. As a Black African-born Francophone educational leader, I am uniquely positioned to reflect on building an identity that integrates the French language and culture with the rich, diverse African Francophone heritage. This journey bridges cultural divides, challenges historical narratives, and expands the concept of being part of the Francophone world.

More than a linguistic endeavor, bilingual education within diverse, multicultural schools is a powerful medium for students to develop a nuanced understanding of global perspectives. It nurtures intellectual growth while fostering social and emotional development through meaningful engagement with cultural diversity. In this essay, I explore how bilingual schools can cultivate a robust Francophone identity by centering African and diasporic voices in the Francophone narrative while addressing the challenges of reconciling cultural diversity with linguistic equity.

Francophone Identity as a Lens for Bilingual and Cultural Perspectives

Francophone identity is multifaceted, encompassing much more than fluency in the French language. It represents a shared cultural and historical experience that unites diverse communities across the globe, including regions in Africa, the Caribbean, Canada, Asia, and beyond. In the context of bilingual education, this identity is deeply rooted in the cultural richness of its members. It is a powerful lens for exploring global issues such as migration, identity, and cultural exchange. It also provides a critical avenue for students to engage with their heritage, whether they come from French-speaking families, are learning French as a second language, or come from other linguistic backgrounds. Integrating Francophone identity into bilingual education enriches the curriculum by acknowledging the complexities of language acquisition and cultural identity.

   A critical component of this broader perspective is the African-centered approach to French language education, including how it reflects the continent's contemporary cultural context and the rich linguistic and cultural history of the French language in African nations.[90] Such an appropriation aligns with Tétu's assertion that "chaque peuple peut légitimement adapter le français à sa culture et à sa civilisation."[91] This African-centered approach highlights the importance of integrating the cultural depth and historical context of Francophone Africa into French language education. It ensures that students move beyond simply learning the language to gaining a nuanced understanding of the complexities and vibrancy of the Francophone world.

---

[90] Joslin, 2015.
[91] Tétu 1997. "Each people can legitimately adapt French to their culture and civilisation." p. 57.

By positioning French as more than a linguistic skill, this approach seeks to decolonize language learning, fostering multilingualism and global citizenship to "transform education at the school site into learning experiences interconnected with the individual and collective reality or realities of the learner."[92] This framework broadens the diversity of texts, prioritizes the learner's perspective in the reading process, and celebrates African and African American heritage alongside the triumphs of Black leaders and communities. Central to this vision is engaging students with narratives reflecting Francophone cultures' richness and diversity worldwide. These efforts aim to cultivate pride, empowerment, and a sense of belonging, transforming language and culture into powerful vehicles for self-discovery and global connection.

Bilingual education should be academically rigorous, culturally affirming, and socially transformative for Francophone identity to be celebrated as a living, evolving part of students' lives. My African heritage, advanced studies in African literature, and deep commitment to the South's epistemologies justify these epistemological orientations and my argument for the centrality of African Francophone culture and identity in bilingual education. Integrating African literature, music, and art into the curriculum enriches students' understanding of the Francophone world. It fosters a profound sense of pride and empowerment among students from African and diasporic backgrounds as they embrace their heritage. This approach challenges entrenched stereotypes, provides a nuanced understanding of Africa's diverse histories and cultures, and positions students as active participants and contributors to the global Francophone community.

Bilingual Schools:
Spaces for Linguistic Equity and Global Opportunity

Bilingual schools have the unique potential to bridge linguistic and cultural divides, fostering global competence, inclusivity, student proficiency in two or more languages, and a deep appreciation for the cultures those languages represent. In American contexts, where English

---

[92] Dei, 2002, p. 338.

often holds more prestige and utility, ensuring linguistic equity is essential. Equitable treatment of both languages is crucial for bilingual schools emphasizing French and English to create a balanced and effective learning environment. I advocate for the transformative 50/50 Dual Language Immersion model, a comprehensive program to celebrate linguistic diversity and cultivate biliteracy, cultural competency, and academic excellence. In this model, instructional time in elementary grades is evenly divided, with students spending half their day immersed in the target language (e.g., French) and the other half in English. Two highly skilled teachers lead the program, one exclusively instructing in the target language and the other in English, ensuring students build strong linguistic foundations and cognitive flexibility. A balanced curriculum with equal exposure to English and French empowers students to master both languages without bias.

Researchers and practitioners[93] have underscored the cognitive benefits of bilingualism, such as enhanced problem-solving, multitasking, and memory skills. These advantages are particularly significant for African and diasporic students, opening doors to academic and professional opportunities. Proficiency in English and French grants access to elite schools, international job markets, global diplomacy, and business and NGO careers. By equipping students with expert-level language skills, bilingual schools prepare them to thrive in an interconnected world, unlocking pathways to success far beyond the classroom.

An Emphasis on Francophone African Culture

While building a Francophone identity in bilingual schools is promising, it has challenges. The French language is spoken across so many different cultures and regions that it is difficult to present one monolithic version of what it means to be Francophone. The traditional French culture has often dominated the discourse around Francophone identity, often overshadowing the contributions of African, Caribbean, and other Francophone communities. Furthermore, schools in predominantly

---

[93] Brann, 2024; Cherry, 2024; Marian & Shook, 2012; Poarch & Bialystok, 2015.

English-speaking countries may struggle to integrate non-European Francophone cultures into their curriculum authentically and meaningfully. The challenge lies in reconciling the different cultural narratives and ensuring that students from various Francophone backgrounds feel seen and heard in their educational journey.

As an African-born Francophone educational leader, I bring a distinctive perspective to the discourse on Francophone identity. To me, Francophone identity transcends the traditional associations with French culture. It moves beyond stereotypes like the Eiffel Tower, the tricolor flag, or the enduring classics of French literature by Molière, Voltaire, Hugo, and many others to embrace a more inclusive understanding of being Francophone. It is a living, evolving identity encompassing diverse voices across the African continent and its diaspora. With its complex relationship to the French language, Africa's colonial history has given rise to a vibrant and distinctive Francophone African culture that deserves to be celebrated within bilingual education.

Francophone African culture encompasses a rich tapestry of traditions, customs, and contributions, spanning literature, music, politics, and art. Countries such as Senegal, Ivory Coast, Cameroon, Mali, Guinea, Congo, and Rwanda have produced some of the most influential writers and intellectuals in the Francophone world. Several Francophone African writers have been honored with prestigious French literary awards, such as the Prix Renaudot, further underscoring the significance of their works.[94] These writers and their works are indispensable in helping students understand the multiplicity of

---

[94] Notable examples include Prix Renaudot winners: Malian writer Y. Ouologuem 1968 for *Le devoir de violence* [*The Duty of Violence*], which critiques colonialism and explores Africa's complex history; I. A. Kourouma 2000. for *Allah n'est pas obligé* [*Allah is Not Obliged*], about child soldiers caught in the chaos of civil war. Congolese author A. Mabanckou 2006. for *Mémoires de porc-épic* [*Memoirs of a Porcupine*], a darkly humorous and philosophical novel exploring African identity; G. T. Monénembo 2008. for *Le roi de Kahel* [*The King of Kahel*], a historical novel set in colonial West Africa; Rwandan author S. Mukasonga 2012. for *Notre-Dame du Nil* [*Our Lady of the Nile*], a poignant and evocative story set during the Rwandan genocide.

experiences within the Francophone world and seeing themselves authentically represented in their education. For too long, African Francophone cultural, historical, and social voices have been sidelined and silenced, with traditional European perspectives dominating educational spaces. Incorporating African narratives reframes the narrative, addresses historical inequities, validates students' identities, celebrates their heritage, and inspires a sense of agency.

Advancing Representation and Inclusion Through Literature and Leadership

As an African-born Francophone leader, I contribute to the shift toward greater representation and inclusion of African Francophone culture. I authored *Regards sans complexe: Vingt-six mots pour célébrer l'enfant africain* [*Uniquely You: A Celebration of the African Child*].[95] This book unapologetically affirms African children's singularity, visibility, and humanity. It empowers young readers to embrace their uniqueness, heritage, and culture with pride and confidence, reshaping the narrative surrounding African children's representation in literature. I have led professional development workshops to equip educators with strategies that foster inclusive, student-centered learning environments and celebrate student diversity in French language classrooms.[96] Multiculturalism has been a guiding principle throughout my professional journey, evident in scholarship, classroom practices, and larger collaborative projects.[97] In 2024, I received the New Leaders Roberts Award Grant for *Francophone Arts Integration at NYFACS*, a project to enrich students' cultural and linguistic experiences. Earlier, in 2010, I was awarded the Maryland Foreign Language Association (MFLA) Escola Teacher Incentive Grant for a project that utilized digital media to bring the richness of diverse Francophone cultures into the classroom.[98]

---

[95] Tchoumi, 2024b.
[96] Tchoumi, 2024a.
[97] Tchoumi, 2020a, 2020b.
[98] Tchoumi, 2010.

Building on this foundation, I have worked with renowned Francophone authors—including Hashley Auguste, a Franco-Haitian writer, and Fanta Marena, a Franco-Senegalese author—to introduce literature that celebrates the richness of Francophone diversity. I also hosted figures such as Kadiatou Diallo, a Malian youth writer, and Felix Djandja, a Cameroonian bilingual school founder and traditional leader, providing students with inspiring narratives highlighting African and diasporic experiences. Felix Djandja served as the guest speaker at the 2023 Grade 8 graduation, where he challenged students to embrace responsibilities, use knowledge to transform their futures, and positively impact their communities both in the United States and abroad. By bringing these Francophone voices to the forefront and fostering inclusive instructional practices, I aim to empower students to embrace their identities and envision a more equitable and inclusive world.

My journey with the French language exemplifies its transformative power. From journalist to teacher to school leader, French has been a bridge to personal and professional growth, enabling me to engage in global dialogues and foster cross-cultural connections. This journey has opened doors to extraordinary opportunities, including leading dual language immersion schools, hosting two French ministers of African descent, collaborating with international policymakers and diplomats, co-founding a Dual Language Immersion Charter School, and receiving the 2024 AATF Outstanding Administrator Award. These experiences have deepened my conviction that bilingual education transcends language acquisition; it is a gateway to understanding the interconnectedness of global communities.

The Francophone community plays a crucial role in shaping and advancing Francophone identity at NYFACS, where parents are deeply committed to preserving and strengthening their children's connections to the Francophone world. They view the school as a vital space where their language and culture can thrive because NYFACS serves as a bridge to maintain their cultural heritage in a new environment. This commitment is evident in their enthusiastic participation in cultural celebrations like Multicultural Days, where they proudly showcase their heritage by sharing traditional dishes from their homelands. Additionally, many parents enrich the school community and deepen students' cultural experiences with African dance sessions for parents and students. In contrast, others facilitate workshops on healthy eating habits or offer arts integration classes. These contributions highlight the collaborative spirit of the Francophone community at NYFACS and underscore their role in fostering a vibrant, inclusive, and culturally rich environment that honors the African Francophone legacy and its future for all students.

Cultural Diversity and Advocacy for African Francophone Culture

Fostering cultural diversity in education demands a deliberate, sustained effort to advocate for African Francophone culture as more than an academic exercise; it is a critical movement toward creating inclusive learning spaces where African cultural expressions are celebrated and meaningfully integrated into the curriculum. By embracing African Francophone perspectives, educational institutions can give students a broader, more representative worldview than traditional dominant European narratives.

One of the most impactful ways to integrate African Francophone culture and identity into bilingual education is through literature, a gateway to diverse experiences and perspectives. Writers, including wa Thiong'o and Adichie, argue that literature is deeply intertwined with language and cultural identity, preserving narratives of a people's resilience, history, and aspirations.[99] They stress the need to counter stereotypes and embrace the richness of African cultures. In her discussion of the "danger of a single story," Adichie highlights the importance of offering diverse, multifaceted narratives—particularly those that reflect African experiences and identities.[100] Within this context, African literature is vital for fostering a strong cultural consciousness, empowering students to embrace their heritage and better understand their place in the world.

This is especially significant for Francophone identity, where literature in French, often enriched with African experiences and

---

[99] Wa Thiong'o, 1986; Adichie, 2009.
[100] Adichie, 2009.

traditions, offers an invaluable opportunity to explore linguistic and cultural dimensions, reinforcing pride in one's roots and heritage.[101] Students are exposed to literature and authors who share their background, such as Hashley Auguste's *Little Nappy: Quand je serai grande* [When I Grow Up] and *Little Nappy: Quand maman nous apprend l'histoire du cheveu crépu* [When Mommy Teaches Us the History of Curly Hair], which empower children by celebrating the beauty of natural hair and cultural heritage. These vibrant stories portray diverse professions—president, filmmaker, farmer, astronaut—paired with stylish Afro hairstyles, delivering an inspiring message: all dreams are valid and achievable (see Figure 1).

As the first Black animated heroine created in France, *Little Nappy* symbolizes dual-cultural pride, diversity, tolerance, and self-acceptance, nurturing these values in children from an early age. Literary works like this are essential tools for preserving and promoting Francophone identity.[102] Stories that reflect the richness of African and diasporic experiences challenge stereotypes, affirm cultural pride, and inspire young readers to see themselves as integral to the Francophone world. These texts are transformative in their ability to strengthen connections to students' heritage while cultivating a global perspective, making them invaluable for the future of Francophone culture.

---

[101] This perspective is exemplified by works like *The Dark Child* by C. Laye 1954., *So Long a Letter* by M. Bâ 1981, and *Comme un million de papillons* [*Like a Million Black Butterflies*] by L. Nsafou 2017, a poetic celebration of self-love and healing, served as a catalyst, raising awareness of the lack of racial diversity in French children's literature.

[102] In the same vein, F. Marena's 2020. *Naturelle et Heureuse!* [*Natural and Happy*] champions the embrace of natural beauty and self-confidence. Both authors share a similar motto: Hashley's character, Little Nappy, embodies "Natural and Happy," while Fanta Marena's motto is the French equivalent, "Naturelle et Heureuse."

> **Je peux tout accomplir**
> *I can accomplish anything.*
> **Je suis fort(e)**
> *I am strong.*
> **Je suis courageux(se)**
> *I am courageous.*
> **J'ai le droit d'être moi-même**
> *I have the right to be myself.*
> **Je m'aime comme je suis**
> *I love myself as I am.*
> **Ma différence est ma richesse**
> *My difference is my wealth.*

Figure 1: *List of Six Affirmations.* Hashley Auguste developed these affirmations and read them to students during her workshop at NYFACS. They are also displayed in French immersion classrooms, serving as a resource to reinforce cultural pride and inclusivity in the learning environment.

Equally transformative is the inclusion of resources like Adinkra. This digital platform addresses critical issues of identity and representation by offering digital children's books featuring African characters and promoting African culture through the lens of African history. This initiative complements the works of African Francophone authors by fostering a sense of pride and belonging among students while helping them connect with their roots. Together, these literary resources celebrate students' uniqueness and humanity and challenge a world that too often marginalizes their stories.

Music, films, and dance from Francophone African countries preserve the continent's cultural heritage while telling powerful stories that connect individuals across generations and geographies, making them invaluable tools for education and cultural advocacy. For example, students might delve into the rich symbolism of Adinkra patterns from Ghana, uncover the wisdom preserved through the oral storytelling traditions of West African griots, or examine the profound contributions of African leaders to global history. During Black History Month celebrations, Francophone historical and contemporary figures take center stage, showcasing the enduring impact of Francophone Africans across history and into the present day. Classroom discussions can delve into themes of identity, community, and resilience, as portrayed in African Francophone works, encouraging students to analyze critically and appreciate diverse cultural perspectives.

Films can also exemplify the power of storytelling to inspire and educate. Based on the true story of William Kamkwamba, *The Boy Who Harnessed the Wind* portrays a Malawian boy's ingenuity in building a windmill to save his village from famine, highlighting themes of resilience and innovation.[103] Similarly, *La Petite Vendeuse de Soleil* [*The Little Girl Who Sold the Sun*], directed by Diop Mambéty (1999), tells the story of Sili, a young paraplegic girl and beggar in Dakar, who overcomes societal barriers to become a newspaper vendor, showcasing themes of determination and equality. These films connect students with narratives of empowerment and provide a deeper understanding of African ingenuity and resilience. Incorporating such works into educational settings broadens students' global perspectives and encourages critical thinking about the challenges and triumphs of the African experience.

Hands-on encounters with African music and dance help foster a deeper appreciation for the Francophone world's cultural richness while promoting creative expression and an immersive cross-cultural opportunity to engage with diverse traditions that reinforce Francophone identity. At NYFACS, Yahaya Kabore, a master drummer from Burkina Faso, and the talented dancer Yacouba Badolo led an interactive cultural session, sharing the rich history and cultural significance of traditional drumming and its vibrant dances. Through this session, students explored the rich cultural context and engaged actively by participating in drumming and dancing, transforming the experience into a dynamic educational journey. Before Kabore's visit, Nkumu Katalay, an accomplished Congolese drummer, had led NYFACS's after-school drum classes for several years, providing

---

[103] Kamkwamba, 2009.

students with ongoing opportunities to connect with African rhythmic traditions. These performing arts initiatives complement and amplify NYFACS's broader efforts to integrate Francophone arts into the curriculum.

To extend these efforts, bilingual schools can host cultural events that bring African traditions to life to foster a sense of inclusion and belonging. An inclusive curriculum must reflect the narratives and experiences of Francophone communities worldwide. By exposing students to the literature, history, and art of regions like Senegal, Haiti, Morocco, and the Democratic Republic of Congo, alongside France, bilingual education enables students to appreciate the interconnectedness of the Francophone world. They gain insight into the values, struggles, and triumphs that define this global community, equipping them with the cultural competence and critical perspective to navigate an increasingly interconnected world.

Through these deliberate and multifaceted efforts, educational institutions can celebrate African Francophone culture meaningfully, bridging cultural divides and empowering students to embrace diversity as a strength and asset. By integrating literature, arts, and cultural events into the curriculum, schools ensure that African Francophone voices and traditions are visible and deeply valued, allowing students from diverse backgrounds to see themselves reflected in their education and the richness of a global community. These initiatives foster empathy, understanding, and respect and prepare all students to thrive in a globalized world. In celebrating African Francophone culture, programming at NYFACS shifts the narrative from marginalization to empowerment, ensuring that students recognize the value of their heritage in their education and the world.

Francophone Identity Integration for African and Diasporic Students

For African and diasporic students, integrating into a bilingual school that emphasizes Francophone identity can be both empowering and challenging. Schools can implement various strategies to support these students and foster a deeper connection to their bilingual education.

Building Identity and Belonging
Through Culturally Aligned Educators

Hiring educators and administrators who share their students' cultural backgrounds is crucial for ensuring cultural and identity congruency, which helps students feel understood and valued. For Francophone students in a bilingual program, in particular, having educators who understand the language and cultural context of their experiences fosters academic success and social-emotional well-being. These educators can serve as cultural translators and role models, positively influencing students' academic expectations and aspirations.[104] As I discussed in my works,[105] cultural congruency in leadership is not just symbolic; it has tangible benefits. Minority leaders who empathize with students' lived experiences can shape their academic perspectives, reinforcing the importance of seeing leaders with similar cultural experiences. This connection is compelling for Francophone students, who benefit from seeing their linguistic and cultural heritage reflected in the classroom, strengthening their sense of identity and belonging.

When such culturally congruent educators are unavailable, teachers and administrators need to challenge preconceived notions and embrace students' cultural differences as assets. This unlearning process ensures that educators view students' cultural diversity through a positive lens rather than as deficits. Additionally, hiring administrators who share the cultural experiences of their students fosters trust, mutual respect, and alignment between school climate, curriculum, and policies. Diverse leadership can improve the school community's culture and student achievement, as minority leaders often act as change agents to disrupt inequities and drive positive change.[106] Ensuring diverse leadership is crucial for creating an inclusive and equitable educational environment for all students, especially Francophone students who face unique challenges related to cultural representation.

---

[104] Sanchez et al., 2009; Williams & Loeb, 2012.
[105] Tchoumi, 2020a, 2020b.
[106] Dantley, 2009; Loebe, 2004.

Fostering Identity and Inclusion with Culturally Relevant Learning Materials

Instructional materials must reflect students' diverse cultures and identities to promote an inclusive learning environment. This is rooted in Ladson Billings' conceptualization of culturally relevant pedagogy, a framework that bridges cultural identity and academic success.[107] Textbooks, literature, multimedia resources, and classroom activities should represent various cultural perspectives, particularly those of African and diasporic students. This ensures that students see themselves in their learning materials, fostering a sense of pride and belonging. Culturally relevant instructional materials empower students to make connections between their personal experiences and academic content, improving engagement and motivation. They also positively impact students' "self-esteem, socio-emotional well-being, empathy, and a greater appreciation for cultural differences."[108]

In addition to the academic and non-academic benefits highlighted above, the representation of diverse identities in educational materials plays a pivotal role in shaping how students view themselves and the world around them.[109] This underscores the significance of educators' choices in the materials they select and the message they convey about identity, belonging, abilities, and potential. Educators must strive to move beyond a one-size-fits-all approach and instead tailor teaching methods to reflect their students' varied backgrounds and experiences. By integrating culturally relevant materials and practices into everyday instruction, educators validate students' identities, sense of self-worth, and cultural pride while fostering an environment that values and honors diversity.

---

[107] Billings, 1995.
[108] Reed Marshall & Rodick, 2023, p. 4.
[109] Adukia, 2024, as cited in Brannon, 2024.

Honoring Home Languages in Schools

Valuing students' native language development has deep roots in educational research. The Intercultural Development Research Association [110] argues that maintaining a child's first language is critical to their identity and contributes to a positive self-concept related to culture. Minority children succeed when their native language is valued and developed.[111] Effective schools encourage the active use and development of students' home languages in academic and social contexts, creating a sense of belonging and promoting success.

NYFACS implements these research-based practices by fostering an environment where students feel comfortable speaking their home languages with teachers and peers. This supports their identity and promotes acceptance within the community. We also provide language support during math testing in students' home languages, ensuring equitable access to learning and assessment. Initiatives like NYFACS' Multilingual New Year Wishes, where students send greetings in their home languages, celebrate linguistic and cultural richness. The 2025 edition showcases the vibrant diversity within our community, reinforcing multilingualism as a cornerstone of Francophone identity. NYFACS supports academic success by valuing home languages and nurtures a globally aware school community.

Engaging in Culturally Enriching Activities

Bilingual schools are vital in celebrating African and diasporic cultures through dynamic, creative events. Activities like multicultural days, National French Week, African dance performances, and poetry slams allow students to explore their identities and appreciate their heritage. In celebration of Black History Month 2025, NYFACS students, in collaboration with schools in Ontario, Canada, participated in two webinar workshops on creative writing led by Yao, a renowned Canadian slam poet and musician born in Côte d'Ivoire. The

---

[110] IDRA, 2000.
[111] Hamayan et al., 2013.

workshops, themed *Ce que nous apportons, ce que nous transmettons*, encouraged students to explore self-expression through poetry. Yao will curate and weave together powerful sentences from students' work into a collective slam piece. This initiative provides students with a meaningful platform to share their voices, exchange perspectives, and celebrate African Francophone excellence through spoken word. They will also develop poetry techniques while engaging with themes of identity and heritage. By fostering artistic expression and cross-cultural collaboration, this project highlights how the creative arts can unite communities and inspire students to embrace diversity as a strength.

Inspiring Students Through Francophone Authors-in-Residence

Bringing authors from African and European Francophone communities into schools provides invaluable opportunities for students to engage with diverse Francophone voices' stories, experiences, and histories. Authors share cultural contexts and creative processes behind their works through workshops, book discussions, and meet-and-greet events, enriching students' education and inspiring critical and empathetic thinking. At NYFACS, the partnership with Made in France has allowed the school to host renowned European Francophone authors and illustrators, collectively known as *Les Troubadours*. These modern troubadours—Andrée Prigent, Orianne Lallemand, Éléonore Thuillier, Alex Cousseau, and Hervé Le Goff—have brought their unique artistic perspectives to life in interactive sessions with students. Events featuring authors such as Clotilde Perrin, Édouard Manceau, Philippe Lechermeier, and Sylvie Joseph-Julien exposed students to diverse literary styles and themes. Similarly, collaborations with African Francophone authors, including Kadiatou Diallo, a Malian youth writer, and Felix Djandja, an award-winning Cameroonian author, have amplified Francophone voices that resonate deeply with African and diasporic experiences. These initiatives deepen students' understanding of the Francophone world, inspire creativity, and emphasize the importance of diversity and representation in literature.

Building Bridges Across Borders

Partnering with schools in Francophone African countries and other regions fosters cultural exchanges that enrich students' global perspectives. These collaborations allow students to work on shared projects, exchange ideas, and gain insights into each other's cultural and historical contexts. In Spring 2023, NYFACS hosted students from Ma Aiye Middle School in Apatou, French Guiana. These students performed *aluku,* a traditional dance of the Aluku people, and engaged in discussions about their heritage and Francophone identity. Such exchanges broaden cultural horizons, promote dialogue, and highlight the value of global connectivity in education.[112]

Cultural Immersion and Community Engagement

To build a strong Francophone identity, schools should integrate academics with cultural exploration and offer meaningful opportunities for students to immerse themselves in the Francophone world:

- Cultural Activities: Students immerse themselves in the language and culture through visits to museums, Francophone festivals, French libraries and bookstores, theaters, and science fairs in Francophone countries—either in person or through virtual tours.
- African Francophone Cuisine: Schools can introduce students to African dishes from the Francophone world through cooking classes and potluck events. Potlucks, organized with the support of families, can be held before or after major civil or religious holidays, creating a communal celebration of culinary heritage.

---

[112] At the time of writing, NYFACS is establishing a partnership with Auxence Contout Middle School in Cayenne, French Guiana, set to begin in September 2025. This collaboration will connect students through written and video exchanges in the first year, followed by a weeklong student visit to NYFACS in the second year, fostering Francophone identity and global cultural ties.

- Freedom of Dress: Schools can encourage inclusivity by allowing students to wear traditional attire from their culture. Cultural dress days during Spirit Weeks or dedicated fashion shows offer students opportunities to share their heritage with peers proudly.
- Collaboration with Families: Engaging families in cultural activities and providing educational resources strengthens the sense of community and supports students' Francophone identity.
- Travel Abroad Programs: Offering opportunities for students to visit Francophone countries enhances their linguistic skills and cultural awareness. These trips could include homestays, school partnerships, cultural tours, and language immersion experiences. Travel abroad programs allow students to experience everyday life in a Francophone context, deepening their understanding of the language, customs, and traditions.

These strategies create an enriching school environment where students are empowered to connect with their Francophone heritage, build global competence, and embrace their identities as part of a vibrant international community.

Conclusion

Building a Francophone identity in bilingual schools requires intentionality, creativity, and a commitment to honoring the diversity of Francophone cultures. As a Black African-born Francophone educational leader, I have witnessed how language and culture intersect to shape students' academic journeys and their sense of self and belonging. This essay reflects on the strategies, partnerships, and initiatives that foster a vibrant Francophone identity within bilingual schools, emphasizing the need for inclusivity, representation, and celebration of the wealth of African and diasporic contributions to the Francophone world. Through cultural exchanges, immersive experiences, and the integration of diverse narratives, bilingual schools can become spaces where students are empowered to engage with a global Francophone community.

Sustaining and expanding bilingual programs presents opportunities and challenges, requiring thoughtful approaches to ensure long-term success. Policy reforms that prioritize bilingual education funding and advocacy for including African and diasporic Francophone narratives in curricula are critical steps toward addressing gaps in representation and accessibility. Equally important are partnership models that leverage community resources, engage local stakeholders, and build bridges between schools, cultural organizations, and Francophone leaders. By fostering collaboration and maintaining a focus on equity and cultural authenticity, bilingual programs can continue to thrive, nurturing generations of students who are proud of their identities and prepared to contribute to a diverse and interconnected world.

Looking toward the future, the role of bilingual schools in shaping Francophone identity is more critical than ever. By creating environments where African and diasporic voices are visible and celebrated, educators enrich students' educational experiences and affirm the importance of inclusion and representation in building resilient, interconnected communities. This work is a testament to the profound impact that education can have in shaping a more equitable and culturally responsive world—one student, one story, and one celebration at a time.

9. Weaving Haitian Roots into the U.S. Francophonie: A Personal Journey
Elcie Douce

I grew up in Port-au-Prince, where I attended Catholic school from kindergarten through 12th grade. In my school, French was the primary language of instruction, and speaking Haitian -Creole was strictly prohibited. Consequently, French became my dominant language for communication, while my connection to Haitian culture was nurtured at home and in my community. This dual exposure gave me a rich, blended perspective of French and Haitian cultures, shaping my identity and worldview. In 1997, I moved to the United States to join my husband and complete my university studies. Inspired by my linguistic and cultural background, I pursued a career in education and earned my French teaching license in 2004. Since then, I have taught French to both English speakers and Heritage French speakers. This role has allowed me to share my language and culture with students while expanding my understanding of the Francophone world. Through teaching, I have deepened my appreciation for the diversity of French-speaking countries and cultures, connecting my Haitian roots to a broader global context. Bilingualism has enriched my personal life and opened up professional opportunities, demonstrating the value of language in personal and professional growth.

Living in the U.S. has further enriched my relationship with Franco-Haitian culture and created the need to cherish and nurture it. Engaging with Haitian communities, participating in cultural events, and maintaining traditions—such as cooking Haitian dishes, which are a mixture of African, Spanish, and French cuisine, and celebrating essential holidays—have helped me preserve my heritage while integrating into a multicultural society. These experiences have strengthened my ability to celebrate and navigate the intersection of my Haitian and Francophone identities personally and professionally. The Haitian immigrant population in the U.S., concentrated in areas like

Florida and New York and neighborhoods like Miami's Little Haiti and Brooklyn in New York, plays a vital role in preserving and evolving Haitian cultural and linguistic identities. Their connectedness and ongoing cultural evolvement have been crucial in maintaining connections between folks living inside and outside Haiti. Since moving to the U.S., I have lived on Long Island, but I frequently attend church in Brooklyn, where services are conducted in French, Haitian Creole, and English. This multilingual environment has been instrumental in shaping my identity, providing a space where cultural and linguistic traditions are celebrated and shared.

Spending time with fellow Haitians and Haitian Americans has deepened my connection to my roots. Culturally, I have bonded with Haitian traditions through music, dance, and literature. Linguistically, I have expanded my ability to navigate between French, Haitian Creole, and English, often blending the languages to communicate in diverse settings. These interactions have enriched my ability to express myself and strengthened my sense of belonging within the diaspora, fostering a sense of unity and shared cultural narrative among us all. Brooklyn's Haitian community has also made it easy to access essential cultural elements, such as ingredients for iconic dishes like Soup Joumou (Squash soup) and Diri ak Djon Djon (black mushroom rice), as well as French-inspired pastries like tarte à l'oignon (Ognon pie). Traditional remedies like lwil maskreti (castor oil) and unforgettable delicacies like kassav (cassava bread) are readily available, further connecting me to the cultural practices I grew up with. For the broader Haitian diaspora, these tight-knit communities serve as hubs for cultural preservation and innovation. They allow immigrants to maintain their heritage while adapting to life in the U.S., creating a dynamic interplay between tradition and modernity. These spaces keep Haitian culture alive and enrich it through interaction with other cultures, strengthening the diaspora's identity and fostering a sense of unity among Haitians worldwide.

The Haitian community is pivotal in preserving and promoting the French language and culture within the broader U.S. Francophonie. Haitians emphasize passing on the French language to the next generation, encouraging their children to learn French as a World

Language in schools and through community programs. This effort ensures that Haitian Americans maintain a connection to their roots while contributing to the broader Francophone landscape in the United States. The community's active advocacy for the importance of French and its historical and cultural significance is a source of pride and inspiration for us all. What sets Haitian cultural, linguistic, and social dimensions apart is the unique identity shaped by Haiti's history as the first Black independent nation. Haitian culture reflects a rich blend of African, French, Spanish, and Indigenous influences, creating a distinctive Francophone identity. This multifaceted heritage is expressed in vibrant music, dance, literature, and cuisine, reflecting Haiti's diverse roots while maintaining strong ties to the French-speaking world. At the same time, the Haitian community intersects with other Francophone communities in shared linguistic and cultural spaces. Events, organizations, and institutions celebrating the French language often unite Haitians and Francophones, fostering collaboration and mutual appreciation. However, the Haitian community's unique historical and cultural pride, particularly in its legacy of resilience and independence, adds a distinct voice to the U.S. Francophonie, enriching its diversity while fostering a shared sense of connection across Francophone groups.

Language Teaching and Cultural Transmission

From my experience, Haitian parents place great importance on ensuring their children learn French for several key reasons. Primarily, they want to maintain effective communication within the family, preserving the ability to share experiences, stories, and traditions in the language that connects them to their heritage. Even when Haitians speak primarily Haitian-Creole, French remains the language of business and transpires a certain level of social status in the Haitian community. Therefore, French serves as a bridge for parents to teach their children about their culture, its values, and its significance, ensuring that younger generations feel rooted in their identity when they visit Haiti or engage with the broader Haitian community. Moreover, this linguistic connection fosters a sense of belonging and solidarity, strengthening the ties between the diaspora and the homeland. Additionally, for those who may choose to return eventually to Haiti to reside, fluency in French is an essential tool for professional and social integration, allowing them to contribute meaningfully to the country's development. Ultimately, these parents view French as a language of communication and a vital link to their cultural heritage and potential future opportunities.

Children in Haitian immigrant households often navigate multiple identities—Francophone, Haitian, and American—while grappling with the complexities of language acquisition and cultural integration. Haitian immigrants are typically proud of their multifaceted cultural background, which is passed down to their children. In households with well-educated parents, children grow up with strong bilingual or trilingual abilities, speaking English, French, and sometimes Haitian Creole, depending on the predominant language at home. This multilingual environment helps children develop a rich sense of identity, balancing their Haitian heritage with the American context in which they are raised. Over time, there has been a noticeable shift in language acquisition patterns among Haitian children, particularly in light of the political instability in Haiti over the past decades. The turmoil has disrupted the education system in Haiti, especially in the capital city of Port-au-Prince, which has, in turn, affected the educational backgrounds of children who immigrate to the U.S. Children from families that came to the U.S. in recent years may face challenges in their academic achievements due to the lower education standards in some public schools in Haiti. As a result, these children may enter American schools with varying levels of academic preparedness, which can complicate their language and educational integration.

However, despite these challenges, many Haitian children still reconcile their identities through language acquisition. They adapt and learn to navigate their roles as Haitian-Americans, often becoming fluent in English while maintaining a connection to their French and Haitian-Creole roots. Language acquisition helps these children bridge the gap between their Haitian heritage and American surroundings, allowing them to foster a sense of belonging in both communities. Over time, as these children integrate into American society, they increasingly become more comfortable with their bilingual or multilingual identities, using language as a key tool for maintaining cultural ties while advancing in the broader American educational system. Schools, community organizations, after-school programs, and cultural associations are critical in transmitting the French language and Haitian heritage to younger generations. In well-resourced areas, bilingual and immersion programs tailored explicitly for French native and heritage speakers offer robust support. These programs often provide culturally relevant books, events, and classroom activities celebrating Haitian culture while strengthening students' French language skills. Schools with English as a New Language (ENL) teachers with a French or Haitian Creole background are particularly effective. These educators help students bridge linguistic gaps and view their home language as a valuable cultural asset. These organizations and cultural associations also contribute to hosting workshops, storytelling events, and cultural festivals that teach younger generations about Haitian traditions, history, and language. Churches and after-school programs often act as hubs where children can engage in French or Haitian Creole activities, such as choir, theater, and language lessons. These initiatives not only preserve linguistic and cultural heritage but also create spaces for children to connect with their peers in the diaspora.

However, challenges remain, particularly in resource-limited communities or areas with few native or heritage speakers of French. In these contexts, the burden often falls on parents to support language acquisition and cultural transmission at home. Many parents lack access to resources, time, or knowledge about advocating for their children's needs. Additionally, some immigrant parents may not be aware of available educational initiatives or may face language barriers that limit their ability to navigate school systems effectively. Best practices include creating accessible resources, such as digital libraries or online platforms, and building partnerships between schools and community organizations to ensure cohesive support. Schools and organizations can also provide workshops to educate parents about available resources and empower them to advocate for their children's educational and cultural needs. Addressing challenges in resource-limited contexts requires a collaborative approach, including targeted funding for programs, training for educators in culturally responsive teaching, and outreach efforts to ensure all families have access to the tools they need to preserve their linguistic and cultural heritage.

My Role and Impact

As a French teacher, Haitian immigrant, and proud Francophone, I have always felt a profound responsibility to share my language and culture while helping fellow Haitians maintain their roots. Over the years, I have undertaken several initiatives to promote the French language and Haitian culture within my communities, significantly impacting language retention, cultural pride, and community cohesion. One of my primary efforts has been ensuring that French language programs remain robust and engaging. I encourage students to continue their French studies beyond basic graduation requirements by creating pathways for advanced coursework. This includes establishing French Honor Societies at middle and high school levels, offering dual language credit courses, and advocating for students to earn the Seal of Biliteracy in French. These opportunities celebrate students' linguistic achievements and validate French's cultural and academic value, especially for heritage and native speakers.

To promote cultural pride, I have organized French cultural festivals, participated in events like Le Grand Concours (National French Contest), and facilitated cultural activities such as movie screenings, culinary explorations, and trips to Francophone regions. These initiatives expose students to the richness of the Francophone world, including Haiti's unique contributions, and foster a deeper appreciation for their heritage. Additionally, I have worked to build connections within the Haitian diaspora by collaborating with local organizations, churches, and community groups. These partnerships help create platforms to celebrate Haitian traditions, language, and history, strengthening community bonds and encouraging younger generations to embrace their cultural identity. The impact of these efforts has been significant. Promoting French language and culture in educational and community settings has expanded program participation, instilled a sense of pride among French native and heritage speakers, and enhanced equity for multilingual learners. By showcasing the richness of Haitian and Francophone culture, I have helped students and community members see their language and heritage as assets contributing to a broader multicultural narrative.

Over the years, I have received overwhelmingly positive feedback from students, families, and institutions I have worked with. Many express gratitude for my impact on French programs and students' educational experiences. Former students often share how my efforts inspired their continued study of the French language and their appreciation for Francophone culture. Families have highlighted how my initiatives, such as cultural events and honor societies, have enriched their children's lives and helped them connect more deeply with their heritage. Recognizing the socioeconomic constraints many families face, I have worked to make cultural and linguistic programming accessible to all students, regardless of their financial situation. For example, I have forged strong relationships with community members, local organizations, and more affluent families to secure resources and support for the French program. These partnerships have provided funding for scholarships, waived fees for events and trips, and supplied materials like books and cultural artifacts to ensure that no student is left behind due to financial limitations.

These feedbacks have been instrumental in shaping my approach. They have reinforced the importance of inclusivity and equity in education and pushed me to advocate for students from lower-income households. I have also implemented strategies like hosting free or low-cost events, offering flexible trip payment plans, and integrating accessible cultural activities like movie nights or virtual exchanges with Francophone communities. By listening to the needs of families and institutions, I have been able to design programs that not only sustain language and cultural education but also foster a sense of belonging and pride among students from diverse socioeconomic backgrounds. These efforts have helped bridge gaps and create opportunities for all students to thrive, regardless of their economic circumstances.

Perspectives on the Future of an Evolving Francophonie

The ongoing political and social turmoil in Haiti has significantly impacted Haitian families and students, both in Haiti and in the U.S.

Many families have been forced to leave the country due to insecurity, seeking refuge through Temporary Protected Status (TPS), family reunification programs, or initiatives like the Biden administration's parole program. While these programs provide a lifeline for immigrants by offering a safer living environment, they also introduce challenges, including limited resources for integration and, in some cases, stigmatization of newcomers. Despite these obstacles, the Haitian community in the U.S. remains resilient and deeply proud of its roots and cultural heritage. Haitian Creole is a unifying language for many, fostering a strong sense of identity and connection to their homeland. At the same time, French plays a significant role in maintaining ties to the Francophone world, particularly in cultural and educational contexts. This dual linguistic identity—anchored in Haitian Creole and French—helps sustain and transmit Haitian culture across generations.

As U.S. immigration policies evolve, they will likely influence the long-term preservation of these languages and cultural identity in several ways. Policies that promote family reunification can strengthen cultural transmission by enabling families to stay together, creating opportunities for children to learn Haitian traditions, language, and values directly from their parents and elders. However, the strain on community resources and social services means that intentional support—through schools, community organizations, and cultural associations—is essential to preserve these traditions. Advocating for increased funding for bilingual education and programs celebrating Haitian culture will be crucial to addressing these challenges. Establishing after-school programs, cultural workshops, and language classes in Haitian-Creole and French can help bridge the gap for newcomers.

Additionally, fostering partnerships between Haitian organizations and local governments can create pathways for better integration while preserving cultural pride. In this evolving policy landscape, the resilience and adaptability of the Haitian community remain key. By leveraging its strong sense of cultural and linguistic identity, the Haitian diaspora can continue to thrive and contribute to the multicultural fabric of the U.S. In an era of globalization and rapidly advancing digital technologies, the francophone identity among young Haitian Americans is poised to evolve dynamically. The digital age has opened up unprecedented opportunities for Haitian-Americans to stay connected to their roots and culture, fostering an environment where language and cultural exchange thrive.

Through platforms like social media, music streaming services, online videos, and virtual communities, Haitian Americans and their counterparts in Haiti, Canada, and France can easily access and share cultural content such as music, dance, literature, and art. These technologies blend languages and cultural expressions across borders, influencing how French is spoken and understood within the Haitian diaspora. Young Haitian-Americans, for example, can interact with peers from various Francophone regions, exchanging language, ideas, traditions, and contemporary trends. This interconnectedness allows for a fluid evolution of the French language, adapted and enriched by diverse influences, including Haitian-Creole, American slang, and global digital trends. Moreover, the digital world allows young Haitian-Americans to explore and celebrate their unique cultural identity globally. They can connect with Haitian communities worldwide, share their experiences, and collaborate on projects that promote Haitian culture and language. This profoundly affects the retention and evolution of the French language, as it becomes part of a broader global conversation that includes traditional forms of expression and modern, digital forms of communication.

As francophone identity becomes increasingly multifaceted, young Haitian-Americans will likely continue to navigate and redefine what it means to be both Haitian and francophone in a digital, globalized world. Blending languages, engaging with francophone cultures globally, and accessing resources online will further shape their sense of identity, making it more inclusive and adaptive to the changing landscape of language and culture. To strengthen Haitian Francophonie in culturally rich metropolitan areas such as Miami, New York, and Boston, community leaders and organizations must consolidate their resources and collaborate on initiatives that support the preservation of Haitian language and culture. By working together, these leaders can create a unified effort that amplifies the impact of their programming and ensures that Haitian heritage remains vibrant within the U.S. Francophone community. One key strategy is regularly showcasing

Haitian culture through various engaging cultural activities. Organizing Haitian book fairs, art and music festivals, language contests, and cultural exhibitions can provide a platform for artistic expression and an opportunity to celebrate Haitian achievements. These events foster pride in the Haitian community and educate the broader public about Haiti's rich cultural contributions.

Educational initiatives are also essential. Schools and after-school programs can offer bilingual education, French language classes, and Haitian history and culture elective courses. By providing students with the tools and support to become fluent in both Haitian-Creole and French, these programs ensure the continuity of the language across generations. Additionally, creating scholarships and opportunities for higher education in French and Francophone studies can incentivize young people to pursue academic paths that connect them to their cultural heritage. Intergenerational initiatives, such as mentorship programs that pair young Haitian Americans with older community members, can also play a critical role in passing down traditions, stories, and knowledge. These initiatives help bridge the generational gap, ensuring cultural practices are preserved and adapted meaningfully. Finally, hosting community events like Haitian book fairs and cultural festivals allows people to unite, share their stories, and celebrate their unique identities. These gatherings strengthen community bonds, promote linguistic diversity, and help the Haitian diaspora maintain a strong presence within the larger fabric of the U.S. Francophonie. By emphasizing education, cultural promotion, intergenerational collaboration, and community events, we can foster a resilient and future-oriented Haitian presence in the U.S. Francophone landscape, ensuring that the Haitian language and culture thrive for future generations.

Reflections

As someone who has lived through the immigrant experience, I am a testament to how the Francophone culture can be a pillar of strength and guidance in navigating life in a new country. Since arriving in the U.S., my French and Haitian Creole background has provided me with a unique perspective that has been instrumental in my personal and professional success. These languages, alongside my cultural heritage, have been vital in helping me adapt to the American context—whether in academia, building a family, or overcoming various challenges. My experience as a Haitian immigrant has allowed me to bridge both worlds, using the resilience and adaptability embedded in my Francophone roots to achieve my goals. I also take immense pride in raising two wonderful Haitian-American daughters deeply connected to their heritage. They are proud of their language and culture, and I have worked hard to instill the same resilience and appreciation for their roots. My story is not just my own—it is the story of countless Haitian immigrants who have navigated the complexities of language, culture, and economics to thrive in the United States while remaining grounded in their heritage. Through my contribution, I aim to provide readers with a deeper understanding of U.S. Francophonie, specifically Haitian Francophonie, by shedding light on the resilience and cultural richness of the Haitian community. My experiences as a Haitian immigrant in the United States underscore how linguistic and cultural heritage—particularly the French and Haitian Creole languages—are not merely survival mechanisms but vital sources of pride and identity. These elements have helped me, and countless others, navigate life in a foreign country while maintaining a connection to our roots.

My narrative will help readers appreciate Haitian identity's complexity and evolving dynamics in the American context. Haitian immigrants in the U.S. often face challenges that require a delicate balance between preserving one's heritage and integrating into a new society. Yet, precisely, this blend of cultural and linguistic influences enriches the broader landscape of U.S. Francophonie. By highlighting the values and cultural foundations instilled in me early on, I hope to convey that our identity is not defined solely by our circumstances or location. Still, the cultural and familial values we carry with us continue to develop. My contribution aims to offer a richer, more nuanced perspective of Haitian identity, emphasizing how it adapts, survives, and thrives in the American context, contributing to the broader narrative of U.S. Francophonie.

10. New Speakers of French in Louisiana: The Future of a Regional Minority Language
Jonathan Olivier

Two moments in the 20th century shaped the future of Louisiana French and the people who speak it. The first was in 1921 when the state constitution made English the official language of instruction in public schools. French had already begun to decline in favor of a dominant language, English, in a "language shift." In the following decades, the state's new policy precipitated this linguistic transition and ensured that intergenerational transmission of French at home would virtually cease. At the same time, the prestige of French further weakened.[113]

This language shift and the prospect of "language death," or the disappearance of Louisiana French, led to the second moment. In 1968, the Council for the Development of French in Louisiana (CODOFIL) was formed to preserve and advance the language. Since children had stopped learning French at home, CODOFIL was charged with reintroducing it at school to reverse this language shift or, at least, prevent language death. The regional and demographic variability of Louisiana French presented obstacles to writing and teaching it. So, the variety of French that CODOFIL chose as the pedagogical standard for second language classes was highly standardized, academic, and detached from an actual speech community—in this chapter it will be called "standard French." CODOFIL hired teachers from France, Belgium, Canada, and Africa to instruct in second-language classes without any resources to teach Louisiana French at the time. In the 1980s, CODOFIL began implementing French immersion in schools that utilized standard French. There are now around 35 of these programs in the state, with more than 5,500 students enrolled.

---

[113] Dajko, 2012.

Today, we sit at a convergence where the implications of these two moments are becoming more apparent. The last generation of native speakers who learned Louisiana French as their first language at home and used it daily in a social setting will soon disappear. Meanwhile, the first generation of the state's immersion participants who were instructed in standard French is now in their 30s and 40s with children of their own, and many others have learned as adults. This has established a new generation who learned French as a second language, not a primary one, and in an academic setting, not at home.

Similar situations exist worldwide as minority languages have shrunk over the last several decades. While it has long been tempting for Louisianans to look to Canada's French-speaking minority communities as a source of inspiration, those regions have retained intergenerational transmission of the language, it is used socially, and federal language laws protect it. Louisiana's linguistic situation more closely resembles that of European regions, where there are efforts to sustain languages such as Gaelic in Ireland and Catalan in Spain through immersion programs. In these regions, there is a reduced population of native speakers of a regional minority language, and there has been a significant language shift. The intergenerational transmission of these regional languages is also weak. Research shedding light on these revitalization efforts denotes a person who learns a regional minority language as a second language as a "new speaker." This is someone "with little or no home or community exposure to a minority language but who instead acquire it through immersion or bilingual education programs, revitalization projects or as adult language learners."[114] Although Louisiana French is a dialect of French, not its separate language like Gaelic, it is a minority language in a region that has experienced a language shift and a virtual halt in intergenerational transmission, accompanied by a revitalization movement. In this context, the new generation of Louisiana Francophones are new speakers.

Throughout the 20th century, scholars focused heavily on Louisiana's native speakers, which intensified as language revitalization

---

[114] O'Rourke et al., 2015.

efforts took off in the 1970s. This was primarily a result of the wave of pride in Louisiana French that swept the region at this time, as people rushed to define and record a language that had been marginalized for decades. Despite a generation of new speakers that now exists, the conversation about French in Louisiana often remains focused on the past without offering a clear vision for this demographic in the future. This emphasis on the native speaker is a common practice in European regions with a minority language, as they are upheld as speaking the language purely and perceived as the ideal model for language revitalization[115]. When new speakers were mentioned in scholarly articles about Louisiana French in the '80s and '90s, they were often used to display the rift between native speakers and second language learners, a representation of the failure to teach children the region's local dialect. The new speaker label attempts to stray from this strict concentration on "nativeness" and performance-based indicators, like "non-fluent speaker," "imperfect learner," or "second-language learner."[116] The new speaker label seeks to identify "new forms of language and modes of communication."[117] By analyzing new French speakers in Louisiana through this approach, we can better focus on the future and evolution of French in the state.

While scholars such as Joshua Fishman have argued that reversing language shift should be achieved by restoring intergenerational transmission of the minority language as a mother tongue, others assert that the existence of new speakers now challenges this notion, with some even questioning if a native speaker community has to exist at all for a language to survive.[118] Suzanne Romaine examines new ways a minority language can function within a society, suggesting that "the main value for many small languages in the future may well be symbolic and cultural rather than practical. That is to say, many will not be widely used, if indeed at all, in everyday communication; they will cease being grounded in continuity of practice and instead become primary vehicles

---

[115] O'Rourke et Walsh, 2015.
[116] O'Rourke et al., 2015.
[117] O'Rourke et Walsh, 2015.
[118] O'Rourke et Pujolar, 2013.

for articulating identity."[119] Romaine notes that many languages are surviving like this already, such as in Spain, where more children learn Basque through the education system than at home.[120] Immersion schools in Ireland have provided a functional knowledge of Irish, acquired later in life and used as a second language. Still, these programs haven't "led to its spoken use in everyday life, nor its intergenerational transmission."[121]

Scholars have long concluded in Louisiana that it is too late to reverse the language shift and that preserving French as a native language is a "far-fetched dream."[122] Many new speakers of French in Louisiana are "passive bilinguals" who may be unable to transmit the language proficiently to their children.[123] It appears that speaking French in Louisiana exists similarly to Romaine's observation of a "symbolic" or "cultural" practice, and it assists in expressing one's identity.[124] As is the case with Gaelic and Catalan, the transmission of French in Louisiana comes from the education system and not at home (except in isolated, rare cases); thus, its survival isn't dependent on a native-speaking population. However, unlike in Europe, the notion of minority language revitalization in Louisiana isn't as clear, given that new speakers learn standard French and not Louisiana French. In Louisiana, survival of the French language, no matter the variety, has become the ultimate goal.

While many scholars have suggested that teaching standard French to children and the disappearance of intergenerational transmission will lead to the extinction of Louisiana French, the new speaker model challenges us to explore how the language will persist in innovative ways instead. Many individuals have used standard French to learn the basics of the language and then gone on to learn facets of Louisiana French. In his observations of young French immersion students in Pierre Part,

---

[119] Romaine, 2006.
[120] Ibid.
[121] Ibid.
[122] Blyth, 1998.
[123] Ancelet, 1988.
[124] Romaine, 2006.

Louisiana, Carl Blyth witnessed the emergence of this sort of "hybrid dialect" in which new speakers have French, Belgian, and Louisiana characteristics present in their language use.[125] Instead of precipitating language death, new speakers are the crux of language resiliency, using Louisiana French in new ways and new spaces and thus equipping it with the tools needed to remain for future generations.

Despite the importance of new speakers to the future of French in Louisiana, there has been little inquiry into their language use or their identities as Francophones. Thus, little is known about who they are or how they use the language. As a graduate student in the French department at the University of Louisiana at Lafayette, I conducted an independent study to respond to this lack of analysis, resulting in an introductory evaluation of this little-studied group. In 2022, I investigated motivation, identity, and sociolinguistic issues among a group of 24 new speakers by using questionnaires, in-depth interviews, and a translation task, culminating in a report called "New Speakers of French in Louisiana: An Introductory Analysis of Identity and Motivation." What follows in this chapter has been selectively pulled from portions of this study, illustrating telling data points that inform notions of language use, identity, and the issues these new speakers face. I hope this chapter will lay the groundwork for an increased interest in this demographic and foster a shift in discourse about what they mean to the future of French in Louisiana.

The Group of Participants

Requests for participation in my study were sent to a population of new speakers born in Louisiana. They learned French as a second language, with many concentrated around Lafayette, Louisiana. Most of these participants are engaged in language revitalization efforts and participated in an adult immersion program. They were between 18 and 40, with a mean age of 29.6, and divided between 16 females, seven males, and one non-binary person. A majority of the respondents self-identified as White, which represents a limited sample demographic.

---

[125] Blyth, 1998.

The level of French language proficiency included 14 participants who self-identified as advanced, nine as intermediate, and one as basic. Although efforts were made to include a diverse group of participants, those who were ultimately selected agreed to participate and were available. In contrast, others were not included due to lack of time or interest. Therefore, these results are an introductory analysis, and these participants do not represent all new speakers of French in Louisiana.

A Shift in Identity

When asked to elaborate on the type of French they spoke, the six participants in the narrative portion of the study shared sentiments that their French was variable or hybridized with elements of Louisiana French. The following participant, Blake, views his dialect as hybrid and part of a larger evolution in Louisiana French, comprised of the regional dialect but heavily influenced by standard French.

> Je parle le français louisianais. Je suis louisianais, je parle français […] mais c'est un peu mondialisé aussi. Parce que je parle pas comme mon grand-père […] Donc, le français louisianais d'aujourd'hui, ça a changé et je crois que c'est plus comme moi, je suis après parler asteur, vraiment. Donc, un mélange du français standard, disons, ou globalisé, et le français d'héritage qu'on a ici.
>
> *I speak Louisiana French. I am a Louisianan, I speak French […], but It is a little globalized, too. Because I don't speak like my grandfather […] So, Louisiana French of today, it has changed, and I think it is more like I'm talking now, really. It is a mix of standard French, let's say, or globalized, and our heritage French that we have here.*

In this response, it is clear that Louisiana French had an influence. For example, he uses the Louisiana grammatical structure "être après" to emphasize an action in progress instead of the standard "être en train de" and the Louisiana French "asteur" to indicate the present moment. Blake labels his dialect as Louisiana French because he is a Louisiana

Francophone, not necessarily because he uses French precisely as it has historically been spoken in the region.

Kate had a decade of standard French instruction, and she reported that after taking a college class about Louisiana French, she wanted to talk more like her family. The class allowed her to find the value in "sounding" like a Louisiana French speaker.

> J'ai dirais que une mélange de français louisianais. Donc je veux dire que je parle avec un accent louisianais, mais le dialecte standard [...] Mais j'ai pas tout le vocabulaire. Et j'ai pas d'habitude de parler avec « vous-autres » et « nous-autres » et tout ça. Je pense pas que je peux juste changer comme ça, *like* dix années de français que j'ai dans ma tête.

> *I'd say that it is a mix of Louisiana French. I want to say that I speak with a Louisiana accent, but the standard dialect [...] And I'm not in the habit of speaking with "vous-autres" and "nous-autres" and all that. I don't think that I can just change like that, like ten years of French that I have in my head.*

Kate views her French as a hybrid due to her Louisiana-specific accent and not because of regional grammatical rules. In her interview, she discussed changing her use of the guttural "r" to the rolled "r" of Louisiana French to feel more belonging to the regional speech community.

These responses reflect a change in what has constituted identity in south Louisiana since at least the early to mid-20th century. Typically, among native speakers, Whites self-identify as Cajun and report they speak Cajun French even if they speak Louisiana Creole. In contrast, African-Americans have self-identified as Creole and reported they speak Louisiana Creole even if they speak Louisiana French, commonly called Cajun French.[126] For new speakers in my study, although most respondents (50%) self-identified as Cajun and 8.3% self-identified as Creole, only 16.7% said they speak Cajun French, and 12.5% reported Louisiana French. The majority of respondents (29%) reported speaking

---

[126] Dajko, 2012.

standard French, and 25% reported speaking a mix of dialects, with responses such as "Louisiana/Standard/Parisian," "mix of standard and Cajun," "Contemporary Metropolitan Louisiana French," and "Standard and Louisiana French."

These results suggest that for these new speakers, Cajun and Creole may no longer represent an intertwined ethnic and linguistic identity. Instead, other identities have emerged. For example, 33% of new speakers self-identified as *Louisianais* or *Franco-Louisianais*. These terms have gained popularity recently, functioning as a way to represent one's identity as a Francophone and a Louisianan, regardless of race. The *Louisianais* identity remains rooted in French, and the *Franco-Louisianais* marker explicitly references a Francophone identity. This is markedly different from the contemporary Cajun and Creole identity markers that Anglophones widely use to express heritage and ethnicity and no longer reference a French-speaking identity.

Native speakers in Louisiana are likely unfamiliar with the *Louisianais* identity markers, which call to mind European contexts where new speakers call themselves by new terms, such as *neofalante* to describe new speakers of Galicia in Spain or *neo-bretonnant* to describe new speakers of Breton in France.[127] New speakers of French in Louisiana have different linguistic and societal experiences; thus, this shift in identity is expected as they create their connections with the language.

Linguistic Mudes

Researchers who have studied new speakers of Catalan in Spain have identified key points in the Second Language Acquisition (SLA) process, specifically dealing with the meaning of adopting a new language in social life, which are moments called "linguistic mudes."[128] These key moments where the second language gets socialized can often work as turning points in the SLA process that profoundly shape a person's experience. A linguistic muda allows a new speaker to project

---

[127] O'Rourke et Pujolar, 2013.
[128] Pujolar et Puigdevall, 2015.

a new, additional, or different linguistic persona distinct from their maternal language.[129]

A muda might appear in primary school, high school, or university, getting one's first job, establishing a new family, and becoming a new parent.[130] Unlike Spain, where Catalan speakers number in the millions, French speakers in Louisiana are far fewer and represent a fraction of the state's total population. Although there are opportunities to use the language, virtually all services and activities are conducted in English. Therefore, daily socialization in the language is impossible in many contexts. My study participants were far more likely to experience a linguistic muda outside of Louisiana during an immersion program in a Francophone country. One of the most common ways was through the summer immersion program at Université Sainte-Anne in Nova Scotia, Canada. Out of the 24 total participants in the study, 13 attended an immersion program at Sainte-Anne, three worked in France via TAPIF, and 10 generally studied abroad (some attended more than one program). Of the six participants who engaged in the in-depth interviews, four attended Sainte-Anne, and one attended after the study was concluded. An experience at Sainte-Anne catapulted Blake's abilities in French and set him on the trajectory to master the language in a way that would have been impossible in Louisiana.

> Mais j'ai vraiment voulu apprendre le français. Et c'est pour ça que je suis allé à Sainte-Anne dans le programme d'immersion, à l'Université de Sainte-Anne. J'ai passé cinq semaines pour leur session d'immersion. Et c'est vraiment là où j'ai trouvé la volonté et la passion pour [...] pas juste apprendre la langue mais être capable de m'exprimer d'une manière plus profonde.

> *But I really wanted to learn French. And that's why I went to Sainte Anne in the immersion program at the University of Sainte Anne. I spent five weeks there in the immersion program. And it is really there*

---

[129] Ibid.
[130] Pujolar et Puigdevall, 2015.

> that I found the desire and the passion for [...] not just to learn the language, but to be able to express myself in a more profound way.

Michelle went to Sainte-Anne when she was a teenager. Up to that point, she had taken French as a language elective and only used it in a classroom setting.

> Mais je dirais que la première fois quand j'avais dix-sept ans, quand j'ai été à l'Université Sainte-Anne, c'était probablement l'évènement le plus marquant dans ce trajet d'apprendre le français.
>
> *But I'd say that the first time when I was 17 years old when I went to the University of Sainte Anne, it was probably the event that impacted me the most in this trajectory of learning French.*

Due to these linguistic mudes in Francophone countries, new speakers of French in Louisiana can experience changes that "bring about a reorganization of one's linguistic repertoire that has significant implications in the ways that individuals present themselves to others."[131] Even though linguistic mudes are powerful tools for new speakers to learn the language and create new identities, when they return to Louisiana, opportunities to express those identities are often limited. For example, 100% of participants reported that they would like to spend lots of time speaking French, and 87.5% reported that it is essential for them to speak French. Yet, 66.7% of respondents reported that they are the kind of person who makes great efforts to speak French, and even less (58.3%) responded that they are working hard at speaking French as much as possible. While this represents a question of individual motivation, these results are likely due to the limited number of French speakers in Louisiana. If that is the case, increasing French language services in Louisiana would provide this demographic with valuable opportunities to use the language in daily life, thus expanding the use of French in Louisiana.

---

[131] Pujolar et Puigdevall, 2015.

Louisiana French Speech Community

New speakers often desire to sound like a native speaker. So, they employ local words or expressions in an attempt to model their idiolects based on what they perceive as an authentic way to speak the language.[132] Emily's following response displays the conflict when hybridized language forms prevent someone from functioning within Louisiana's native speech community.

> Y a des jours où j'ai honte parce que je suis en train de parler avec quelqu'un de ce tit village de l'autre coin de l'état et je parle pas comme lui [...] Et j'ai un peu honte que je peux pas être assez louisianaise pour cette personne.
>
> *There are days where I'm embarrassed because I'm talking with someone from this little village on the other side of the state and I don't talk like him [...] And I am a little embarrassed that I can't speak the same variety of French as this person.*

In this example, Emily uses *être en train de* to indicate actions in progress instead of *être après*, which is the Louisiana form. She goes on to say that when speaking French, the first word to express herself that comes to mind is the one she'll use, whether it is in standard French or a more Louisiana variant. Her hybridized language use conflicts with the localized and regional variants found among native speakers in Louisiana.

Another respondent, Kate, reported having similar experiences with native speakers, notably her grandfather. Since she sounds different and uses unfamiliar words, she has been singled out as speaking oddly. For her, this has created a clear distinction between her French and their French.

> Et même avec mon grand-père. Et peut-être c'était juste moi où j'étais au lycée. Mais je ne voulais pas parler avec lui parce qu'il était un de ces gens qui disait quelque chose comme, ah, ton

---

[132] Mcleod et O'Rourke, 2015.

> accent c'est différent et mais moi je parle ce français. Ok. Je veux juste pas parler.

> *And even with my grandfather. And maybe it was just me, where I went to high school. But I didn't want to speak with him because he was one of those people who said something like, ah, your accent is different, and I don't speak this French. Ok, I just don't want to talk.*

Kate's response reflects a divide between native and new speakers, which raises the issue of the authenticity of her French and of her belonging to Louisiana's French speech community as it has historically been described.[133] Since the native speaker is often seen as authentic, this "has been found to deter newcomers to the language and sometimes prevent them from using it altogether," as described in Kate's response.[134]

Still, many new speakers in this study reported having limited interactions with native speakers. They are left to forge their own linguistic identities as Louisiana Francophones. Many of their identities have been established in the classroom, which function as powerful speech communities.[135] So, although some new speakers may have trouble integrating into the native speech community of Louisiana due to differing fluency and communicative competence levels, they can excel within academic settings where a more standard variant of French is valued. Those who learned standard French as children in immersion programs—taking science and math classes in French, for instance—have obtained a vocabulary that is not available to native speakers in Louisiana who lack the terms in French for these academic topics. This can provide an "alternate source of linguistic legitimacy or capital" for new speakers.[136] Thus, new speakers are better equipped to use the language in their professional or academic life, highlighting French as an asset in a globalized world.

---

[133] Mcleod et O'Rourke, 2015.
[134] O'Rourke et Pujolar, 2013.
[135] Romaine, 2006.
[136] McLeod et O'Rourke, 2015.

When a minority language is relocated into new spaces, transformations in its use and the forms of language used often occur.[137] Today's new speakers of French in Louisiana no longer have the same relationship with the language as previous generations. French is not a primary method of communication but an academic one or a cultural one that can open new doors—whether that is an advanced education, opportunities to travel, or a connection to one's heritage. New speakers express themselves differently than previous generations, using various globalized words with differing accents. Even demographically, new speakers are strikingly different— a French immersion classroom can be comprised of Hispanophone children from Central or South America alongside Louisianans who have generational ties to the region. As this continues, the French of Louisiana, being relocated to novel spaces, will sound differently than some are accustomed to. This evolution, a common thread for all languages, will ensure the survival of French in Louisiana.

---

[137] O'Rourke et Walsh, 2015.

11. Observing and Understanding Language Contact Among French Migrant Children in the United States[138]

Valérie Barrau-Ogereau

Human history is closely linked to population movements, and international migration has never been as widespread and facilitated as it is today. Whether seeking political asylum, family reunification, or academic and economic opportunities, people from elsewhere shape the United States. My personal story is part of this migratory dynamic.

At the start of 2016, my husband was offered an international relocation. Eager to leave the Paris region and give our children a chance to learn a new language while experiencing life immersed in another country, we moved quickly to Massachusetts, near Boston. Before long, I realized that continuing my job as a flight attendant would be difficult. After working in the aviation industry for 15 years in France, I decided to return to my studies and train to become a teacher of French as a Foreign Language (FLE). My children were two and five years old then, so finding a career that would fit their schedules and the local job market was essential. Additionally, teaching French provided me with an excellent opportunity to preserve and develop my own children's French language skills, as I had great educational ambitions for them, centered on a perfect mastery of both French and English.

Although I had a clear, straightforward vision of how they would acquire two languages, reality turned out differently. Their learning difficulties, neurodevelopmental challenges, mixing of languages, frustration, tension, and occasional rejection of French as their heritage

---

[138] Reflections of a mother on introducing a second language to her children, the observed learning difficulties, and possible remedial approaches based on plurilingual methods.

language all led me to watch French relegated to "second language" status, much to my dismay.

This linguistic shift happened over a few years. I was enrolled in an online curriculum for a University Diploma (DU), then a Bachelor's, and finally a Master's in FLE. My Master's track in Digital Technology and Plurilingualism helped me observe and understand how my children's linguistic evolution took place. Above all, it enabled me to recognize their polyglot profiles better and to foster a plurilingual, transdisciplinary competence in them.

Observing the First Steps in a New Linguistic and Cultural Environment

As parents of young children, my husband and I were determined to expose them to early bilingualism: French would be the language spoken at home (the "source" language), while English (the "target" language) would be used in society. More than just wishful thinking—and simply because of our situation—it was imperative that our children acquire the vehicular language (English). Their linguistic and social immersion essentially took place in the local education system. At the same time, an opportunity arose for me to teach French after school at a community organization, which seemed like the perfect way to balance exposure to both languages, academically and socially.

The Preschool (Day Care) Setting

When we arrived in the United States, my son was 4 years and 10 months old. Because he would not turn five before the next school year, he attended a daycare, a private facility that blends elements of a daycare center and preschool—what I might call a "children's garden." It enrolled children aged 21 months to five years.

In France, preschool (école maternelle) provides academic instruction from the age of three, following a national curriculum.[139] Children learn the basics of reading (letter recognition, simple and then

---

[139] Blanquer, n.d.

complex graphemes), cursive writing (fine motor skills, spatial orientation on lined paper, sizing of uppercase and lowercase letters), and mathematics. This approach ensures a smooth transition to first grade (Cours Préparatoire, or CP in France, equivalent to 1st grade in the U.S.).

In contrast, daycare centers in the U.S. have varying educational goals. Like many others, the one my children attended focused on social-emotional development and learning through individual and group play. Children are encouraged to manage their own emotions and those of others and to interact with their peers—preparing them for elementary school, as social-emotional learning is given as much importance as academic readiness. An entire section of elementary school report cards is dedicated to social-emotional progress.

After two years of preschool in France, my son started at this American daycare. I was more anxious, wondering how he would navigate this new environment: How would he communicate with his teacher and classmates? How would he express his basic needs? Much to our relief, his teacher, Anne, happened to be from Martinique—a French Caribbean island. Having lived in the U.S. for several years, she was American and French. Thanks to Anne, my son's transition went smoothly, and after three months, he felt at ease in his new life. He had picked up the vocabulary needed for the social and learning rituals appropriate for his age.

The American cultural calendar is full of celebrations: Indigenous Peoples' Day, Veterans Day, Halloween, Thanksgiving, Christmas, and more. While Christmas is celebrated on both sides of the Atlantic, in those first three months, my son dove headfirst—often playfully or festively—into a new culture, which accelerated his acquisition of American English. Since he began being exposed to English at age five, his bilingualism could be described as consecutive: his first language (L1) was French, and his second language (L2) became English.

My daughter, who was two then, started attending the same facility twice a week in the mornings, gradually moving to full-time attendance from age three to five. Naturally sociable and talkative, she navigated this new environment quickly, making herself understood and meeting her needs efficiently. French, English, "franglais," or simple baby talk—

words and bits of sentences flowed in whatever language she happened to grab onto. Sometimes we could understand her, and sometimes not. She would speak with such enthusiasm and a smile that it was both endearing and amusing. I have fond memories of that time, witnessing her natural language acquisition. Because she was too young to differentiate linguistic codes, mixing them in a highly fluid way, it was impossible to separate her L1 and L2 strictly. So, for her, I would say that her bilingualism was simultaneous until she entered elementary school at age five.

American Elementary Schooling and Learning Disorders

My hopes for a perfectly balanced, "ideal" bilingualism were challenged in the following years—roughly my children's "middle childhood," from ages six to eleven. This is when fundamental academic skills, such as reading, writing, and math, are typically acquired and consolidated. Since we are French and speak French at home, both of my children were automatically enrolled in the English Language Learner (ELL) program, which provides language support for students whose first language is not English. Although they were already comfortable speaking English, the program helped them strengthen their reading and writing skills, which proved incredibly challenging for both.

From kindergarten through 3rd grade, my son struggled with what I call a "mirror vision." He saw things in reverse, horizontally (right to left) and vertically (bottom to top). As a result, letters like *b* could be interpreted as *d*, *q*, or *p*. This issue caused delays in his acquisition of reading and writing skills, as he would sometimes write letters backward. While his classmates were reading chapter books from children's literature and writing with ease in English, my son began to lose confidence, exhibiting what can be described as linguistic insecurity. Concretely, he preferred relying on comic strips' illustrations rather than reading books with chapters and would struggle to write ten words when asked to compose a paragraph. Fortunately, by around age nine, this mirror vision faded, and thanks to personalized ELL support at school, he caught up relatively quickly. After that, his schooling proceeded normally.

My daughter started kindergarten at age five. Outgoing by nature and with her preschool background, she began elementary school on a strong note. Then, in March 2020, COVID-19 upended our lives, and her classes went remote via videoconferencing. Suddenly, I could "enter" her classroom virtually and see firsthand the gap between her level, the program's expectations, and her classmates' abilities. She had significant difficulties with memorization, conceptualization, and time markers, leading to significant delays in literacy. When confinement was extended into the following year, I observed her falling further behind despite my best efforts to support her at home.

It was not until 2nd grade when she could return to in-person classes, that I requested the school evaluate her for an individualized education program. Specialists diagnosed her with a neurodevelopmental disorder: Attention Deficit Hyperactivity Disorder (ADHD). She then received daily personalized support in addition to ELL services and her regular classes. Over the following years, thanks to the dedicated educational team, she gradually caught up in her fundamental academic skills.

After-School French Classes

While developing fundamental academic skills in English (the language of immersion) was laborious for my two children, we were fortunate to enroll them in an after-school community program that offered French classes twice a week for children from francophone backgrounds. Around 80 students were enrolled, forming a vibrant community of kids who were immigrants themselves or living in a migration context. Classes were taught in French, focusing on developing reading and writing skills. This emphasis on written language was also a priority for the families, especially those considering a return to their home countries once their visas expired.

Each class had an average of six to eight students, an ideal size for classroom management and differentiating instruction. Teachers followed a curriculum inspired by France's National Education guidelines, using materials designed for native French speakers (Français Langue Maternelle, FLAM). Because France has a strong grammatical tradition, children start learning grammar concepts (conjugations, syntax, etc.) very early, from around age six (1ˢᵗ grade). They use grammatical terminology and engage in exercises that analyze the language system: verb conjugation tables, orthographic and grammatical drills, etc.

French children learn writing skills this way, but American students typically develop these abilities mainly through exposure to language rather than explicit analysis. Given these educational differences—and the absence of French reinforcement in American elementary schools—French quickly appeared "too hard." French classes became burdensome for my children, who were already struggling to learn English. My son soon grew discouraged, protesting that French was useless in the U.S. and "too complicated." Meanwhile, despite her inherent enthusiasm, my daughter could not grasp—and therefore remember—the grammar rules. She struggled to perform the mental operation of turning a nominal subject group into a personal pronoun, then identifying the verb and its "group," and finally applying the correct ending. It was overwhelming for her.

However, the program offered much more than just language study. Many families came from various Francophone countries, and the curriculum also featured activities celebrating Francophone culture. This cultural component spotlighted diversity and the local Francophone community's plural identities—an aspect my children appreciated. Yet COVID-19 eventually forced classes online. Many teachers and families returned to their home countries, and the program's campus ultimately closed.

Despite our efforts to develop equal proficiency in both languages, an enduring imbalance emerged in favor of English. English became their L1, and French receded to an L2.

Understanding Language Contact

Just as I came to terms with the idea that my children might not become perfectly bilingual, I entered a Master's program in FLE. Over two years of coursework—including classes on "Theories of Plurilingualism," "Plurilingual Situations," "Didactics of Plurilingualism," and

"Migrations and Plurilingualism"—I realized that all was far from lost. Different didactic approaches exist, and I tested them on my children.

Translanguaging

Although it has been difficult to develop my children's written French, my husband and I continue to maintain the language orally at home: we speak French to them exclusively, watch French-language TV programs, and talk with our family in France over video calls in French. In short, we do our best to maximize every oral channel for transmitting this linguistic heritage. Ideally, our home language is French, and our social language is English. While this may sound straightforward on paper, reality is more nuanced because English (their L1) heavily influences their oral production in French (their L2). These shifts—sometimes subtle, sometimes noticeable—can be seen at three levels:

> Lexical: Borrowings from English are easy to spot. The children may slip English words into their French speech for various reasons. Sometimes, it is because of a "gap" (they don't know the French word):
> - "Maman, j'ai oublié de prendre mon *retainer* au *sleepover* hier soir." ("Mom, I forgot to take my retainer to the sleepover last night.")
> - Other times, if the listener can understand English, they may not bother finding the correct French term:
> - "Ma mère viendra *pick me up* après la répétition." ("My mom will pick me up after rehearsal.")

I have also observed that when my children are overwhelmed by emotion (stress, anxiety, excitement), they switch to English when speaking to us. We correct them as much as possible to avoid fossilizing these habits, but in emotional moments, we let them speak whichever language they need.

> Syntactic: They often transfer English grammar rules into French speech. These are also quite noticeable. I have heard literal translations:

- "Je suis fini." for "I am finished." (instead of "J'ai fini.")
- Or English word order: "la blanche robe" ("the white dress") rather than "la robe blanche."
- A common one is dropping "ne" in negative phrases—"Je sais pas"—mirroring the English contraction (don't, can't, won't, etc.).

Phonetic: The influence of English is more subtle but still present, particularly in prosody. In French, a statement has a falling intonation, whereas in American English, it often rises at the end (the so-called "uptalk"). To a French ear, it can sound like the speaker is trailing off when, in fact, they have finished their statement. My children also frequently use drawn-out pauses or hesitation words. One could attribute that to their incomplete grasp of French, but American English has a slower rhythmic structure than French. It is also worth noting that while silence and hesitations may be deemed awkward in French, they are not necessarily so in American English. For a native French speaker (especially for parents of teens!), these phonetic features might be mistakenly perceived as laziness or lack of interest, leading to misunderstandings.

Thus, the two languages blend despite having distinct communication contexts (French at home and English outside). At times, any of us (adults included) may consciously switch languages out of a need for simplification – "On va au playground?" ("Should we go to the playground" [one word in English, three words in French for *aire de jeux*])—for emphasis or mutual understanding ("S'il te plait maman, *pretty please?*"), to show cultural identity (choosing a "donut" vs. a "chocolate croissant" in a French bakery) or simply for stylistic flair ("*Okey-dokey!*"). In all cases, communication draws on elements from multiple linguistic codes because these codes make up a single plurilingual repertoire. This is what is known as translanguaging.[140]

---

[140] Grosjean, n.d.

Embracing Plurilingualism

Being bilingual does not mean being "twice monolingual." Plurilingualism implies having language skills in at least two languages, with varying degrees of proficiency. According to the Common European Framework of Reference for Languages,[141] plurilingualism is "an uneven and evolving competence [...]. Plurilinguals have a single, interdependent repertoire combining their general competencies and various strategies to carry out tasks."

In short, all linguistic codes present (languages, dialects, etc.)—regardless of the user's level—are considered and drawn upon for communication. A plurilingual individual develops plurilingual competence, which can manifest in various ways:

- "Switching from one language or dialect to another;
- Speaking in one language while understanding someone speaking another;
- Drawing on knowledge of different languages to comprehend a text;
- Recognizing words in a new form that come from a shared international vocabulary;
- Mediating between individuals who share no common language (or have only partial knowledge of one);
- Employing a complete linguistic "toolkit" by trying out a range of possible expressions;
- Using paralinguistics (facial expressions, gestures, mime)."[142]

As parents, this means accepting instances of interlinguistic interference, conversational intercomprehension (parents speaking French while the children reply in English, for example), and the creativity inherent in language mixing (like "Maman, tu peux *viendre?*" [nonstandard French for "Mom, can you come?"]). It primarily means continuing to pass on our home language and encouraging its use in all forms.

---

[141] CEFR, 2021: 30.
[142] Ibid.

Introducing a Foreign Language and Plurilingual Approaches

Of all the language skills, the only one my son has not fully mastered in French is written production. Given his early struggles in reading and writing, I was hopeful he might get a new perspective from secondary school since U.S. curricula generally include studying a foreign language starting in 6th grade. Unfortunately, he had to choose a different language because French is not considered a foreign language for him. So, his linguistic biography now includes Spanish.

Having a negative memory of learning French, my son finds Spanish much easier to learn, understand, and memorize. This is hardly surprising, given that French and Spanish belong to the Romance language family. Maurer & Puren, relying on data from ethnologue.com, provide these lexical similarity coefficients:[143]

- French – Spanish: 0.75
- English – French: 0.27
- English – Spanish: –

Beyond vocabulary, French and Spanish also share significant syntactic similarities. Without going into detail, sentences are often structured similarly, and the metalanguage (grammar terminology) is almost identical. My son's Spanish teacher says he learns quickly and easily grasp linguistic concepts. He said, "Spanish is easier because it's like French and reminds me of French class." In reality, he has instinctively developed plurilingual learning competence, applying strategies of analysis, intercomprehension, and transfer.

One might think it is less feasible to use English to learn French. True, the lexical similarity coefficient between English and French is 0.27. However, Bernard Cerquiglini estimates that "more than a third of the [English] vocabulary is French in origin. If we add words derived from Latin, it surpasses 50%."[144] He attributes much of English's lexicon to "abstract vocabulary, commerce, administrative terms, legal and

---

[143] Maurer & Puren, 2019: 254.
[144] Cerquiglini, 2024:10.

political concepts").[145] Thus, it is indeed possible to draw on English to learn French (and vice versa). Beyond vocabulary, Maurer & Puren have identified "about ten strictly identical syntactic patterns shared by both languages."[146] Practically, more so than my son's Spanish class, I use his English science and social studies lessons to spark his renewed interest in written French. Drawing on one language to learn another is part of a plurilingual didactic approach, the Integrated Language Didactics.[147] Tapping into other academic subjects as well makes it transdisciplinary.

Conclusion

The theory of plurilingualism helped me realize that imperfection in plurilingual children does not signify failure or confusion but underscores their evolving linguistic flexibility over time, shaped by age, language exposure, and life experiences. My journey as a parent of plurilingual children has led me to believe that learning a language is a lifelong endeavor. If young children struggle academically, we must give them time, show patience, and remain confident. Beyond developing plurilingual competence, our immersion in a new society led our entire family—children and parents alike—into new cultural arenas: celebrating new holidays, commemorating local historical events (Martin Luther King Day, Patriot Day, Independence Day), discovering new foods, and more. We learned to shift our perspective away from our usual cultural benchmarks and incorporate others. Boston is an international city, so we also encountered customs and traditions from Ireland, India, Mexico, and Egypt. In turn, we happily shared some of our own French traditions: *la galette des Rois* for Epiphany, *les crêpes de la Chandeleur*, and so on.

My children are French and American—both. More than just learning languages and developing plurilingual skills, I have seen them acquire values of respect, tolerance, and openness. I look upon them with affection and pride, watching them flourish in a multicultural environment, and I have come to see them as citizens of the world.

---

[145] Ibid.
[146] Maurer & Puren, 2019: 257.
[147] Candelier, n.d.

12. My journey within the field of Francophone studies: From Africa to America
Emmanuel Kayembe

My love for the French language was born from contact with my primary school teachers, who made me discover and love the childhood literature of Ernest Pérochon (1885-1942), a local writer born in Courlay who knew how to give relief to his fictional characters, whose simplicity evokes a profound dimension of his native Poitou. This ancient relationship with French culture was the spark that ignited in me a taste for literary studies. At the end of my secondary studies in philosophy and Latin, I had to enroll at the University of Elisabethville-Lubumbashi. Finally, I obtained a double baccalaureate in classics and French language and literature. This went against the wishes of my parents, who wanted me to become a lawyer or a medical doctor at a time when the promotion of science, technology, economics, and legal sciences, as well as studies of engineering and mathematics, occupied the center of discussions on the future of Africa. With all due respect to my family, who only saw studies in terms of immediate profitability, I had to earn a doctorate in French language and literature to find myself, one thing leading to another, a teacher-researcher at the University of Elisabethville-Lubumbashi first, then at the University of Cape Town, and, a little later, at the University of Botswana, where I taught for four years French as a foreign language and Francophone cultures, including the North American Francophonie, after a brief stint at the American Council of Learned Societies (Carnegie Corporation of New York). This long adventure, far from reaching its conclusion, has transformed me into a nomad and a tireless advocate of classical humanities and French language education.

François Guilbert, a specialist in Plautus, taught me the tricks of classical philology and introduced me very early to reading French novels of ideas. Robert Baudry, a renowned medievalist, taught me to love the Arthurian cycle, the quest for the Grail, and its marvelous structure (my childhood dreams are full of Percival and Vermeil!). Paul de Meester de Ravestein initiated me into the hidden beauties of Francophone literature, which offers a suggestive shortcut to major contemporary questions relating to global identities. I am no longer African through and through. Belgium and France constitute my second homelands. From my former masters, I perhaps got my passion for French and Francophone letters, which allowed me to take part in numerous research projects, financed in particular by the French Institute of South Africa and the University Agency of the Francophonie. Starting from the University of Southern Maine, my interest became increasingly focused on French Canadian heritage in the United States as it relates to Franco-American identity, working on a collaborative project that aims at allowing Franco-American or French-Canadian Heritage organizations to know each other better, to enhance their mutual institutional visibility by sharing their resources, projects, and expertise, and by providing data that can be easily accessed in the USA and beyond.

Exact Sciences and Technological Studies Or Letters and Human Sciences?

In the aftermath of African independences, the problem of training national elites capable of contributing to the development of Africa became acute. Moreover, well before at the end of the Second World War, Cheikh Anta Diop, Senegalese historian, anthropologist, and physicist, already underlined the role of exact sciences and technological studies in the development process of the black continent: "Africa, he said, will have a huge need for atomic scientists, solar energy specialists, engineers with a scientific culture related to the works of art that they will have to build on a continental scale, during its independence"(Diop 16, my translation). However, while insisting on introducing young Africans to the mysteries of scientific and technical studies, the first African academics highlighted the need to "humanize" technology, to consider humans as the ferment of all real progress. They, therefore, denounced the dangers and abuses generated by any technological practice that does not integrate the ethical values from ancient traditions.

Many educators and politicians believed Africa needed writers, linguists, and executives keen on humanist culture. This educational position, it should be emphasized, ultimately led to a discussion on the judicious uses and the harmful uses of technology and the integration of the studies of cultures and languages in the development projects of the black continent. In Africa, in general, and in the Democratic Republic of the Congo, the definition of the intellectual as an agent of social transformation thus considered knowledge of languages an essential formative element, among others.

> Indeed, first and foremost, and as a priority, our country [the Democratic Congo] urgently needs doctors, engineers, a competent administration, and industrialists. All of these expect adequate and highly specialized training, which begins best in the scientific Sections. However, shouldn't it also be necessary for the country to have well-trained executives in a humanist style? (De Meester 5, my translation).

Let us refer here to the reflections of Leopold Sedar Senghor on the place of classical studies and the importance of the teaching of Latin in Senegal, reflections that show how the United States and the Federal Republic of Germany, two technologically advanced countries, have nevertheless integrated into academic curricula the study of Latin and Greek as a catalyst for human and economic development. Moreover, in a communication entitled "Le français, langue de culture," published in 1962 in the journal *Esprit* (pp. 837-844), Senghor highlighted the usefulness of learning and teaching French as a vehicle of culture and a tool for international communication, which allows Africans to express themselves in world circles, while keeping their languages for local exchanges:

> Most African states are French-speaking, and, [at] the UN, a third of the delegations speak French. In 1960, after the massive entry of new African states into the International Organization, Habib Bourguiba logically concluded that strengthening the teaching of French in Tunisia was necessary. Hassan II did not apply another policy. Morocco alone has 8,000 French teachers, and more than half of those serve abroad (Senghor 837, my translation).

This point of view of Senghor was in line with a policy of continental unity, likely to allow a good number of African countries to communicate among themselves and with the outside world, given the strong linguistic heterogeneity of the black continent. Indeed, at the height of the debates on the linguistic decolonization of Africa, politicians and educators supported the importance of keeping foreign languages as official languages, although imposed on Africa through colonization, and this despite the opposition of some prominent intellectuals, including Cheikh Anta Diop, author, among others, of a work which caused a stir, *Les Fondements économiques et culturels d'un État fédéral d'Afrique Noire*, published for the first time in 1960 in Paris by Présence Africaine and translated in English in 1987 by Harold J. Salemson (*Black Africa: The Economic and Cultural Basis for a Federated State*). When I enrolled at the University of Elisabethville-Lubumbashi in 1982, all these questions still dominated the Zairian political and intellectual fields (the Democratic Republic of the Congo was called Zaire from 1971 to 1996). Africa's development projects were then at the crossroads of cultural and economic issues. However, despite recognizing the role of so-called soft sciences in building young African nations, many families steered their children towards more technical training, which was considered more profitable on the job market. I will never forget my father's dismay when I told him I had enrolled in literature and the humanities! He quickly called a family meeting to bring me back to reason. We lived in a society in complete transformation, where educational strategies had replaced patrimonial strategies. Indeed, our peasant societies had sold to the colonists and missionaries the ancestral lands inherited from a long tradition for the benefit of symbolic capitals.

We had then submitted to a process of acculturation where the prestige of diplomas and medals measured social success. Like Ferdinand Oyono's hero in *Le Vieux nègre et la médaille* (1956; *The Old Man and the Medal*), our destiny was now linked to "privileges socially conditioned in merits or personal "gifts" (Bourdieu). Our parents had raised to the pinnacle the social benefits that came from studies whose economic profitability was apparent. They no longer spared us the possibility of becoming teachers, a profession that, in their eyes, would only lead to extreme poverty. My choice to study French and Latin was thus considered pure provocation! We had at least one reason that pushed us towards literary studies: our prestigious masters, whose nascent international reputation already fascinated us. Among the most prominent Congolese teachers was Valentin Yves Mudimbe, born, like me, in Jadotville-Likasi in the Belgian Congo. For political reasons, Mudimbe left his native Congo in the 1980s and later became the William R. Kenan Professor of French, Comparative Literature, and Classics at Stanford University, then Newman Ivey White Professor of Comparative Literature at Duke University. Mudimbe is Ruth F. DeVarney Professor Emeritus of Romance Studies and Comparative Literature at the same University. Impressive, the cultural capital of Mudimbe left no one indifferent. Apart from the fact that he mastered a dozen modern languages, including French, Italian, Spanish, Portuguese, German, Dutch, and Russian, he already enjoyed considerable international fame from Congo well before his American exile, as evidenced by the numerous visiting professorships he held in Europe, at the University of Louvain in Belgium, and the University of Paris-Nanterre in France.

He was, strictly speaking, one of our most culturally gifted professors, who spoke French without an accent, except for Dr. Wansanga Mukendi, a geographer and economist trained at the University of Paris-Sorbonne, who was a Visiting Associate Professor at Amherst College. All those who attended the University of Elisabethville-Lubumbashi in the 1970s and 1980s will remember this joke by Dr. Mukendi: "In this entire University, there are only two people who know how to speak French, my friend Valentin Yves Mudimbe and I."

We were looking for intellectual models capable of justifying our choice of French, among other things, as a subject of university specialization. To Valentin Yves Mudimbe, whom the book *The Invention of Africa* (1988) revealed to the scientific world, we willingly opposed another Congolese Professor, Dr. Georges Ngal, author of a brilliant thesis on Aimé Césaire defended in 1968 at the University of

Fribourg in Switzerland.[148] From the 1980s, Ngal traveled the world to teach as an Associate Professor in several universities in France, Germany, Belgium, Canada, and the United States: Middlebury College in the United States, Universities of Montreal and Sherbrooke in Canada, University of Liège in Belgium, Universities of Nice, Sorbonne, Bordeaux, Grenoble III, Nanterre Paris X, Sorbonne Paris IV in France and University of Bayreuth in Germany. At that time, two antagonistic groups of students were on the Élisabethville-Lubumbashi campus: those who claimed to be followers of V.Y. Mudimbe and those who swore only by Georges Ngal! In 1975, Mudimbe did not stop himself from taking Ngal to court for defamation following the publication of a novel entitled *Giambattista Viko ou le Viol du discours africain*, of which the latter is the author.[149]

Around 1970-1980, the University of Élisabethville-Lubumbashi constituted a true microcosm of the French-speaking world, where teachers from the four corners of Africa, Europe, and Asia came together. Théophile Obenga, poet, linguist, and historian from Congo-Brazzaville, currently Professor Emeritus at San Francisco State University, represented with much more rigor the Afrocentric current of Egyptology initiated by Cheikh Anta Diop, who conquered the hearts of the Congolese during a series of conferences organized in Élisabethville-Lubumbashi. Paulin Hountondji, a Beninese philosopher trained at the École Normale Supérieure of Paris and the University of Paris Sorbonne, brought grist to the mill of discussions on the existence and definition of an African philosophy. Bogumil Jewsiewicki-Koss, currently Professor Emeritus at the University Laval in Canada, nicknamed "Radio-France Internationale" because of his volubility in French, was already laying the foundations for his research on Congolese cultural history and social memory that he will develop within the Centre de recherche Cultures, Arts et Sociétés in Laval.

---

[148] *Aimé Césaire: Un homme à la recherche d'une patrie*.

[149] This novel has been recently translated into English in the 2023 Modern Language Association's "Texts and Translations series" by Dr. David Damrosch, a native of Maine, who is Ernest Bernbaum Professor of Comparative Literature at Harvard University.

Professor Tran Hong Cam, originally from Vietnam, commanded the admiration of his students with his extensive knowledge of French linguistics. Robert Baudry, born in Sallèles d'Aude in the Occitane region of France, generously took charge of the direction of my honors thesis following the unexpected death of my master François Guilbert at the Saint-André Abbey in Bruges in Belgium. Baudry later became a Research Associate at the Literary Research Center of the University of Angers in France and collaborated on the *New Encyclopedia Arthuriana*, the world reference work on the Arthurian world. His works *Graal et littérature d'aujourd'hui*[150] and *Le Mythe de Merlin*[151] constitute the sum of his research on the marvelous in French literature initiated from the University of Elisabethville-Lubumbashi.

Discovering the Classic French Novelists of the 20th Century

At the end of three years of study, the programs of the University of Elisabethville-Lubumbashi required that each student present a short essay on a specific subject approved within the department in which they were enrolled. One of our Professors, François Guilbert, who had a good disposition towards me, suggested that I conduct a semantic study on the word "forest" in Latin in Seneca's *Tragedies* (the concept of forest is subsumed by four words, *silva, lucus, nemus,* and *saltus*), whose semantic difference can only be understood about the context in which they appear. But at the same time, he advised me to read the entire works of the major French novelists of the 20th century, including François Mauriac, André Gide, Antoine de Saint-Exupéry, André Malraux, and André Maurois, beyond the French text analysis course, which only included selected pieces from authors. Guilbert explained that he had detected in me a vocation as a researcher and university teacher and that I needed to prepare myself for a career as a comparatist scholar in literature. These recommended readings were only a logical extension of the exercise in semantic categorization to which he had subjected me by inviting me to begin a vocabulary study on one of Seneca's works.

---

[150] Dinan: Terre de Brume, 1998
[151] Dinan: Terre de Brume, 2008

From a limited semantic decoding, I thus opened myself up to the methods of a broader textual understanding. I discovered the role of the reader in the recreation of textual meaning. As Wolfgang Iser,[152] who was part of our required reading, points out, this meaning only becomes apparent when we manage to combine sociological-historical reading methods and theoretical-textual approaches to grasp both the social meanings of the literary work and the aesthetic effects it produces on us. Reading is truly an adventure that leads us to unknown lands, an activity that broadens the horizon of our knowledge and enriches our inner being.

Thérèse Desqueyroux by François Mauriac introduced me to the romantic universe of spiritual anxiety. Pure love, nourished by innocent country virtues, transforms into incomprehensible hatred! Thérèse, the heroine, loathes the countryman she loved and married. She goes further: she plans to poison him! Oh, unfathomable recesses of the human heart! The magic of Mauriac's style seduced me, and it was with eagerness that I devoured *Le Mystère Frontenac* by the same author. This time, a hymn to the family is at stake; it is the family united by mysterious bonds, where tradition and respect for the name appear to influence the essence of the relationship between its members. My interest shifted from novels of love and family affection to more serious works that illustrated human greatness and the drama of the human condition. *Terre des hommes* and *Vol de nuit* by Antoine de Saint-Exupéry taught me, practically, self-improvement and a sense of duty. The same ideal, transformed into a political and ideological fight, is thematized in *La Condition humaine* by André Malraux. André Maurois and his masterpiece, *Climats*, completely disorientated me, plunging me into the chaotic world of marital relationships. French literature radically transformed me. It taught me to know myself in depth and to understand others. As Roland Barthes so aptly put it, "L'exercice jamais clos de la lecture demeure le lieu par excellence de l'apprentissage de soi et de l'autre" (The never-ending exercise of reading remains the place par excellence for learning about oneself and others").

---

[152] *L'Acte de lecture. Theorie de l'effet esthétique*, Bruxelles: Mardaga, 2nd ed., 1985

Damourette and Pichon
or the "sexuisemblance" in the French Language

My recent reading of Céline Labrosse's *Pour une langue sans sexisme* (Montreal: Fides, 2021) brought back old memories. It was in 1982. We took a mandatory course in contemporary French grammar and enrolled in the first French and Latin studies cycle at the University of Elisabethville-Lubumbashi. The course instructor, Pierre-Claver Ntamunoza, a disciple of V.Y. Mudimbe who died in Australia in 1992, constantly invited us to read books by good authors, including *Les Nourritures terrestres* by André Gide and *La Chute* by Albert Camus. Still, at the same time, he urged us to convert to linguistics: "Convert, comrades, convert to linguistics, you will go to heaven!" Beyond his frequent jokes, which helped us relax, Professor Ntamunoza taught us the prolegomena of the great currents of modern linguistics. From him, we learned the fundamental concepts of grammar, from Ferdinand de Saussure, the founder of modern linguistics and structuralism, to Noam Chomsky, the father of generative and transformational grammar, through Ferdinand Brunot, the author of *La Pensée et la langue* (1922) and the precursor of psycholinguistics. We wondered what the "Chomskian revolution" was called at the time. Chomsky illuminated the innate structures of the "language faculty." He assumed that children are innately aware of the fundamental grammar shared by all human languages, suggesting that every language is a form of limitation. He referred to this innate knowledge as "grammaire universelle." He asserted that using formal grammar to express language knowledge explains its "productivity." Given a finite number of grammatical rules and a finite set of terms, people can create an infinite number of phrases. He said there are and always will be words that have never been spoken. Proponents of this theory contend that it is difficult to explain why children pick up languages so quickly unless they are born with a natural aptitude for language acquisition.

However, the most interesting part of the course taught by Pierre-Claver Ntamunoza concerned the question of "sexuisemblance" in the French language raised by Jacques Damourette and Édouard Pichon in *Des mots à la pensée. Essai d'une grammaire de la langue française* (1930-

1956). According to these authors, the French nominal noun is based on three concepts: the base (i.e., the degree of determination), the quantity (i.e., the number), and the "sexuisemblance." This last idea, which does not fall under linguistic logic, extends the sexual difference between men and women to things. Why were objects and ideas given sex in French? For Damourette and Pichon, this fact is part of the French national imaginary and is the mark of the most refined languages. In *Pour une langue sans sexisme* (2021), Céline Labrosse, lecturer and research and teaching associate on women at McGill University, reintroduces the debate to the heart of the University and speaks out in favor of a French language that is "vivante, fertile, enrichissante et infiniment plus égalitaire." She criticizes the first grammarians and accuses them of making women "invisible and mute." According to Labrosse, gender is not universal since some languages, notably Finno-Hungarian, Turkish, Mongolian, and Chinese, do not have genders. Even if such a project seems legitimate, it is nevertheless to be feared that it will lead to the total disfiguration of a language whose beauty has spanned the ages despite the sexual character of the French national imagination, which is a legacy of Latinity. This beauty, which makes French a place of discovery *par excellence* of oneself and others, inhabits and keeps transforming me. It is always with passion that I have been committed for decades to promoting it, especially in regions where it is a minority language.

Promoting French in a World Dominated by English: From South Africa to America through Europe

The post-apartheid period allowed South Africa to open up to the world and Africa. The massive immigration of French speakers from sub-Saharan Africa to South Africa created a need for knowledge exchange and collaboration in the educational, cultural, and commercial fields from a global perspective. In this context, the French Institute of South Africa was born, and its mission is to strengthen bilateral relations between France, southern Africa, and the world. In this sense, faced with the increasingly pressing challenges of the "transcultural" phenomenon that emerged in major South African cities, the University of Johannesburg and the French Institute of South Africa believed it necessary to organize an international conference on transculturalism in French-speaking African literature and culture in 2005. I was privileged to speak at these crucial meetings sponsored by the French Embassy in South Africa and the French Institute of South Africa. The French Embassy generously covered the travel expenses, the board, and the room and granted me a *per diem* of 800 rands per day for personal needs (the equivalent of USD 100 per day). Intercultural and transcultural are part of understanding cultural and racial differences today. They have a close relationship with the identity processes of belonging, integration, and exclusion. Intercultural identities are based on the reality that no one is locked into a single culture, like in a bubble, isolated from the world. No one is monocultural. We all wear several identity hats, which we often use opportunely. We are in permanent identity negotiation.

Interculturality (or intercultural) encourages exchanges between cultures and facilitates their integration within a specific society. In this way, it helps to avoid discrimination and promote social cohesion. This is thanks to intercultural dialogue, mutual respect, and the desire to preserve all cultural identities. Therefore, The objective is not to impose one culture on another but to create shared values. The diversity of identities, whether cultural, religious, etc., is highlighted in interculturality. However, it also considers the dominant culture of the host country to avoid excessive integration of individuals with a different culture. Everyone must have the same rights. The transcultural or transculturality, on the other hand – this concept was coined by the Cuban anthropologist Fernando Ortiz Fernandez – defines us as men of passage, prisoners of the passage, involved in a permanent process of identification with several different cultural poles. It is strictly a crossing of cultures towards a hybrid culture, formed of a skein of different identity threads.

What can be learned from these critical discussions on contemporary identity dynamics is that they allowed me at the time to insert myself into a network of researchers on French-speaking literatures and cultures of the world. I will never forget these kind words from my colleague and friend, Heidi Bojsen, Professor of Francophone literatures at Roskilde University in Denmark: "Well, dear friends, we are now part of the same family." Our identities were then defined more in terms of existence than essence, about others and to ourselves, without falling into the identity extremism of Gilles Deleuze: "Le désert, l'expérimentation sur soi-même, est notre seule identité, notre chance unique pour toutes les combinaisons qui nous habitent" ("The desert, the experimentation on oneself, is our only identity, our unique chance for all the combinations that inhabit us," my translation).

This meeting with colleagues worldwide strengthens my vocation as a defender of the French language and Francophone literature and my passion for comparative literature. Thanks to mobility scholarships from the Agence Universitaire de la Francophonie and the University of Botswana, I had the opportunity to take part as a speaker in important conferences and to contribute to works on emerging identities, notably at the University of Kwazulu-Natal in Pietermaritzburg, the University of Galati in Romania, the Universities of Lorraine and Bordeaux in France, Laval University in Canada, Furman University, the College of Charleston and the University of Puerto Rico in the United States, apart from a research invitation from the University of Melbourne, among others. I want to mention here the debt I owe to Professor Paul de Meester de Ravestein of happy memory, who, even though he was a specialist in classics, made me discover the hidden beauties of Francophone literatures and encouraged me to undertake research in this field, starting by directing my interest towards *L'Aventure ambiguë* by Cheikh Hamidou Kane.

Teaching North American Francophonie
at the University of Botswana

After earning my Ph.D. in Francophone Literatures and Cultures at the University of Cape Town, where I taught French as a Foreign Language for three years, I went on to be a Research Fellow at the American Council of Learned Societies (Carnegie Corporation of New York) for one year and then joined the University of Botswana. At this institution, my primary assignment was to teach the French language at all levels, the cultures and civilizations of the French and French-speaking world, and Francophone and French literature. Despite the many classes I oversaw, I had set myself the priority of developing two courses, French 314 and French 214. French 314 introduced ways of life, social structure, law, politics, attitudes and mentalities, and other facets of French culture and civilization pertinent to studying literature and language. Students could study French language and literature and had a greater appreciation for French civilization. As didactical material, we used texts from television shows, movies, newspapers, journals, and other media that provided students with a foundational understanding of French culture and civilization. French 214 was an introduction to French-speaking culture and Civilization. This course aimed at exploring facets of French-speaking civilization and society that are important for studying literature and language, as well as a genuine introduction to social structures, politics, law, and other areas of daily life. A survey of French-speaking countries' civilizations used real resources about politics, social life, and economics. Students got the chance to contrast various facets of French-speaking civilization with those of their own.

It is essential to underline that I devoted one chapter of French 214 to what we call "la francophonie invisible," namely the North American Francophonie. When it comes to teaching about the American Francophonie of the US, the teacher is faced with a glaring shortage of teaching materials unless he makes a considerable effort to turn the disparate sources into a coherent whole. A few texbooks, however, appear here as an unexpected solution to this documentary gap, even if they often only offer short passages relating to limited aspects of the French-speaking world in the United States.

- *Civilisation progressive de la Francophonie* (2003) by Jackson N. Njiké,
- *À l'Écoute des Francophones d'Amérique* (1991) by Nicole Maury and Jules Tessier, and
- *Je me souviens. Histoire, culture et littérature du Québec francophone* (2014) by Elizabeth Blood and J. Vincent H. Morrissette.

Njiké presents a global anthology of the Francophonie, which includes West Africa, Central Africa, the Great Lakes of Africa, the Indian Ocean, the Arab countries, Southeast Asia, the Pacific Ocean, the Caribbean, North America, and Europe. Of the American Francophonie, the Cameroonian author unfortunately only includes Louisiana, New Brunswick, and Quebec. Not a word about New England! Njiké briefly addresses Louisiana's musical culture, one of the most accomplished forms of which is jazz – a music that originated from the songs of enslaved Black Africans brought into captivity in America and which was made famous worldwide by Louis Armstrong – and Cajun music illustrated by Zachary Richard. Maury and Tessier devote a paragraph to the history of Franco-Americans, descendants of Quebec immigrants who chose to emigrate to New England in search of better-paid jobs – and who, to resist cultural assimilation by the United States, organized themselves into small agglomerations called "Little Canadas." Blood and Morrissette consider the history of Franco-Americans as an appendix to the history of French-speaking Quebec. They ultimately sacrifice Franco-American specificity by classifying, without any taxonomic concern, authors whose nationality nevertheless poses a problem, namely Honoré Beaugrand (*La Chasse-galerie*, 1900), Louis Hamon (*Maria Chapdelaine*, 1916), and Lucie Therrien (*Mémère*, 1992). In any case, the teaching materials for a course on the Francophonie of New England are not abundant, and the teacher is often obliged to compose his notes. The teachers' handbook published by the University of Maine at Orono in 1981 is a valuable tool that can provide teachers with the opportunity to develop curricula on Franco-American studies (see Stanley L. Freeman and Raymond J. Pelletier, *Manuel du Professeur pour introduire les études franco-américaines. Initiating Franco-American Studies. A Handbook for Teachers*, Orono: University of Maine). Unfortunately, this book is not available on the international market. Perhaps it should be considered for updating and publishing by Editions CLE, Hachette, or Hatier in Paris.

In total, my courses in French 214 and French 314 allowed me to introduce students to key questions relating to the concept of diversity in France and Francophone literatures and cultures and to the notion of identity, which has been widely integrated into the field of human and social sciences for decades and now seems essential for understanding in depth the conflicts, tensions, and crises that are shaking the world.

Building Bridges Between French Heritage Societies in the U.S.

My commitment to Francophone studies extends beyond instructing students in French and Francophone cultures. Numerous services to the profession, the university, and the Francophone communities are also involved. Recently, I have been working on building bridges between French heritage societies in the US. My collaborative project aims to allow Franco-American or French-Canadian Heritage organizations to know each other better, enhance their mutual institutional visibility by sharing their resources and expertise, and provide data easily accessible in the USA and beyond. It is designed to reunite in a national interactive platform board members, teachers, researchers, and amateurs from diverse origins and cultures who are interested in the history and culture of Francophone Canadian immigrants from regions along American borders and Acadians, who were brutally deported from their homeland. Apart from Acadians whose exile was forced, those people, as I said, were attracted by better employment opportunities in mills and shoe manufacturers of New England, farms, lumber companies, and mines of the Midwestern United States (Minnesota, Michigan, Illinois, Missouri).

The history of Franco-Americans or French-Canadians in the USA is also a history of mutual ignorance. With time, French heritage societies have been splintering increasingly, every group working separately in its corner. Therefore, one of their shortcomings is the near total absence of a platform of concertation and coordination when it comes to common strategies for preserving French-American history and culture. In this regard, laying the foundations for a common strategic platform seems urgent. This place could serve as a framework for consultations, exchanges, discussions, and collaboration about major questions devoted to the protection, preservation, and promotion of the cultural heritage of the Franco-American population in the United States of America and beyond.

The second project I am currently working on is a community-based French program. The growing influx of French-speaking African immigrants to Maine has resulted in a French-language renaissance in Lewiston, Auburn, Portland, and surrounding areas. We are far from the period when a law passed in 1919 prohibited the use of the language of Voltaire in the schools of Maine. These have now become multilingual places at the crossroads of various cultures. As a result, we are witnessing a renewed interest in French, especially among Franco-Americans. More and more young Franco-Americans who want to reconnect with their linguistic and cultural roots are choosing French as an optional subject, especially at the University of Southern Maine, where I have been teaching for a few years. These young students, recognizable by their French-sounding surnames (Beaudet, Beaulieu, Leblanc, Lévesque, Paquette, Pelletier, Saint-Onge, etc.), reinforce the need to create programs in French as a community-based language not only for Franco-Americans but also for Francophone immigrants.

13. Collective Action to Protect our Future – Creating a Sustainable Franco-American Path Forward
Timothy Beaulieu

I have volunteered and organized in the Franco-American world for over a decade.[153] Currently, I organize PoutineFest in New Hampshire and Maine—events that celebrate the French language and Francophone culture in their respective communities.

Like many United States ancestral groups, we are siloed in the communities in which we live. We say phrases like, "I am a proud Maine Franco" or "I am a Westside (of Manchester, New Hampshire) Franco." These are great things to be proud of; our ancestors did amazing things in the communities we settled during our mass migration to the United States between 1860 and 1930. While that local pride is commendable, it raises an important question: Is it serving us here in the present? What would our ancestors think of this? After all, did French-Canadian mill workers go on 19th-century Zillow to find the best neighborhoods?

This chapter will delve into some pressing urgencies and potential solutions for preserving our culture, highlighting the urgent need for immediate action.

French is in danger

As I have become more involved and aware of the Franco-American world, I have noticed that we have a "closing of the mill" on our

---

[153] For this chapter, think of the Franco-American world as the New England states (Upstate New York and parts of the Midwest). Also note a Franco-American in this chapter is someone who identifies as a descendant of French Canada living in the United States.

horizon, and none of us can see it. This is not a distant threat; it is a reality that is unfolding before us. Maybe it is a little denial; maybe we see a good story or two, and confirmation bias begins to kick in. But the truth is, we are at a critical juncture where our language and culture are at risk of disappearing within a generation if we don't take immediate and substantial action.

Regardless of the reason, the stark reality is that French and French education will disappear in New England within my children's lifetime without some real action. Sure, we will have small pockets and French expats in Boston, but that is it. You might think, "That is not possible; we have many organizations doing various things." However, for the record, it is not enough. It is just simply not enough. We have become complacent with the reality I describe, and it feels like we are going through the motions a little bit. Every time I read my local news online (newspapers are disappearing, too), it is another story of a school district cutting its French program. It is somewhat challenging to advance in French in many school districts in northern New England.

This is the trickle-down effect of the decline from the 1990s. Finding teachers is complex, and since school districts cannot find teachers, they pull the plug altogether. Relying on local municipalities to promote *notre langue* through school districts is not working. This prompts us to ask: What can we do differently?

Is French still important?

The short answer is absolutely. Even though the recent Franco-American renaissance is mainly in English, French fingerprints are all over it. That is not bad; being fully part of American culture is a massive strength. It allows us to ensure our culture is not forgotten and remains part of our corner of the United States.

However, in my travels and the time I have spent getting to know the Québécois, many do not understand our very American concept of culture: if you cannot speak French, you are just American. I am not a huge fan of that attitude, but that thought process does exist in the motherland. It highlights the cultural disconnect that has developed over time. It is hard for folks outside the United States to understand why the language has disappeared in most Franco-American families. Fortunately for us, many Québécois get it and are more than willing to offer language learning advice and listen to ideas. If our Franco-American world continues, having a strong bond with Québec is very important. This bond can help bridge the cultural gap and reinvigorate interest in the French language.

The Foundation is Being Set

First, let's acknowledge that we're in this for the long haul. Preserving our Franco-American culture is not a quick fix but a sustained effort that requires us to shake off complacency and recognize the groundwork already laid.

Some glimmers of hope are beginning to emerge. All over New England, there are grassroots and organized efforts to make our culture more visible. You can start a podcast, organize a food festival, host virtual cultural events, or initiate open communications among all the different Franco groups in New England. We are more connected than ever, and each one of us can contribute to this movement in our own unique way.

Many of these projects did not exist ten years ago; consider what things could look like ten years into the future if we act on French now. As these projects mature (some already are), we must decide what to do with that success. Success can be quantified in dollars and cents for some projects, but the true measure is the cultural impact. This leads us to consider building upon this foundation to address the challenges ahead, with a hopeful outlook for the future.

The Silo Problem

As I began working across New England, I noticed many good organizations working in their communities. However, that impact needs to be amplified beyond local boundaries. For example, in the fall of 2024, I gave a presentation to some students at the University of Massachusetts Lowell. Lowell, Massachusetts, is Jack Kerouac's hometown and a historic Franco mill town. It is less than 100 miles from

Maine PoutineFest in Portland, Maine, and 17 miles from New Hampshire PoutineFest in Merrimack, New Hampshire. Yet, not one of the students I spoke to knew what a Franco-American was or whether there were any institutions still carrying on parts of the culture. It was like we were extinct.

Once I explained the story of French-Canadian immigration to New England and how poutine fits into our modern story, the students became very interested. We had a nice dialogue, and I left that meeting feeling like I had helped keep our story going. However, I also left with some pressing questions. How is it possible that students at a university in New England had no idea about the Franco history of the area? This underscores the silo problem we face.

The Franco Bubble

The story of French-Canadian immigration is not taught in New England schools; we are a footnote. But we are doing things here in the present. So why are we still unknown? Some of this comes from the Franco bubble. As mentioned before, Franco organizations tend to be small and only operate in their local community. Good feelings can come from a handful of small activities, but what is the long-term plan? Is staying small sustainable?

The short answer is that this model is not sustainable. If you are not growing, you are dying. If you are drawing small classes or crowds in a local community, that is a concern. Instead of having many scattered, smallish organizations working in a bubble, why not come together a little more? By uniting our efforts, we can create a larger impact and reach a wider audience.

Gagnon's Dream

This brings us to Ferdinand Gagnon's vision. In the 19th century, early Franco-American journalist Ferdinand Gagnon envisioned an international union of French-Canadians in the United States and Canada. He thought this idea would eventually come to fruition; unfortunately, it did not in his lifetime. By the middle of the 20th century,

French-Canadians in Québec and the United States began to drift apart. In the 21st century, that drift has hit the point of forgetting our connections.

Some are beginning to wake up, but it is a slow process. In 2024, PoutineFest had volunteers from Québec at both the Maine and New Hampshire events. All these connections came through social media, specifically the Facebook group Le Rêve de Gagnon – French-Canadians in Canada and the United States. It is remarkable what can happen when cousins reconnect.

Perhaps French-Canadians in the United States should collaborate more on large events and projects. I see the same issues in Lewiston, Maine, as in Nashua, New Hampshire. Could sharing best practices regularly ensure our culture continues? By embracing Gagnon's dream, we can forge stronger ties and reinvigorate our cultural heritage.

Franco Talent Collective

Building on this idea, some Franco-Americans are already starting to break out of those silos and begin working on projects. A number of us from New Hampshire, Maine, and Massachusetts make up a group of like-minded Franco-Americans who get together and help each other on projects. We have had meetups in Manchester, New Hampshire; Lewiston, Boston; and Salem, Massachusetts. To me, it is very reminiscent of what Ferdinand Gagnon envisioned. While we have grown up in separate communities, we ignore those boundaries and work together.

Perhaps my favorite part of the Franco Talent Collective is hearing new ideas and sensing a similar sense of urgency. We recognize that time is of the essence. Fifty years ago, finding a group of Franco-Americans to get together like this would have been far easier. Perhaps there would be thirty to forty people interested; at the moment, there are about ten of us. While we are a small group, I will take ten motivated people over a larger group of folks who may not be as motivated. Together, we can serve as a catalyst for broader change.

How To Bring Us Together

This has puzzled me. As I look across the Franco-American landscape, the most apparent gap appears to be seeding the future. We need to find ways to engage the next generation. We tend to get together to talk about the past—a lot. One of the biggest complaints I hear is that no young people are coming to these events to discuss what is becoming a distant past.

Getting younger folks to attend events is hard, but we constantly miss the why. The key issue is that we have not been seeding the future. The only way to get the next generation to care about this Franco-American stuff is to meet them where they are. Everyone can take a break from the past and focus on the present and future!

Ideas to Seed the Future

To address this challenge, here are some actionable ideas:

- Reward students

There are many headwinds for students who choose to study French these days. School districts seek to cut the language for sport, never mind the friendly competition with Spanish. Lastly, we have not done a great job advocating for the language. You can do a lot with French and Québec, which is only a few hours from most parts of New England; the opportunities are endless.

We must reward students for taking French to hit home that they have made the right choice studying the language. There are several easy ways to do this. The easiest one is a big language contest with prizes for the kids to react to. It may be money, trips, or opportunities to study abroad. It should be a contest that kids hear about before signing up for a class. Imagine students saying, "I am taking French because I can win an opportunity to study in France."

Another idea is job fairs and gatherings of French students. This taps into defeating some of the voices students may hear when taking French. They may hear, "You will never use that language." Imagine a student being able to reply, "Well, there is a job fair for French students every winter, so maybe you are wrong." The job fairs can help college students and people who already speak the language and reinforce the decision of high school students to take French. Many French and Canadian companies in the region can help; they need to see something happening.

Lastly, there need to be gatherings of French students. It is hard to see value in doing something when only a handful of kids in your school do it. Why not open it up to bring lots of students together? This is another way to reinforce their decision to take French and build a community.

– Reward teachers

Equally important is supporting our educators. We need more recognition for our French teachers. Many of these educators fell in love with the language of our ancestors and dedicated their careers to it. If you stop and reflect on that for a minute, that is a huge gamble and commitment.

In today's budget-cutting climate, we have far fewer French teachers than in the past. Franco-American institutions should bend over backward to help them. Some easy wins are sponsoring classroom supplies, offering to cover professional development classes, holding free conferences, funding trips to Québec, and, last but not least, the annual Teacher of the Year awards. Some of these ideas have happened in the past, but many seem to have fallen by the wayside. Making teachers feel valued and appreciated can go a long way; we need them. It is time we started acting like it.

– Regional family events

The culture must be visible to reach a wider audience. Having a conversation group with our same old friends will not do it. We need to get out there and engage with the community at large. Parents love to bring their kids to minor league baseball games, jump parks, soccer and hockey tournaments, and get ice cream. We need to be visible in these places.

Whether sponsoring a family night at the ballpark or setting up a fun family soccer tournament to benefit the culture, these are potential markets. The kids come and have fun, and our knowledgeable organizations engage with those parents. Offer the parents discounts on classes, free French swag, give away a few nights in Montreal—anything to spark an interest in the culture. You never know what the spark will be.

- Summer camps

Another avenue is to provide summer camps with a French influence. The reality of modern parenting is that most parents work full-time, and in this post-COVID-19 pandemic, most white-collar workers are required to be onsite a lot. The scramble to put kids in camp during the day begins in late winter and early spring. There are rarely enough spots for every kid to attend a camp.

I have seen a few tiny and lightly advertised French day camps for kids in New England. Maybe there is no market for them? It is hard to tell at this stage in the game. Perhaps there is an opportunity to pool resources and develop a few regional camps near high-population areas. These day camps do not have to be entirely in French but could have French influence. If parents see something that is 1) safe, 2) helps their kids learn, and 3) is fun, they will give it a shot. This could be an effective way to introduce children to the culture in an engaging environment.

- Document your family's successes

An easy win here is to change the narrative. I grew up away from the culture. In all the Franco communities I visit, we are either invisible, or the story is a little doom and gloom. Let us be clear: it is okay to mention the bad stuff sometimes, but let us celebrate some of those wins! It has not been all losses.

Americans love an underdog success story. Instead of saying, "We were oppressed in the mills and lost our language," control the story a bit more. How about, "Our ancestors came to this country and had a rough start in the mills, but we are still here and succeeding because of their sacrifice." Strong statements like that instill pride in children.

I mentioned our immigrant story to my kids but avoided the doom and gloom. I played up our successes and PoutineFest. Being French-Canadian is fun, and they are very proud of it. By documenting and sharing these success stories, we can inspire others and foster a positive cultural identity.

Burn The Ships

In conclusion, it can be scary to take some risks, but playing to "not lose" has caught up with us. We must finally stop aiming small, burn the ships, and go all in.

We have been aiming way too low for far too long. There are no right or wrong paths here, but doing something is better than doing nothing. Let us embrace the challenges ahead with courage and determination. By uniting our efforts, supporting our educators and students, and engaging with the broader community, we can ensure that the Franco-American culture survives and thrives for future generations.

14. Exploring the Intricacies of Franco-American Artistry
Melody Keilig

When you think of a culture's artistry, what comes to mind?

The visuals that instantly pop into my head are items I remember from childhood, like tea towels embroidered with folk art flowers, beer steins collected by my father during his military service abroad in Germany, and cultural clothing from this country and many others, or as I saw them portrayed in books, TV shows, and movies. I still think of these things and the various forms of visual art expressed through the clothing, writing, and artwork of cultures worldwide.

In sixth grade, my class had two elective classes to take before moving on to seventh grade, one of which was a culture class. It quickly became my favorite class and what I looked forward to at the end of every school day. I loved learning about different cultures; seeing how they expressed themselves visually and artistically was awe-inspiring.

At that point, I knew my maternal side was of some French heritage, but I could not exactly pinpoint it. Saying we had roots in France seemed foreign, yet I did not understand how I had a mémère and a pépère born and raised in the United States who spoke French.

When my interest in genealogy grew around that time, I finally asked my mother what kind of French heritage and culture her side of the family was called: if we could not consider ourselves as French as people in France, then what kind of French were we? That's when I finally heard her say "Franco-American" about French-Canadian heritage rooted in Quebec.

After that, it finally clicked. I was on a mission to learn as much as possible about Franco-Americans.

I could never find much when searching for Franco-American or French-Canadian visual expression in my culture textbook like I could with other cultures. My online research over the years to see how other

Franco-Americans expressed themselves artistically never resulted in anything besides some French-Canadian history.

Fast-forward to 2020, around the time of launching my blog, Moderne Francos. I once again began researching the cultural expressions of Franco-Americans, specifically those like me of French-Canadian descent from Quebec. However, I still came up short of finding cultural clothing and visual artwork. Everything that popped up was Canadian mountie uniforms or historically accurate clothing from New France.

When I searched for visual culture in online Franco-American groups, I only found discussions of the language, music, and food. These are significant parts of our culture, but I wanted to see more visual expressions through cultural clothing, artwork, and writing.

However, I did not have a picture in my mind of what exactly French-Canadian and Franco-American culture looked like regarding recognition as a cultural group in the same way I recognized an Oktoberfest celebration by attendees drinking out of beer steins while wearing dirndls and lederhosen.

Eventually, I found French-Canadian depictions of the long coats (capotes), hats (tuques), and woven belts (*ceinture flechées*) worn by "the voyagers" or *les voyageurs* of New France. These main clothing items are worn today in French-Canadian festivals and at the Quebec Winter Carnival by the mascot, Bonhomme, and some attendees.

I refer to this concept as "visual culture" when we recognize cultural groups through their visual art and other outward expression. With these forms of artistry, I believe Franco-Americans can become more of a recognized cultural group in the U.S. and beat our fears of the French language and our unique culture being quietly forgotten by ourselves.

Let's point this toward visual culture and expression to answer the question that could help our culture represent itself.

What is Franco-American artistry? To find out, I spoke to three Franco-American artists who tie specific themes, stories, and experiences of themselves and their families into their creative work.

Tanja Kunz

Tanja Kunz is an interdisciplinary artist whose works explore the healing capacity of art. She uses paint, textiles, metals, sounds, light, performance, and digital media to address spirituality, medicine, ancestry, labor, and justice.

When asked how she envisions the future of Franco-American artistry, she replied, "The short answer is, we must write our best stories with our great great great grandmother's pen. The longer answer requires an understanding that the arts are an expression of culture. And further, to explore the difference between 'culture' and 'living culture.'"

Kunz further explained that culture is defined by the customs, arts, social institutions, and achievements of a particular nation, people, or other social group. She added that it is often viewed as fixed and unchanging; the way things "used to be" is who we are, which is necessary to an extent because it establishes the cultural group.

"It creates the 'we'. This is the framework for the way we define ourselves. But to engage the arts today, we need a 'living culture' which requires we expand this framework," she said.

Going further into Kunz's concept of 'living culture,' she said the term implies the active passing of ancestral practices, knowledge, and skills through generations. This 'living culture' is not a static entity but a dynamic and evolving force that keeps a culture alive. To keep it thriving, 'wisdom keepers' must transmit cultural knowledge. Who are these leaders, exactly?

"These are our community leaders, our spiritual leaders, our artists and historians, our language keepers, our laborers, our mémés and scholars. All of these transmitters of culture connect us to the old ways, while also providing us a map to claim and grow our culture today," she said.

According to Kunz, all of this goes into the continued growth of Franco-American culture and artistry.

"In other words, to grow Franco-American artistry into the future, we must understand, respect, and honor our ancestors. We must learn from our mémés and other wisdomkeepers. And with all this in mind, we must do our best work, from where we are today. Can we write our best stories with our great great great grandmother's pen?" she said.

To present examples of Franco-American artwork, I asked Kunz if she could share a specific piece of art of her creation inspired by her Franco-American background.

Kunz describes her piece, *Lucien's Cloth*, as relating to her Franco-American ancestry and other Franco-Americans with ancestors who worked in mill towns. Lucien's Cloth is a textile-based work consisting of interlocking phosphorescent threads. Instead of making it with a loom, Kunz developed a process that held the threads in place as her sewing machine repeatedly "warped and wefted."

"The result is a delicate filigree of interconnections, like family, like community, like the way we come together," she said, adding that the piece speaks about the presence of Franco-American labor in the Northeast.

"Much labor, as we know, is made invisible through systems of oppression. This was especially true during the height of the textile industry in Maine, with its unrelenting economic pressures and inherent classism. Worker narratives were rarely captured. The cloth seems to barely hold itself together, yet took hundreds of hours to produce," she said.

Accompanying *Lucien's Cloth* is Kunz's poetry, which she considers both personal and social. By retelling his story, she honors her great-grandfather, Lucien, to whom the piece is dedicated.

"His hands are 'un-erased' by my own. His story, told with light-responsive thread, manifest and liminal," Kunz said.

Below is Kunz's writing as part of *Lucien's Cloth*:

> Lucien, my great-grandfather,
> whose name means 'light,'
> Never told me his stories.
> It is thought he worked his whole life as a
> textile laborer in Lewiston, Maine.
> I imagine his hands, expertly working
> through mine,

> weaving this changing cloth,
> without a loom.
> Cloth,
> made of only warp and weft.
> Over and under, through and through.
> Built from hundreds of points of connection.
> The way we speak our stories,
> has the power to transform them.
> Past is changed by the words we speak today.
> Light changes the darkness.
> The changing cloth.

Steven Riel

Speaking of Franco-Americans writing poetry, I wanted to speak with Steven Riel about written words and identity. Riel is a poet and the Editor-In-Chief of *Résonance,* a Franco-American online publication.

In speaking with these Franco-American artists, I wanted to find out how much of their heritage and culture plays into their work (if at all). So, I asked Riel what aspects of his Franco-American heritage have influenced his artistic expression.

"My Franco-American identity certainly has some impact on what I write about because I think about issues related to this identity quite a bit, especially now that I serve as the Editor-In-Chief of *Résonance,*" Riel said.

Riel's perspective reflects a deep connection to Franco-American identity, revealing how it shapes not only his poetic themes but also his approach to language. By prioritizing clarity and relatability in his poetry, Riel strives to write about his personal experiences so readers can engage with his words clearly and concisely.

"One way in which my Franco-American identity affects my poetry is that I want my poems ultimately to be accessible and understandable. I am not interested in unnecessary obscurity or with playing intellectual word games for their own sake. Perhaps this aesthetic stems from an underlying utilitarianism or practicality deep inside someone whose grandparents were working class. My paternal grandparents met while employed in a corset factory, after all," he said.

Although Riel wasn't raised in a French-speaking home, his grandparents spoke French to his parents. He began studying French in eighth grade and continued taking French classes during and after college.

Backed by this French education, Riel sometimes incorporates the language into his poetry. He also said that other aspects of his family's history, such as his forebears enduring poverty primarily throughout the Great Depression, have found their way into some of his writing.

"French appears in some of my poems. In some, a few French words (*piton, mémère*) get sprinkled in as singletons because those are the words used in my family for what the speaker is describing. In some poems, I introduce a greater amount of French when the core of the poem concerns Franco-American experience. Also, I've written one poem about my relationship with the French language ("*Deux Langues*")," he said.

Riel's Franco-American upbringing has influenced some of his poetry, but another influence has more strongly affected his creativity, inspiration, and expression.

"The aspect of my heritage with the greatest impact has been Roman Catholicism," Riel said, adding that he left the Catholic Church as a college student at Jesuit Georgetown University. However, Catholicism stuck with Riel and his artistic expression before and after this religious departure.

"The strong language of hymns and the liturgy made a powerful impact on me as a child. I believe that influenced my deepest relationship with language — how and why I love language. The stanza in my poem '*Monson, Mass.*' that mentions the words 'redemption, manna, myrrh' relates in part to this," he said.

Talking about the Church brought me back to a past Le Rassemblement I attended virtually—the first time Riel and I spoke to each other. The Franco-American Programs in Orono, Maine, hosts this gathering of Franco-Americans to share artwork, writing, research, or other projects and connect as a community.

After giving my presentation on the "visual culture" of Franco-Americans, Riel responded by sharing the Catholic visuals of his Franco-American upbringing. He shared his memories of the crucifix at home and praying with rosary beads. Beyond religion, Riel's poetry also addresses more introspective topics.

"Catholic imagery, situations, and psychology appear in several of my poems, but what might be much more significant is the absence of belief in an afterlife in poems that try to address the death of my younger brother, who died of AIDS at the age of 28," he said.

When asked in what ways his Franco-American identity shapes his creative process and artistic vision, Riel said it makes him compare it to the impact of his gay identity on his written work.

"My gay identity has had a far greater effect on my overall output as a poet. This is because the shame, stigma, harassment, and condemnation I faced as a gay boy and young man were profound. As a poet, I had to begin working through that burden first," he said.

Three years after graduating college, Riel took a French class that raised his consciousness about his Franco-American identity. He got more out of it than he anticipated, seeing the parallel between how gay people and Franco-Americans faced shame in New England.

"However, differences existed in the severity and manifestation of the two oppressions. At least in Southern New England, where, by the time of my childhood, Franco-Americans often lived in relatively assimilated communities, gay people met with much more destructive oppression than Franco-Americans did," he said.

With this theme of assimilation, Riel expressed it further in a poem inspired by his Franco-American heritage titled "*Dandelions That Sprout in My Yard Know I'm Franco-American.*" Riel said its inspiration came from two different experiences linked by a metaphor.

"On the one hand, I knew how clean and tidy my extended family was. Cleanliness certainly was related to Godliness in our minds. Yards needed to be well taken care of, too — they were the family's public face. How dandelions that sprout in such strictly tended yards try to avoid weeding became the vehicle of the metaphor because strategies of the plants to adapt to their micro-environment seemed akin to how Franco-

Americans tried to blend into American culture in New England to flourish," he said.

Through his poetry, Riel illustrates that the journey of incorporating cultural narratives into his work is both intentional and spontaneous. Each poem serves as a testament to the interplay between family history, personal identities, and artistic expression, enriching his understanding of what it means to be Franco-American.

Abby Paige

I spoke with another artist in the New England Franco-American community to explore other forms of Franco-American artistry. Abby Paige is a writer and theater artist whose work is rooted in the cultures of northern New England, Quebec, and eastern Canada. Through her solo shows, she delves into the impact of French-Canadian and Franco-American culture on New England's life and identity. Her latest work, a one-woman show titled "*Les Filles du QUOI?*" delves into her experience as an American immigrant to Canada, the country of her ancestors. Paige performed the bilingual show in 2022 at the Lost Nation Theater at Montpelier City Hall Arts Center in Montpelier, Vermont.

Regarding how her Franco-American heritage influences her creative work, Paige replied that it is about cultural connection and discovering how we came to be.

"Ancestry is fundamental to how I think about my creative work. By that, I don't only mean ancestry in genealogical terms, although that feeds into it, too. I mean being connected to a lineage of people who are makers or thinkers, being part of an intergenerational, human conversation. For me, art is about communication and relationships," she said.

Paige expresses that she learns from the author whenever she reads something and allows that person's thinking to become interwoven into hers. She does this to uncover, understand, and honor connections to where she and her ideas come from, her connection to what came before her, who she learns from, and how to honor what they have taught.

"I'm interested in how we become who we are. My work is trying to sort that out," she said. Addressing this thought further, she shared her belief in the importance of an oral culture for Franco-Americans more than a literary one.

"So, when I think about my ancestors, I think about farmers, loggers, and factory workers. The women in my family, particularly, worked in textile mills, weaving, and sewing. I think about how my work is in conversation with theirs, how their creativity lives in me. When you use the word 'artistry,' I think of them, of how they brought creativity into their labor and their living since they did not have the freedom to pursue art the way that I have," she said.

In telling these stories, especially with "*Les Filles du QUOI?*" on my mind, I had to ask Paige how she incorporates Franco-American themes and narratives into her work.

"Living in Canada is one of the things that pushed me to write about my family history. Growing up in Vermont, my family always defined ourselves as French-Canadian, and so when I moved to Quebec in 2008, I had this vague idea that I was returning. But living in that environment, I suddenly had to figure out my relationship to Quebecois culture," she said.

Paige asked herself what it meant that her family was "from" Quebec, so she said most of her writing at that time was her trying to sort out her relationship to places, history, language, and everything that had taken place between her ancestors' move south to the United States and her move back north. These themes surface in her work, notably in Paige's solo shows, where she attempts to figure out those ideas in various ways.

However, she never declared herself as a "Franco-American artist." Instead, Paige's opinion on that label is that an audience has to "claim its artists." In her case, other Franco-Americans appreciated her work and claimed her.

"It's not my role as an artist to promote or even necessarily to represent the culture, except insofar as my work represents my own human experience, including my heritage and identity. I'm not trying to attract people to Franco-American culture. I am trying to create artifacts of my and my ancestors' existence, and when I perform, I want to create experiences that connect people to their humanity," she said.

Additionally, Paige is extremely grateful that her work has resonated with the Franco-American community and feels a sense of belonging. Along with that feeling of community, Franco-American artistry can also preserve cultural heritage and foster community engagement.

"Sometimes, we talk about culture as though it is something we're outside of when, really, it is us and everything we do. It is like talking about the traffic when you're in a car in the middle of it. We are the traffic. Culture is how we are together, the things we make, the things we talk about, and how we talk about them. We're doing it right now! I think it is helpful to our thinking about 'cultural preservation' to consider our living cultural project," she said, adding that this might be clearer for other people with children because she knows what she wants to pass down to her kid.

"That transmission happens mostly through my behavior — the ways we cook and eat together, the way we mark milestones and celebrations, the language we use in our house, the ways we express affection or demonstrate our values. That's all cultural," she said.

In advising aspiring artists who want to explore Franco-American themes in their creative pursuits, Paige said to look for answers from their ancestors, elders, mentors, and creative peers.

Whether you can learn from them in person or study the work they left behind, think about who is making or has made the things you admire – the things that excite and inspire you.

"Put yourself in conversation with those people, literally or figuratively. Aspiring artists often think they have to have some original idea, some approach that no one's ever thought of before. But new ideas can only come from really steeping yourself in what's already been done. None of our ideas or our work are ours alone. We make better work when we cultivate and honor those connections," she said.

Conclusion

Through each of these three artists, I have thought more about my role in telling Franco-American stories through my artistry – writing for my blog, Moderne Francos.

Kunz's question from earlier, "Can we write our best stories with our great-great-grandmother's pen?" immediately made me think of using my mémère's maiden name to author my blog posts. It was a fun idea at the time when I became inspired to share my thoughts and ideas for the future of Franco-American culture.

It felt right to me to take on that persona, that "what if" scenario where I was born with a French-Canadian name that I had thought about when reading through documents revealing more of these surnames on my maternal side. I remember making business cards with Microsoft Word for my future photography business, which I dreamed of having during my younger teenage years.

Even then, I took on a different persona as I typed my name as variations of "Mel Deschenes" and "Melody Desjardins." I am unsure if I was trying to escape my authentic self, express my passion for the culture, or both. But taking on these pen names was my way of feeling closer to my Franco-American background, and that's what I did for Moderne Francos.

I am proud to have taken on the Desjardins name to share my Franco-American artistry through writing, sharing personal stories of my mémère whom I did not get to know that well and my pépère whom I did not get to know at all. However, documenting my Franco-American experience will contribute to our culture as an archive for future Franco-Americans to expand our understanding of our culture and where it can go. What more can we do, and what can we create to express ourselves and our culture?

In June 2024, I published a blog post on Moderne Francos and *Le Forum* (a Franco-American publication by the Franco-American Programs at the University of Maine in Orono, ME) about Le Rassemblement 2024. In this post, I discussed how Franco-American culture and my personal experiences of being Franco-American inspire my writing and creativity. It shows that our culture can inspire us, and whether or not we consider ourselves artists, we can express Franco-American culture creatively. We can reach people through our visuals and words, so if you feel inspired, create and share your artistry with us.

We will all be here to witness and embrace it as part of our Franco-American story.

15. Documenting the Francophone Contribution to American Music
Scott Tilton

New Orleans. 1910. Basin Street: A fight breaks out at Madame Lulu White's saloon in the red-light district known as Storyville – named after a French-speaking alderman, much to his chagrin. As fists and half-empty glasses fly and the commotion draws the attention of the wide-eyed tourists on the street, a raucous, syncopated sound flows out of the saloon onto the street – more intoxicating than the sazeracs being served. This new sound, jazz - whose name is thought to derive from the French word *jaser* (to chatter) – is making its grand entrance onto the raucous streets of New Orleans and about to ignite the world with syncopation. More surprising for an observer today, even for those millions of tourists who travel to New Orleans each year on pilgrimage in search of "authentic jazz," would be the languages many of the primarily Afro-descendent musicians inside Lulu White's saloon were speaking: French and Louisiana Creole.

French has been spoken longer than English in parts of the modern United States, in places as diverse as Maine, Missouri, and Louisiana. Like English and Spanish, French arrived in North America through forces of European colonization and competition among empires that dispossessed Indigenous peoples of their lands and forced people of African descent to the Americas as enslaved laborers. But unlike English, which became the predominant language, and Spanish, which has become widespread through immigration, French has receded, which makes it easy to overlook. French speakers are often grouped into English-focused narratives about the United States, as many French speakers became English speakers in the 20th century. As their distinct linguistic identities have been erased, the contribution of French speakers to American culture has similarly been erased – as seen in the roots of Jazz in the French language.

This chapter presents one observation: Francophone Americans have contributed immeasurably to the intangible culture of the United States, from cuisine to music and art. Despite this contribution, the intangible culture linked to the French language in the United States is too often relegated to a footnote, prescribed to specific geographies such as Louisiana- or outright forgotten. When we think of quintessentially "American" music forms, we think of the delectable twang of Dolly Parton's country music or the heart-breaking sadness of Americana/Folk and the Blues – very often sung in English. However, the public is far less aware of the French lyrics in the early jazz songs by Sidney Bechet or the Creole lyrics from musicians such as Fats Domino that landed in early Rock N Roll. This chapter will be divided into two parts: an overview of America's rich musical tradition shaped by Francophones and a focus on the need to advocate for an expanded understanding of how minority language communities – not just French speakers – speakers – are too often excluded from narratives about American culture, obscured by the preference for English dominant narratives. I will present in this section an overview of a multimedia project called *Musique(s)!* they are working on through their nonprofit, the New Orleans Foundation for Francophone Cultures (the Nous Foundation), with the Library of Congress, to document and celebrate this important part of America's musical heritage.

As a disclaimer, I am not a musicologist—though I love music deeply. My observations are not meant to imply that the contributions of French-speaking musicians are unknown in the United States. Instead, they arise from misperceptions embedded in our collective memory, where the contributions of minority language communities are too often overshadowed. I recognize that the origins of any musical form result from collaboration among musicians of diverse backgrounds and languages. It would be impossible to single out one individual or community as solely responsible for a form of music in a country as vast as the United States. Instead, I highlight the contributions of many without excluding any community, regardless of origin or language.

The central contention of this chapter is that American music is too vast and important to exclude languages other than English from the sounds that make a country. The focus of this chapter is also on

Louisiana, given that the author proudly calls New Orleans home. This is a practical choice as Louisiana is easily identifiable with the influence of the French language on American music. However, this focus does not intend to eclipse the critical impact that French Canadians had on American music in the North and that the French-speaking peoples of the Illinois Country had on the Midwest. The authors made a practical choice to talk about their knowledge close to home, but the conversation nurtured in this chapter is far more significant than the Crescent City.

So, ready for a little Iko Iko?

Orpheus in America:
Francophones at the Origins of American Music

The Greek god Orpheus may have called Mount Olympus home, but he surely visited the United States at some point. The melding of musical styles from the Scots and Irish to French, German, African American, Indigenous, and countless other communities has produced internationally renowned musical genres that are often synonymous with the country: the Blues, Rock N Roll, Jazz, Americana/Folk to more recent Punk Rock and Rap. Each successive community facing hardship, uplift, and hope brought lyrical expressions and instruments. The blending was sometimes so compelling that people even forgot the origins of quintessentially American music. Think of the banjo, an instrument whose metallic reverberations are synonymous with Folk/Americana but whose origins lie in the enslaved peoples who brought the instrument to the American South from West Africa. While musical genres and instruments we identify with America emerged in different parts of the country – often in simultaneous genesis – the spiritual home of many of these forms of music are in the South, especially for the Blues, Jazz, and Rock n' Roll.

Critical to the emergence of music in the South were French and Creole-speaking musicians spread across the Gulf South, many of whom were of African descent. These musicians lived in a geographic region from Texas in the west through Louisiana to Alabama in the east, standing at a crossroads in the Americas – drawing on sounds from

Europe, Africa, the Caribbean, the rest of the United States, and Indigenous communities.

In the 19th century, the bustling port city of New Orleans was home to French-speaking theaters and opera houses, whose orchestras often were comprised of Afro-Creole musicians who played the latest plays and operas from Europe – which often passed through cities such as Havana before arriving in the Crescent City. Each year, an annual exodus of wealthy New Orleanians would take place as they fled towards cooler climates to avoid the voracious yellow fever epidemics that would kill thousands – a luxury working-class residents and enslaved people could not afford. These wealthy patrons would invariably return to their townhouses in the French Quarter as the opera season would begin again in the fall. So important was opera in the city's cultural life that the entire city would end its summer stupor and roar back to life as many French-language operas would make their American premiere in the city. Many Afro-Creole musicians who played in the opera houses and theater orchestras were from a specific social group called the *gens de couleur libres,* or free people of color. This social group often traced their origins to enslaved relatives freed under Spanish colonial rule in Louisiana (1763-1801). They benefited from select economic rights but were often deprived of political rights in the Antebellum American South. With certain occupations limited to them, many Afro-Creoles became artisans and musicians. This rich tradition of French and Creole-speaking classically trained musicians produced some of America's earliest internationally-renowned musicians, including Edmond Dédé (Afro-Creole) and Louis Moreau Gottschalk (Creole of European descent).

These musicians themselves were inspired by the African rhythms of Congo Square (Place Congo), a public square on the edge of the French Quarter in the Faubourg Tremé, in which enslaved peoples, gens de couleur libre, and Indigenous communities would meet to sell goods they made and dance on Sundays. On Sundays, enslaved peoples were given special dispensation under the draconian French *Code Noir* (Black Code) to have off, which many used to sell wares and meet loved ones at Congo Square – and some enslaved people successfully raised enough funds from selling their goods to buy their freedom and the freedom of their loved ones. Congo Square was influential in New Orleans because it was a crossroads of African music and dance and was prominently positioned in the booming city. Musical styles and dances like Calinda would be played alongside a chatter of dozens of African and Indigenous languages progressively blending into Louisiana's French-based Creole language. In a city already engaged in intense cultural dialogue with the Caribbean, each boat up the Mississippi brought new sounds that people of color often performed at Congo Square. For budding musicians like Jean Moreau Gottschalk and Edmond Dédé, the sounds from Congo Square had an indelible impact on their classical music that set an essential precedent for blending what Eurocentric music norms imposed as technical mastery in Classical music with the equally complicated rhythms and sounds of African and Indigenous music.

After the Civil War (1861-1865) and a brief period of Reconstruction (1867-1877) in which it looked like Americans of African descent would gain full equality, the counter-revolution came as white nationalists passed Jim Crow laws discriminating against Black Americans. In a very short period (1880s-1890s), Afro-Creoles were expelled from the whites-only theaters and opera houses. At the same time, English-speaking former enslaved peoples from across the South migrated to cities such as New Orleans to reunite with families and flee the repressive life of plantations. As this new social environment emerged, history would have it that the city's futile attempt to control vice would lead it to setting up a red-light district called Storyville at the edge of the French Quarter in New Orleans - near the neighborhoods where many Afro-descendent musicians lived. More lax than the rigid Jim Crow white-black color line imposed in posher parts of the city, in Storyville, Afro-Creole and African American musicians started pioneering sounds taken from the Blues, ragtime, and classical music to form jazz. When one looks at early jazz, what's striking is the number of Afro-Creole musicians present, from Lizzie Miles to Sidney Bechet and Jelly Roll Morton, who helped teach a young Louis Armstrong. Many of the early jazz bands named themselves the "Original Creole Dixieland" or variations that were markers of identity and branding to a broader American audience enraptured by this transgressive music emerging from the saloons of New Orleans.

As jazz became mainstream, the origins of the music in French and Creole-speaking neighborhoods of New Orleans were often lost as English-speaking musicians took the spotlight. This is a pattern that would be replicated for other forms of music. Famously, Antoine 'Fats' Domino, who grew up in a Creole-speaking family in New Orleans and sold more than 65 million records, would be involved in developing Rock n' Roll. Musicians like Domino and Allen Toussaint often reprised Creole songs into emerging musical genres like Rock n' Roll or Funk. Still, they sang them in English, sometimes the choice of their record labels or sometimes a practical choice in the America of the 1950s – present in which consumers are accustomed to English-language songs. French and Creole songs such as Iko Iko (recorded by the Dixie Cups) would enter popular American mainstream culture during this period. Mississippi-born Elvis himself – renowned for his star-studded role in the film 'King Creole' - would draw on sounds heard in French and Creole songs that were popular up and down the Mississippi. This tradition of French and Creole-speaking musicians continues today. And like always, the music continues to evolve because people don't live in a vacuum. Grammy-winning musicians such as the Lost Bayou Ramblers and Leyla McCalla and Indie Rock group Sweet Crude continue to experiment with emerging soundscapes in American music while drawing on more readily identifiable 'French' forms of music like Zydeco and Swamp Pop.

While the innovation in French and Creole languages continues in the 21st century, the pressures on musicians to adapt their sounds to audiences that may not understand their lyrics presents unique challenges. In Louisiana alone, the number of French speakers has dropped from an estimated 1.5 million speakers in 1970 to 100,000 today, a greater than 90% drop due to discriminatory laws, pressure to 'Americanize,' and a lack of policy to encourage genuine bilingualism. As French speakers drop from Maine to Louisiana, exacerbated by the loss of native speakers and a national decline in French taught in schools and universities, now is the time to discuss the Francophones' impact on American music. If not now, then the impact of that intangible heritage risks being lost for future generations – no matter what language they speak.

Won't Bow Down, Don't Know How: Documenting the Future of French and Creole Music in The United States

As part of our commitment to the vital task of documenting this important musical heritage, the authors, who run an organization called the New Orleans Foundation for Francophone Cultures, or Nous Foundation, created a project selected for the American Folklife Center at the Library of Congress's Community Collection Grant. This project, called La Musique nous réunit (Music Brings Us Together) or *Musique(s)!* for short, aims to document how a new generation of French and Creole-speaking musicians in Louisiana are transmitting their musical styles to a new generation that lives in a country where English is omnipresent.

Understanding Musique(s)! as a project helps to briefly look at the mission and work of the Nous Foundation. The author, Scott Tilton, met Rudy Bazenet in Paris, where they had the opportunity to launch and spearhead an initiative that saw Louisiana join the *Organisation Internationale de la Francophonie* (OIF from its French acronym) in 2018 as the first U.S. state to join the organization. The OIF is the second largest international organization in the world behind the U.N. and Louisiana's joining, which offered a momentum milestone in recognizing the minority French- and Creole-speaking communities in Louisiana. While working on the initiative, the authors received countless messages from young people who wanted to live their culture but found a lack of resources and community with whom to speak French. Recognizing this dual challenge of visibility and capacity for promoting Louisiana's heritage culture, the authors set up the Nous Foundation in 2020 to create a world-class cultural institution in the French Quarter that would promote French and Creole in Louisiana and raise funds to support our community. In three and a half short years, Nous has achieved several milestones, including the following:

1. the opening of a cultural center at the Historic BK House & Gardens in the French Quarter,
2. the creation of six original films and documentaries that have been featured at festivals such as the New Orleans Film Festival and Cannes, and

3. An original exhibit co-curated with Max Jean-Louis, Haiti-Louisiana: Tides of Freedom, explored the impact of the Haitian Revolution and opened in New Orleans before being displayed at the United Nations.

I often joke that the two things all Louisianans can agree on are music and cuisine. As such, music has been a core part of the mission of the Nous Foundation from its inception, from organizing regular concerts, conferences, and fundraisers to supporting Louisiana roots music. Nous has had the unique opportunity to partner with the Louisiana Philharmonic Orchestra (LPO) on three separate occasions to create postcards (inserted into patrons' playbills) that make the connection between French-language music played by the LPO and the important heritage of Francophone Louisiana. This work with the LPO and numerous talented musicians honed a deep appreciation for how music transcends everyday boundaries and transmits appreciation for culture. In an era in which French and Creole are declining as languages used in everyday conversation, Louisiana roots music is a genre that notably bucks the trend, as musicians have adeptly continued singing in French and Creole and made their music wildly popular. The idea behind *Musique(s)!* emerged in early 2021 with the groundbreaking success of the LPO's live album with the Lost Bayou Ramblers, a two-time Grammy-winning group that sings in Louisiana French. Their album won the Best Regional Roots Album at the Grammy Awards. Seeing the immense success and vision behind that project inspired us to want to continue our work in promoting Louisiana roots music sung in French and Creole to a larger music documentation project that would culminate in Musique(s)!

In August 2024, while dodging hurricanes, we recorded an album with six musical groups at Esplanade Studios, a beautiful former church converted into a recording studio in New Orleans. The groups involved include Grammy-winning musicians such as Louis Michot and Leyla McCalla, Sweet Crude, Sunpie and the Sunspots, the Baby Dolls, and Les Cenelles.

Each group recorded two songs of their choosing in French and Creole. What emerged from the recordings is a snapshot of Louisiana music – both traditional and *avant-garde* – as performed in 2024. The sounds of each musical group are deliberately quite different from one another. For example, we are working with the Baby Dolls, women-led groups whose beautiful dresses are a prominent part of New Orleans's Black masking tradition – a tradition many outside the city know through the Black Masking Indians. The Baby Dolls' go back to the early 1900s, and many of the songs they still sing are directly linked to the Creole songs that informed the emergence of early jazz. To the best of our knowledge and those who participated, this album is the first time the Baby Dolls have been formally recorded, and we are giving the rights back to the group so they can hold onto their music. Alongside the Baby Dolls, we have Grammy-winning musicians such as Louis Michot, who performed traditional 'Cajun' music as performed by his own family, and he even found a lost 1934 track that he re-recorded for the first time in generations.

The album and accompanying interviews that will be put into a vinyl and publication will be stored in the Library of Congress's permanent archives, ensuring the contribution of French and Creole-speaking musicians to American music is documented for generations to come. In addition to this work, through the support of the Create Louisiana grant, we also filmed a documentary on the album's creation, which will premiere at the New Orleans French Film Festival and then be shown worldwide on TV5Monde. Finally, to share the beauty of this music with our community, we will open an exhibit called Musique(s)! that will open in February 2025 – right before the Super Bowl – at the Historic BK House & Gardens.

This project builds on the foundational work of Dr. Barry Ancelet and Dr. Carl Brasseaux to record and document Louisiana French folk music. Drawing on this vital work, we are showcasing the diversity of Francophone music today. Groups such as Les Cenelles, a chamber orchestra, create new music based on the Calinda sung in Congo Square. They aim to bring to the fore the African and Indigenous roots of New Orleans, a place they refer to as Bulbancha, a name derived from the Choctaw term for the region meaning 'land of many tongues.' Les Cenelles' music pays homage to the diverse roots of Louisiana's music while updating traditional sounds with contemporary musical styles - an idea at the core of the *Musique(s)!* project. Music is not static. These musicians have been able to make relevant French and Creole-language music for a new generation because the innovation of their songs speaks to this new generation.

In contrast, the cross-generation dialogue they foster speaks to their audiences' complex identities rooted in Louisiana's heritage cultures. In the past, Louisiana music was portrayed as one-size-fits-all. In reality, it is incredibly diverse, and the different sounds and backgrounds of the musicians today, when viewed as a whole show, speak to communities across Louisiana and the nation. Perhaps this is why a whole Grammy category exists for Louisiana roots music. Fingers crossed, maybe our album will join the canon.

Projects like *Musique(s)!* are essential in documenting Francophone and Creolophone musicians' contributions to American music. Outside this project, phenomenal musicians such as Josee Vachon in Maine are doing similar work to document Maine's rich heritage of French-speaking music derived from Acadian and French-Canadian migration to the region dating back centuries. The gorgeous work of filmmaker and storyteller Brian Hawkins in creating short animations that incorporate the traditional music of Missouri's French-speaking Creoles also preserves the music of a new generation. But the work is far from done.

The United States is home to hundreds of languages, from Louisiana French to Cherokee and Gullah Geechee. The country is also home to hundreds of heritage language communities, such as German whose transmission to new generations is weak. One of the sole exceptions in the country is Spanish, as the country's more than 40 million Spanish speakers have created a whole music recording industry with hubs in Miami, New York, and Los Angeles that have taken the world by storm. No one language has a monopoly on good music. Music is a critical vehicle for transmitting an interest in culture and community – as shown by the prominence of Spanish music among young people, even among English speakers. As a country, it is an integral part of our tapestry and story to hold onto our linguistic diversity. Suppose we want to keep the musical sounds of French and Creole, Navajo, and Gullah Geechee. In that case, we need to invest more resources in supporting musicians' careers when they decide to invest in passing on their language and culture through their music.

One program we have at the Nous Foundation that seems to be making some progress is our le Lab accelerator program, which has raised $250,000 to support entrepreneurial projects for minority language communities. Starting this cycle in November, we will open a spot dedicated to music recording that will support artists. Right now, we're working on a musical called Swell with Chasah & Charliese West, made possible through the support of the We Are Family Foundation.

But beyond this private initiative launched by civil society, nationally, there will be a need for further public funding for musicians in minority language communities. In New Orleans, musicians have a hard time making ends meet due to the lack of insurance, a rising cost of living, and the precariousness of work, as underscored by the COVID-19 pandemic that shut down the city's tourism-based economy. Even under the best conditions, it is hard for musicians to sustain their careers. It is an added burden to ask them to learn the canon of French and Creole music, which is incredibly important to hold onto but can be less identifiable for tourists from the rest of the country. Public grant programs or services helping these musicians could help. For example, in working with the Baby Dolls, we received various grants from the City of New Orleans that have helped compensate the members of the Baby Dolls, who have 9-5 jobs, to participate and relearn the pronunciation of Louisiana Creole for their music.

Also, having specific recognitions and awards for minority languages, such as the Grammy Awards for Louisiana roots music, would be helpful, as it entices musicians to invest in heritage languages. Finally, the age of Netflix and the rise of Spanish-language music underscores that Americans of all backgrounds are open to other languages. Major music and media studios should include other languages in their music. This would be even more interesting as the other languages being spoken are 100% from the USA, which may pique the interest of an American audience.

From the alleys of Storyville to the majestic BK House & Gardens, where our exhibit will open in just a few weeks, the music we are celebrating through the Nous Foundation is a long but short path. From the BK House to the old French Opera House that once stood on Bourbon Street to Congo Square and the former site of Storyville, it would take about a 20-minute walk. Sadly, the French Opera House would burn in 1918, and Storyville would meet an ignominious end in 1917 when it was closed by the American Navy during WWI because sailors were drawn to the neighborhood during their mustering in the city before heading to the Western Front. But standing in the neighborhood is one lone building that used to belong to Madame Lulu White – a testament to the resilience of music. Now, more than ever, to understand America, one must understand its music. And that music is spoken in so many more languages than English. The sounds still linger in the air, gently whispering, "Iko Iko!"

16. A Hard-Won Battle: The Lasting Gift of Franco-American Churches to New England's Built Environment
Eileen M. Angelini and Rebecca P. Sewall

Drive through the mill towns of New England, and you will see them. The grand, cathedral-like churches that loom over the skyscape and dwarf what were once mills and workers' housing. These elaborate churches are the remaining vestiges of the French-Canadian struggle to retain its language and culture as the French Canadians left their farmlands in Quebec to work in the industrial mills of Protestant New England after the American Civil War. Upon their arrival, the French Canadians attended the Catholic churches established by Irish immigrants decades earlier. But steeped in the philosophy of *La Survivance* – a concept that held that the maintenance of the French language, the continuation of the distinct French-Canadian church and French-Canadian customs fundamental for their cultural survival, the French Canadians soon sought to establish their own French-speaking parishes despite the formidable resistance they encountered from the Irish-dominated episcopate. The French Canadians built modest churches until funds were raised to build more elaborate and permanent ones. By the late 1880s, these "temporary churches" were replaced with grand, extravagant ones, many of which could seat more than 1,500 people and cost more than $500,000 to build. Today, these churches provide a visual testimony of the fierce determination of the French Canadians to maintain the French language. This determination has had a lasting impact on the built environment of the mill towns of New England and has survived to this day.

La Survivance

The fundamental importance of maintaining the use of the French language as a key to cultural survival was already well-established when the French Canadians first made their way south to New England as the engines of the Second Industrial Revolution were starting again after the Civil War. The concept of *La Survivance* first emerged as the French in Canada suffered a sound defeat at the hands of the British during the Seven Years' War (1756-1763). While it had been a guiding principle in French Canada in the wake of Anglicizing forces after the war, the concept took on new significance as the French left their failing farms in Quebec to work the industrial mills of Protestant New England.[154]

La Grande Saignée

When New England's factories were gearing up again after the Civil War, the region desperately needed workers. This demand for workers coincided with the steep decline in agricultural production in rural Quebec, and according to one historian, "Quebec stood ready to answer the call."[155] Despite the challenges, the families of Quebec, known for their resilience, were ready to adapt. Between 1784 and 1844, Quebec's population increased by 400%. Acreage available for agriculture became scarce.[156] In the 1840s, poor soil, wasteful farming techniques, and an inheritance system that forced the continuous sub-division of land left family farms heavily indebted.[157] Indebtedness snowballed as the century wore on and soon forced entire families to seek other forms of employment to earn money to save the family farm.[158] With few economic opportunities in Quebec, the farming families went to New England. The proximity of the mill jobs in New England to their farms and improvements in the railway system facilitated what would be

---

[154] Potvin, 2023.
[155] Vermette, 2019.
[156] Bélanger, French Canadian Emigration.
[157] Podea, 1950.
[158] Brault, 1986.

eventually known as *La Grande Saignée*, or the great hemorrhage of French Canadians leaving Quebec.[159]

By the 1880s, the railway system had revolutionized travel between Montreal and Vermont, reducing the distance and cost to a few dollars and hours. This pivotal development played a crucial role in the mass migration of French Canadians to New England, significantly enhancing the accessibility and affordability of the journey.[160] United by their shared experiences and unwavering determination, families immigrated, with women and children seamlessly integrating into the mill economy. As one observer noted, "trainload upon trainload" of French Canadians began to settle in New England, a powerful testament to their unity and shared determination.[161] By 1860, 18,000 French Canadians were working in the textile mill towns of Lewiston, Maine, Manchester, New Hampshire, Lowell, Worcester, Holyoke, New Bedford, and Fall River, Massachusetts. Between 1865 and 1873, emigration from Quebec reached a "fever pitch" as French Canadians settled in the crowded French-speaking enclaves that came to be known as "Little Canadas."[162]

The Quest for French-Speaking Parishes

When they first arrived, the French Canadians attended the established Catholic Churches built by the Irish, who had arrived two decades earlier. Not speaking the same language as the rest of the parish, long steeped in the principle of *La Survivance*, the French Canadians quickly sought to establish their French-speaking parishes organized like those they left behind in Quebec and have the same religious service elements. This was a testament to their perseverance in maintaining their cultural identity, a struggle that many can empathize with.

Regrettably, French Canadians soon encountered resistance from the Irish-dominated Catholic episcopate, which sought to assimilate

---

[159] Lacroix, 2018.
[160] Bélanger, French Canadian Emigration.
[161] Vermette, 2019.
[162] Bélanger, French Canadian Emigration.

them to quell the anti-Catholic sentiment of the bourgeoning nativist movement. By the 1850s, anti-Catholic sentiment had begun to surface, and the Irish, who had initially borne the brunt of it, sought to counter Protestant fears by promoting the swift assimilation of immigrant Catholics into American society.[163] According to one historian, "The Irish believed that rapid Americanization of foreign-born Catholics would ease the anti-Catholic feeling."[164]

Despite the growing number of French Canadians in New England, the Catholic dioceses, primarily dominated by the Irish, were initially hesitant to approve the formation of new French-speaking parishes. Their reluctance stemmed from a fear that rejecting such requests would lead to the French Canadians leaving the church rather than worship in a language other than their own.[165] Even when permission was granted, the Irish-dominated Diocese viewed the French-Canadian parishes as an interim step before the French Canadians would eventually assimilate into American culture and join the existing Catholic "territorial" churches.[166]

The First Wave of Temporary Churches

Despite the Catholic diocese's misgivings about forming French-Canadian parishes, the period between 1860 and 1900 saw an enormous growth of French-Canadian parishes. By 1891, there were 86 French-Canadian parishes in New England, and by 1900, there were more than 100 such parishes.[167] The big French-Canadian centers boasted several French-speaking churches. For example, Fall River had six Canadian parishes, and New Bedford had seven.[168] While immigration had started to slow down by 1900 due to improved economic conditions in Canada, the high birth rates among Canadian families who had arrived earlier

---

[163] Wade, 1950.
[164] Wade, 1950, 178.
[165] Brault, 1986.
[166] Brault, 1986.
[167] Wade, 1950.
[168] Cartier, 1999.

necessitated the need for more French-Canadian parishes.[169] From 1900-1930, sixty French Canadian parishes were founded.

The formation of French-Canadian parishes followed a regular pattern. They would break away from an Irish church and build their modest one until funds could be raised to build a more permanent church. One observer noted that this "was the era of wooden churches, as plain as they were numerous."[170] Because maintaining the French language was fundamental to their cultural survival, French-Canadian parishes soon established a parochial school where instruction would be in French. This was followed by constructing a convent or rectory to house the nuns and male teachers often brought in from Canada. In the larger French-Canadian centers, such as Fall River, New Bedford, Lowell, and Worcester, it was not unusual to see orphanages, older people's homes, and other auxiliary buildings as part of the parish compound.

The Grand Replacement Churches

At the turn of the century, new French-Canadian "nationalist" parishes were still being established while existing parishes were entering a new phase.[171] The historian Armand Cartier notes, "After 1900, once the immigrants were more firmly entrenched in their new environment, many of the wooden churches would be replaced by more impressive structures."[172] He explains further, "In many cases, the modest wooden church dating back to the beginning of the settlement was replaced by an impressive stone temple. This was the start of what might be called 'the age of the cathedral-like churches,' given the size and the majesty of some of these edifices."[173] These "replacement" churches were characterized by their size, cost of construction (many cost between a quarter of a million dollars and a million dollars to build), elaborate Neo-Gothic, Roman, and French Renaissance designs, and the fact that

---

[169] Cartier, 1999.
[170] Ibid. p.17.
[171] Ibid.
[172] Ibid.
[173] Ibid.

French-Canadian architects primarily designed them.[174] Among the grand churches that replaced smaller wooden ones was the new Saint Anne's Church in Fall River in 1906, designed by one of Quebec's well-known architects, Napoleon Bourassa.[175] Also in Fall River was the new Notre Dame de Lourdes, built in 1906. Another Quebecois architect, Louis-G, designed the grand Romanesque cathedral-like church. Destremps who had immigrated to Fall River. Its steeple was almost 300 feet high and "could be seen for miles around."[176] In New Bedford, Saint Antoine's Church was built in 1912. The Montreal architect Joseph Venne designed it in the French Renaissance style.[177] Venne also built the grand Notre Dame church in Southbridge, with its brick and marble façade, in 1916. In Rhode Island, Walter Fontaine built Saint Anne in Woonsocket in 1918.[178] In New Hampshire, the towering Saint Marie church was built in Manchester in 1880, and the grand church of Saint Anne was built in Berlin in 1900.

Tensions Mount

Tensions between Irish and French-Canadians heightened during labor unrest in the 1870s. While the Irish started to strike in response to low wages and dismal working conditions, the French-Canadian priests actively discouraged their congregants from taking up the cause. In 1870, when Irish and English workers were striking in the Flint district of Fall River, the priest of Notre Dame de Lourdes called upon his congregants to break the strike.[179] The French-Canadians obeyed their pastor's wishes. They served as "knobsticks"[180] or strikebreakers, inciting such furor among the parishes' handful of Irish Catholics that they broke off from the French-Canadian parish to start their Irish one.[181]

---

[174] Cartier, 1999.
[175] Ibid.
[176] Ibid. p.102.
[177] Ibid.
[178] Ibid.
[179] Ibid.
[180] Lacroix, 2018.
[181] Silvia, 1979.

The thought that French-Canadian strike breakers were willing to undermine their fellow Catholics brought down a wave of disharmony among already antagonized groups.[182]

Soon after, tensions between the Irish-dominated diocese and the French-Canadian nationalists would again come to a head. In 1874, ten years after its inception as a French-Canadian parish, the bishop of Springfield appointed an Irish pastor to take over Notre Dame de Lourdes in Fall River. The French-Canadian congregants protested against what they saw as the Diocese's attempt to impose an Irish priest on their parish to force their eventual assimilation.[183]

When the first Irish priest appointed left on his own accord, the bishop responded by appointing yet another. The congregants' protests, which had previously been limited to boycotting baptisms and marriages—a regular source of income for priests—became more strident. The new Irish priest was threatened and forced to leave the rectory when bottles were thrown at the window of his new residence.[184] On February 13, 1885, the situation became so extreme that the bishop of Springfield imposed an interdict on the parish. Soon after, both parties appealed to the Vatican in Rome.[185] In March 1886, the bishop named a French-Canadian priest who had already been pastor of the parish.

While the French-Canadian church scored a victory, the conflict between nationalist and assimilationist churches was far from over. In 1887, the group contest was brought to the brink again in North Brookfield, Massachusetts. According to one observer, "The arguments were the same as in the Flint Affair of Fall River, "survivance" vs. assimilation!"[186] French-Canadian congregants petitioned the new bishop of Springfield to establish their parish. When the bishop refused their request, the French-Canadian congregants defied his authority, built a church, and secured their French-Canadian priest. After three

---

[182] Ibid.
[183] Cartier, 1999.
[184] Silvia, 1979.
[185] Cartier, 1999.
[186] Potvin, 2013, p. 59.

years of "bitter conflict," the bishop excommunicated the disobedient parish in 1900.[187]

It was during this turbulent period that a group of French-Canadian parishioners at Saint Leo's in Leominster, Massachusetts, first made their request to the bishop in Springfield (the same one who had just excommunicated parishioners in North Brookfield) for permission to found their own French-speaking parish. After being denied, they made another request in 1899 and were told to wait for the bishop's decision. While waiting, the group organized a boycott of the Christmas services at Saint Leo's to prompt the paster to "see it was hopeless to no longer hold out against them in [their] endeavor to split the church congregation.[188] A newspaper quoted one "separatist" French-Canadian parishioner who explained that "...by doing this, we think perhaps the priest may be made to see the folly of trying to keep us together and will be more willing to acquiesce in giving us what we want."[189]

On January 7, 1900, just weeks after their Christmas protest, the French-Canadian "separatists" of Saint Leo's learned that the bishop had approved their petition. After meeting at a rented music hall in town, the parish soon decided to build their modest wooden church, Saint Cecilia's, until funds could be raised "to erect such a building as they proposed to have in a few years."[190] Not long after, the tenements that housed the French-Canadian community grew around the church, and the neighborhood soon became known as French Hill. In addition to a rectory, the parish grew and purchased a property in 1901 to use as a school and another as a convent to house the French-speaking nuns, first from Canada and then from France, who were brought in to teach the students. A new school building was erected in 1907.

In 1925, just as the parish was poised to start work on the grand church they envisioned replacing the "temporary" wooden one, Saint Cecilia's parochial school was set afire. The fire caused over $150,000

---

[187] Potvin, 2013, p. 59.
[188] Climax in Leominster: French Catholics Omit Offerings: Their First Open Act of Rebellion," *The Telegram* Leominster, December 25, 1899.
[189] Ibid.
[190] Cormier, 2000, p. 24.

in damages and was labeled "suspicious" by arson investigators.[191] By the 1920s, the Ku Klux Klan was making its way to New England, where much of its vitriol was directed at the Catholics, who had by that time started to comprise a sizable percentage of the population. While the target of Klan hate was Catholics in general, the Irish and the Italian Catholics were on a path to assimilation. The French Canadians were not. The day after the fire in Leominster, Saint Anthony Parochial School in Shirley was burned,[192] and "Two days later, another French parochial school went up in flames."[193]

The Sentinelle Affair

While the parishioners of Saint Cecilia's were forced to delay construction of the new church while they rebuilt the parochial school, another conflict between the Irish episcopate and the French Canadian "nationalist" churches was brewing. After nativist sentiments were heightened after World War I, the Catholic episcopate, through its *Call for Catechism Education* in 1922, sought to unite the Catholic Church "through a program of assimilation for all non-English speaking Catholics."[194] To operationalize the new directive, the Providence, Rhode Island, bishop initiated a fundraising drive to build several English-speaking high schools. All parishes were called upon to deliver their quota of funds, and those that did not would be subject to a special tax. Immediately, some vocal French Canadians protested, arguing that French-Canadian parishes should not have to use their parish funds for what they saw as an effort to assimilate them,[195] especially when there was a need to build more French-Canadian schools.[196] The conflict at Saint Ann's in Woonsocket, Rhode Island, soon spiraled throughout New England and Canada.

---

[191] Goldberg, 1983.
[192] Bodanza, 2019.
[193] Bélanger, Franco-Americans.
[194] Ibid.
[195] Cartier, 1999.
[196] Bélanger, Franco-Americans.

Much of the conflict played out in the pages of *La Sentinelle* newspaper, in which the leader of the Association Canado-Americaine started to protest the bishop's ultimatum. It also played out in speeches and gatherings convened by the Association throughout New England.[197] One rally in 1927 attracted roughly 10,000 French-Canadians in Woonsocket who opposed the Catholic episcopate's demands.[198] The Sentinellists, as they became known, eventually sued twelve parishes in Rhode Island for what they claimed was the misappropriation of funds.[199] In 1928, the Sentinellists who had brought the suit were excommunicated by the Holy See, and La Sentinelle was put on a Church index, making it a sin to read it.[200] In 1929, all of those who were excommunicated recounted, and their excommunication was lifted, but the affair had a chilling effect on the French-Canadian community.[201] Many in the Catholic diocese in New England were reluctant to recruit priests from Canada as a result of the affair.[202] While the notion of *La Survivance* may have been still alive in the hearts and minds of many French-Canadians, its overt expression, manifest in its willingness to challenge the Catholic establishment in the region, had faded. After 1930, no new "nationalist" parishes were founded in New England.[203]

The New Saint Cecilia's Church

In September 1931, during the Great Depression, excavation started on the foundation of the long-anticipated new church that would replace the temporary church that the parish had erected thirty years earlier. The new church was designed by French-Canadian architect Donat Baribault, who was active from 1870 to 1943 and specialized in constructing French-Canadian ecclesiastic buildings.

---

[197] Ibid.
[198] Ibid.
[199] Potvin, 2023.
[200] Ibid.
[201] Cartier, 1999.
[202] Potvin, 2023.
[203] Cartier, 1999.

After its completion in 1933, Saint Cecilia's joined the pantheon of other grand French-Canadian "replacement" churches in the region. When it was built, it was one of the largest churches in the Springfield diocese after Springfield and Worcester.[204] Its cost was estimated at between $400,000 and $450,000.[205] The church was built in the Neo-Gothic style, which originated in England during the latter half of the 18th century and had already made its way to rural New England by the 1770s. While in the United States and parts of Canada, the Neo-Gothic style was popular for churches of different denominations, in Quebec, the affiliation between the Neo-Gothic style and the French Catholic Church was established with the construction of Notre Dame in Montreal in 1823-1829 and remained strong throughout the century.[206]

The Waning Days of *La Survivance*

The 1930 immigration law put an end to what had been a steady flow of French Canadians into Massachusetts. In the 1930s, most French Canadians were still living in Little Canadas. The church and school remained the cornerstone of French-Canadian life, but there were signs that its grip had started to loosen. While the early French Canadians saw themselves as citizens of Quebec and viewed themselves as temporary visitors to the United States, by the 1920s, the term Franco-American emerged, suggesting that what were now the second and third-generation descendants of immigrants had a greater recognition of their American identity and were in the United States to stay.[207]

While production during and after World War II invigorated New England's industries, this work's economic and social organization changed dramatically. The war's end brought waves of new immigrants who sought work in the mill towns along New England's rivers. As they were now called, the Franco-Americans were catapulted up the

---

[204] "Bishop O'Leary to Officiate at Leominster Dedication," *Sunday Telegram* Worcester. Sept 9, 1934.
[205] Cormier, 2000.
[206] Clerk and Bergeron, 2024.
[207] Cartier, 1999.

economic ladder by the arrival of more recent immigrants. They started to seek jobs in the white-collar service sector where English was required.[208] French-Canadians started moving out of Little Canadas and into areas where they were not guaranteed to have French-Canadian neighbors.

As they left behind their grand churches that served as the center of their French-speaking enclave, the new churches springing up to serve them in the English-speaking suburbs were not "nationalist" French-Canadian ones. For those who remained in the Franco-American parish, by 1950, young French Canadians were requesting the use of English in their parishes.[209] One commentator says, "Historians have identified the 1960s and 1970s as a period when often 'only middle-aged and elderly' people could speak French in the mill towns of New England."[210] The foundations of *La survivance* had started to crack.

Today, many of the grand replacement churches have been torn down (e.g., Notre Dame des Canadiens in Worcester and Immaculate Conception in Holyoke, Massachusetts) or lost to fire (Notre Dame de Lourdes in Fall River and Our Lady of Perpetual Help in Holyoke, Massachusetts) or neglect. Many, such as the Church of the Immaculate Conception in Lowell, Massachusetts, where author Jack Kerouac once worshiped, stand unoccupied as city planners debate their fate. In contrast, others, such as French-Canadian architect Donat Baribault's Sacred Heart in Concord, New Hampshire, have been adapted for residential use. Those that remain (e.g., Saint Antoine's of Padua in New Bedford, Massachusetts; the Basilica of Saints Peter and Paul in Lewiston, Maine; Notre Dame in Southbridge, Massachusetts; Saint Cecilia's in Leominster, Massachusetts, and Sainte Marie's in Manchester, New Hampshire) stand as a testimony of the strength of *La Survivance* – and the quest of the French-Canadians to maintain their distinct identity as they found their footing in Protestant New England. These churches remain as an enormous source of pride for Franco-Americans – and as any of us who have driven west on Route 2 out of

---

[208] Potvin, 2023.
[209] Cartier, 1999.
[210] French-Canadians in Holyoke 1900-1940 (*Moving Up*).

Boston and seen the magnificent, stone, Gothic Saint Cecelia's church emerge out of the wooded landscape can attest – they continue to provide a source of awe and inspiration for all who behold them. They are the lasting legacy of a fiercely independent people with great faith in New England's built environment. A legacy for which we are forever thankful.

17. The Tapestry of our French-Canadian Ancestry
Joseph Bolton

I was born in Pawtucket, Rhode Island, in 1964, at the twilight of the golden age of French-Canadian culture in New England. My 21-year-old mother, Carol Bolton (née Savoie), was the oldest of eleven children of Roland and Claire Savoie (née St. Goddard). Many older French-Canadians in Rhode Island could and did speak French then. We even had French churches and French Schools in Pawtucket.

I was the first grandchild and was loved and doted on by my aunts and uncles, most of whom were still children themselves. In some of my earliest memories with them, I recall going to midnight Mass at Pawtucket's French church, Saint Cecilia's, and then on to my great-aunt's apartment for a big family Christmas meal. To this day, I still associate the strangely spicy aroma of warm *tourtière* with my great-aunts and with Christmas, in particular.

The rooms in my grandparents' home were decorated with crucifixes, statues, and religious art. My grandmother Claire would gather everyone in for family Rosaries. On rare occasions, I would overhear the playful French banter between my grandfather Roland and his sisters, Jeannette, Rita, and Florence. In many ways, I suspect that, except for the primacy of the English language, my early upbringing was much like what other French-Canadian children experienced in Québec in the early to mid-1960s.

I knew as a small child that we came from Québec. However, as I got older, the way I saw Québec also changed and evolved. In the beginning, Québec was the place of family legends and tales. My great-aunts would talk about their brother Georges Savoie, who, as Brother Donald of the Sacred Heart, taught mathematics in Sherbrooke and Drummondville in Québec and in Central Falls in Rhode Island. My grandmother Claire would tell how her then-childless parents, Adélard and Eva St. Goddard (née Marion), visited the Shrine of Sainte-Anne-de-Beaupré to pray for a child of their own. My grandfather Roland would talk of visiting his cousins at the old Meunier family farm in Québec. They would also talk about how my great-great-grandparents Elphage and Delia Meunier would host Brother (later Saint) André Bessette for dinner at their home.

A bit later, Québec became an adventurous place to visit. My first trip to Québec was a family camping trip in Gatineau, across the river from Ottawa. We visited the Parliament House, and this was when I learned that there were two Canadas: English and French. We also took family trips to Montréal; attending Montréal Expos games was the best.

When my siblings and I were in our early twenties, my brothers David, Peter, and Patrick, fluent in French, would go bar hopping in Montréal. Their French wasn't perfect, though. My brother Patrick still laughs when he remembers being yelled at by a bartender for improper conjugation of the verb *boire*. Suffice it to say that, at this point in our lives, Québec was the place for rowdy adventures.

Poignantly, my last visit to Québec, until 2022, was with my grandfather Roland and my brother David back in 1987. We went to Notre Dame and the Musée des beaux-arts, drove by the old Meunier farmhouse, and then drove a long, dull drive along the flat shore of the Saint Lawrence River for a quick walk around the Plains of Abraham, then on to Sainte-Anne-de-Beaupré. The trip was exhausting, and while I was certainly interested, I felt like an over-scheduled tourist. I feel sad about that now, partly because I miss my grandfather.

Many years later, with the advent of DNA tests and enhanced genealogical tools, I researched our family's history in Québec. The first big surprise came when I gave my mother and five of her siblings a DNA test. As a boy, I was fascinated by the stories about the "olden days" told to me by French-Canadian grandparents and aunts and uncles. At the root of all my questions to my elders was a simple desire to know where I came from. As an adult, with the modern tools of the internet and DNA tests, I discovered our family's *roots in Québec. Knowledge of* names, places, and dates was only the beginning, not the culmination of my journey. I wanted to understand my ancestors as human beings.

Growing up, we were told my mother's family was "100%" French. Well, we are primarily French, but the DNA tests showed that we were spiced with other nationalities, including Spanish, English, and Native

American. Among those Native American gateway ancestors, I have found three so far. One was the Penobscot warrior Madockawando, whose daughter married the irascible Baron Jean-Vincent d'Abbadie de Saint-Castin. Another was a Mi'kmaq woman of whom, sadly, not much is known.

But it was the life of a third Indigenous ancestor, my ninth great-grandmother, an Algonquin woman baptized as Marie Madeleine but born as Miteouamigoukoue, who touched my heart. Thanks to the Jesuits' good record-keeping and the research of the late French-Canadian genealogist and educator Normand Léveillée, who was also a Miteouamigoukoue descendant, we know a lot about her.

In 1652, Miteouamigoukoue was a young woman of the Weskarani band living with her husband Assababich and two young children, Pierre and Catherine, near Trois-Rivières. Her life changed forever when Mohawk raiders from the south attacked the settlement, killing and capturing many Algonquin and French people. Her husband Assababich was killed in the raid, and both of her young children, along with a young Algonquin woman named Kahenta, the mother of future Saint Kateri Tekakwitha, were taken away to the Mohawk village of Ossernenon. She never saw her children again. Five years later, she married French soldier and interpreter Pierre Couc and became my ninth great-grandparent. Her tragedy deeply moved me at such a young age, but more importantly, I admired her strength, perseverance, and courage to live and to love again.

None of my Québecois and First Nations ancestors touched my heart as much as Miteouamigoukoue, also known as Marie Madeline Couc, the Algonquin wife of Pierre Couc. As a young woman in her twenties, she lost her husband and her two children. It was a devastating tragedy that could have understandably made a person despair. Yet many years later, only days after she died, Father Crey in Trois-Rivières wrote of her: *"Miteouamigoukoue lived a full life with dignity, respect, and love. A courageous and loving Algonquin [woman]."* Father Elisée Crey, January 1699

So much is said in a short sentence: whole life, dignity, respect, courage, love. Any person whose life can be transcribed by those words, especially after beginning their lives with such profound loss, must be truly remarkable. Miteouamigoukoue became the hub of the wheel of stories that comprise the Old Grandmother's Tree books. Through the books, I wanted to honor and respect her and the culture that she came from and to acknowledge her connection to us, her descendants, as our Old Grandmother.

Inspired by her story, I began to write a collection of original stories about her life. I wasn't trying to tell a literal true story but a deeper true story through folktales. Folktales are ubiquitous in cultures all over the world. These deceptively simple stories often feature fanciful creatures, and trickster animals entertain and pass on profound moral lessons for living virtuous lives. Each culture's folktales have a particular flavor stemming from their origins. Yet, simultaneously, because they speak to universal themes of human life, they are appreciated far beyond the land of their origin. The result was a two-volume set called Old Grandmothers *Tree: A Collection of French-Canadian Folktales.*

This two-volume set of original French-Canadian folktales has three primary sources. First, I immersed my actual French-Canadian and Native American ancestors into a folklore world of magic, trickster animals, and creatures set in the Québec of the 17th and early 20th centuries. The second source is the inspiration of Algonquin, Abenaki, and Mi'kmaq mythology. The third source is my childhood experience of the significant Québécois diaspora in New England.

In August 2022, I was already well into writing these folktales when I was inspired to return to Québec. Opening a map, I saw a village just over the Vermont border with the intriguing name of Magog. A short four-hour drive later, I found myself the guest of Nicole and Michel, my hosts, at the charming bed-and-breakfast, Au Coeur de Magog.

Honestly, I did not know what to expect, as it was my first visit back to Québec since I was with my grandfather in 1987. Would I be welcome? Would people get mad at me for my imperfect French? Would anyone want to talk to me, a stranger from south of the border? It turns out I had nothing to worry about. The people of Magog were friendly and warm and interested in the story of a French-Canadian coming home from New England. Even my attempts at French were met with benign amusement and encouragement. Thank you, people of Magog, for helping me to discover that the village of Saint-Honoré in Tales of

Old Grandmother's Tree is as close to Magog as possible without being the village of Magog.

On that trip, I remember one warm, early evening on the shore of Lake Memphremagog, watching the sunset over Mount Orford as if I were experiencing Québec for the first time. I did not feel like a tourist, nor was I a stranger, and as I walked over the land touched by my ancestors, gazed at the mountains they saw, and looked upon the people who were my cousins, I felt love for the land and people of Québec.

Learning French has not been easy. Part of the reason is that I started late in life; the other reason is that outside of my tutor, there is no one to practice with. At times, I have been tempted to quit. However, I strive for this because I love visiting Quebec, especially skiing. To give up would reinforce a fear that the ancient land of my ancestors, both Indigenous and Quebecois, was inaccessible to me. Learning French provides a sense of continuity and connection to them.

One of the most fascinating discoveries I made with genealogical websites like Ancestry and Geni is that Quebecois and Acadians are all related. I have researched French Canadians for other people, and I have always been able to find at least one common ancestor with myself. Is that always true? I suspect so, with the founding French populations of Acadia and Quebec being so small. The statue of Dr. Louis Hébert and his wife Marie Rolette in Quebec City stand together watching over their myriads of children as they walk by. In truth, the French-Canadian story is a family story.

It is estimated that there are at least 2 million French Canadians living now in New England. If you look at a census map of the United States, you will see that French Canadians make up the majority of the population in the northern parts of New England. Take away the actual surveyed border between the United States and Canada and you could conclude that Quebec and New Brunswick's real border extends quite far into Maine, New Hampshire and Vermont.

In New England, we love to celebrate our diversity with ethnic festivals throughout the year from Saint Patrick's Day to Cinco de Mayo. Long neglected, French-Canadian celebrations are also becoming more prominent. In my hometown of Leominster, Saint Celecia's Church with many of its parishioners hailing from New

Brunswick, celebrates Christmas in Acadia. In New Hampshire, October brings the Poutine Festival which sells out and brings participants from all over New England and even Canada. Next year, in June 2025, Leominster will host its first French Canadian Cultural Festival.

The future is bright for French-Canadians. With a newly found awareness of our heritage and cross-border connections, we are now seeing a revival of French-Canadian pride and culture.

18. A Heritage Recaptured
John Tousignant

Elle est jolie! Elle sort avec quelqu'un? (She is pretty! Is she going out with someone?)

Thus, I started my personal connection with the French language as an adolescent boy! Language is ultimately a means of communication, and teens will find any means to share their thoughts with peers while keeping their parents oblivious to their deeper motivations. In many New England Franco-American households, the parents spoke French to each other so that the children would not understand. In my house, I spoke French (or some version thereof) with my friends in French class so that my parents would not understand! The journey of French in my home, like the journey of French in our communities, continues to evolve with a view towards the future. Like a young student learning a new skill, we must explore ways to apply it in different contexts while keeping it active and relevant.

Recapturing – The Choice to Reconnect

I have always known that I came from a French-Canadian heritage. My father's family came from Trois-Rivières, Quebec, to work on the NH railroads. My maternal great-grandmother had crossed the border from Stanstead, Quebec, to have her son (my maternal grandfather) in Vermont so he would be an American citizen. Both families looked to the United States as an opportunity for personal and professional success and emigrated there with hope, dreams, and a commitment to hard work.

As in many immigrant families, the French speakers of my grandparents' generation had effectively exhorted their children to learn English as an essential key to upward mobility in their new home. As a result, my parents spoke very little French and raised me in an

Anglophone home. Despite the language differences, the deep underpinnings of French-Canadian culture, traditions, and values were an integral part of the fabric of my upbringing.

Before I had an opportunity to voice any opinion, my parents chose my name – a name that would truly highlight my Franco-American identity: John (English) Tousignant (Quebecois). My father had wanted a hyphenated name: Jean-Paul. My mother said "Jean" would always be pronounced "Jeen," and Tousignant was already too long. Mom won.

My paternal grandfather having passed away when I was barely able to walk, we frequently would visit my grandmother – my Memère – who had become the housekeeper for the pastor at the only French-Catholic parish in the city. Saturday nights consisted of visits while my grandmother and her friends would hold raucous card parties. As they all laughed and teased each other in French, I realized I did not understand them. However, it is a common experience for 4-year-olds not to understand conversations with adults, so I did not pay much attention to the language difference. I learned through my visits that if I said *Bonjour* to her and her friends, they would smile broadly and sneak candy to me while my parents were looking in another direction. The lesson to young John was clear: Using French leads to a sweet result that English doesn't provide!

There was always a wide array of foods at Memère's card parties – nuts, chips, cookies, and "toochay," a meat pie I only learned years later was *tourtière*. Food was central to all celebrations. Many years later, my father explained that his family had been relatively poor when he was young and that his mother's creativity had always kept food on the table. Despite the lack of resources, it was not uncommon for strangers to appear on the doorstep. Working at the rail yard, my Dad's father would come across traveling people – hobos, as they were called at the time - "riding the rails" in search of better opportunities. Often, they would be hungry. He would direct them to his house and tell them that there would be a warm meal for them. Dad shared that his mother was not always thrilled to see them arrive but that they never left hungry.

Both of my grandmothers passed away by the time I was 6, which led to my maternal grandfather moving into our home. I was fortunate to have him living with us until I was 13. I adored my grandfather and enjoyed the evenings he would serve as a babysitter while my parents were out. He taught me to play poker, cheer on the Boston Bruins, and express profound disappointment in terms that would make a sailor blush. The stories of his youth and his unwavering support of my growth live on with me today.

My grandfather had come down to Manchester, NH, as a young man in the early 1900s to work as a shipping manager for a shoe factory. He was short, stocky, and smart, with a quick wit and a fiery temper that likely elicited some fear from his subordinates and ire from the company owner. However, his tough and tenacious exterior was complemented by a charitable side. While he would readily share some of his arguments with his boss, his eyes would soften as he mentioned how he treated his staff, sometimes covering for them so they could get out early to attend to a sick family member at home. He brought some extra food a couple of days before payday for some men who had trouble making ends meet. "Do a good job and feel free to take the credit," he'd say, "but do the right thing because it is right. Then you can look in the mirror and like what you see."

While my father's family had maintained their French connection, my mother's father had all but erased it. He was fluent in French but had assimilated into American culture and rebranded himself as an Anglophone. When I asked him what a French word meant, he often came up with colorful translations that Collins-Robert would have never accepted. For many years, I believed Tousignant translated to "Hole in the ground."

My parents both had styles that put others at ease – my mother through her warmth and genuine interest in others and my father through his broad smile and self-deprecating humor. While these traits are not unique to the francophone world, I have experienced them in many of my dealings with French speakers and often hear those who visit French-speaking regions comment on that different feel. It is that hard to define *Joie de Vivre* that seems to permeate French cultures. I firmly believe it is a piece of who we are and should strive to become.

When I was 14, I had to choose a foreign language in junior high school. It was time for me to move forward in my heritage language journey. Knowing my ancestral roots, there was never a hesitation. Like my grandparents' generation, I would recapture my French heritage and be francophone.

In retrospect, "foreign language" immediately conveyed a sense of being from the outside rather than a language commonly spoken locally. It is good to see that many schools have evolved to use the term "World" languages to show a more equal value and promote intercultural connections. As a junior high school student, though, I learned French as though it were something from far away. Additionally, there were very different standards for the spoken language. The ultimate goal was to speak like you just stepped out of a café in Paris. While I knew that English speakers had different accents, whether from England, Australia or even as close as New York City, I had never sensed a hierarchy of dialects in English. The one exception was when my cousin from Texas commented during a visit, "Y'all talk funny." In French, though, it was clear that to be mistaken for a Parisian would be the ultimate prize and that any failure to achieve that dialect would be a cheapening of one's French mastery.

Despite the heightened emphasis on France, I readily immersed myself in using the language in my community. Finding several friends who also wanted to develop their speaking skills, we would fight through conversations using a mix of French and English that, without us knowing it, mirrored the language development experience of my Franco-American ancestors.

Coming from a strong Roman Catholic background, I soon started to take advantage of the French Mass at our family's parish. One of the advantages of Catholic worship is the typical structure of services regardless of language. Having just missed the post-Vatican II transition from Latin to the locally spoken languages, I had grown up and served as an altar boy hearing English at Mass. Moving to French was an easy transition. Of course, initially, I was a bit lost. I knew that any time I heard *Pour les siècles des siècles* ("for ever and ever"), I should respond, "Amen!" I knew that hearing any number greater than 12 probably meant a song was coming. Most importantly, when the priest said, *Prions le seigneur!* ("Let us pray to the Lord"), it meant "Stop daydreaming and stand up!"

Continuing my high school and college studies, I appreciated many facets of the French language and culture. Although my initial contacts were with the culture of France, I soon came to know my Quebecois and Acadian roots as well as other branches of the Francophonie tree. Traveling to Québec and seeing the language used in daily life made me realize that French was used in more communities than mine and France. Part one of recapturing my heritage was complete: I had made and acted on the decision to learn about French heritage and language.

Recapturing - Taking Past Traditions into the Present

There is a point where the past, with its historical clarity, intersects with the present, with its inherent uncertainties. For each of us, this happens daily as we move through our lives.

Like the "Canadien errant" (wandering Canadian), many of us are forced or choose to reinvent ourselves professionally and personally several times over the years. I chose to do it while maintaining French as a key component of each new situation. Each position offered new opportunities to put my heritage and language skills into practice while contributing to the overall growth of the French-focused community. Each opportunity is available for any of us to pursue, depending only on our energy, motivation, and tenacity.

French teaching is a calling for many who seek to share their love of the language. Falling somewhere between missionary work and stand-up comedy, good teaching takes the content of the language and instills its more profound meaning in the students' hearts. Today's language teachers must also serve as marketing agents for the relevance of their subjects. Where a classical education of the past was expected to include additional language studies, many present-day communities relegate languages to optional, elective status, relying on teachers to continually advocate for their subjects' importance. Fortunately, professional organizations such as the American Association of Teachers of French (AATF) and, in New Hampshire, the NH Association of World Language Teachers (NHAWLT) help to provide professional development and support to this marketing effort.

Beyond the importance of the language itself, people benefit from the sense of belonging that a common language, culture, or heritage provides. Many organizations help to highlight this in our French community, several of which I was fortunate to have been involved in. The Association Canado-Américaine (ACA) was one organization that united people of French-Canadian ancestry or affiliation from Canada and the United States. From 1896 through 2008, the ACA was a key organization providing varied insurance to members while using its profits to promote French-Canadian culture. While the fraternal organization merged with another entity, the ACA Educational Fund still supports U.S. and Canadian students pursuing higher education. Le Club Richelieu, located in many cities internationally, brings together those who want to promote the French language while supporting youth in need. The Franco-American Centre in Manchester, New Hampshire, celebrates the French language, culture, and heritage in New Hampshire and beyond. The worldwide network of Alliances Françaises also deserves recognition for the tireless promotion of the French language and culture in the many local communities it serves. Of course, the list goes on with many other important regional, statewide, and community organizations. However, my involvement in each organization I mentioned increased my sense of belonging in the larger French community.

Before we think about culture, though, we closely examine the economic security in our lives. Until we can provide for our needs, we are unlikely to pay much attention to the value of additional languages or our sense of belonging to a group. Yet, here again, French provides an open door to many potential business opportunities. New England, particularly the Northern states (Vermont, New Hampshire, Maine), directly border the French-speaking markets of Quebec and New Brunswick. In each case, the ability to speak French provides a valuable skill for those working in the tourism, manufacturing, and service industries. As a consultant, I worked with many Canadian companies looking to expand their businesses into the U.S. market. I was often reminded that regardless of their English capabilities, French-speaking contacts provided much-appreciated language and cultural understanding.

Although the common mindset that those who study a language can only use it as a teacher was never really true, it is even less accurate today. As the population ages, particularly among those who were brought up speaking French as a first language, new opportunities have arisen for those who can speak the language fluently or proficiently. Ride shares, meal & grocery delivery services, and providers of home care, recreation, and skilled trades all can benefit from having French-speaking team members.

Recapturing – Building a Future

"What do you want to be when you grow up?"

It is a pretty common question that is asked of young children. As we approach our changing Franco-American cultural identity, it is equally important to ask of ourselves.

As my development has evolved through the years in different arenas, the French language and culture continue to evolve in the 21st century. Just as Franco-Americans have continued to reinvent themselves over past generations, the Franco-American culture must continue to reinvent itself as young people of French heritage seek to combine the sound traditional values of their ancestors with the changing realities of modern life.

What Are the Key Factors Impacting This Evolution?

- Immigration

The face of French is changing. With many French speakers of African heritage, the Franco-American experience will have increasing cultural diversity. While some might find that difficult to accept, we must realize that the large influx of French Canadians in the late 19th and early 20th centuries provided a change that differed from a European-oriented French culture. Future Franco-Americans will adapt and incorporate some Franco-African traits, while the new residents will receive some traditions from North American French culture.

Immigration is a highly-charged topic in U.S. politics at present. Often, the issue of illegal immigration is reduced to simply a broad brushstroke on immigration in general. As a Franco-American culture, we must realize that we were the targets of anti-immigrant sentiment and discrimination in our not-so-distant past. For us to passively accept those injustices today is an affront to our ancestors' experience.

- Technology

As technology expands, our world will continue to shrink, and our interconnectedness will grow. Thanks to the internet, we have been exposed to many more French speakers, performers, and programming from the many francophone cultures of the world. The net result has been a greater acceptance of different dialects and cultural norms. This has helped break down the "Parisian is the only good French" attitude among younger French students, encouraging them to speak more without shame.

Moving forward, we must address the increasing sophistication of translation software and an unknown future using AI. While tools may make it easier to communicate with French speakers, will we focus less on learning French (and other languages) ourselves? If internalizing a language provides a greater understanding of the culture, we will hopefully continue to encourage language mastery.

- Changing sense of identity

Every day, we are all confronted with changing gender norms, religious values, and public (and private) etiquette. Many of the lines in old conventions have been blurred, and new lines that did not exist a few years ago have been drawn.

As we continue exploring our identity – as French speakers, Franco-Americans, and French-Americans – we must reassess what those identities mean. Do these terms mean the same things they meant in the 20th Century? Do they have to? Does it matter?

- A refreshed, welcoming attitude to new expressions of the French language

Understanding the value of a friendly, welcoming attitude when sharing the language is essential. When you ask a group of first-graders, "Who can sing?" they will all reply, "I can!" "Who can dance?" yields the same answer. "Who can draw, play soccer, or build a robot?" will all get positive responses. In youth, we believe that anything is possible.

Unfortunately, this hopeful attitude tends to dissipate as we grow older. People who studied French in their youth turn "I haven't used it in a long time" into "I can't do it." In the same way, those who were told that their French wasn't "good enough" may have taken that to heart and chosen to remain silent.

Those French speakers need to reassess what is most important: Perfection or Communication. Are there people in our lives who have been separated from French and need our encouragement to reconnect with the language and culture?

Being a *coureur de bois* or a 20th-century textile mill worker has no future. However, the tenacity, resilience, and dedication that characterized those ancestors' success can be rechanneled as we meet the challenges of creating a new Franco-American identity and rebuilding this identity for the future.

Recapturing – A Conclusion

"Recapturing" our heritage is more than studying our history and learning the French language. It is developing a commitment to actively participate in this long-term Franco-American historical experience. It is not enough for us to sit back and watch it. We need to channel the energy, vitality, and commitment of our parents, grandparents, and previous generations as we determine where we are going and how we will get there. *Allons-y!* Let's go!

19. Finding Franco-America in Historical Anniversaries
   Patrick Lacroix

Would it not be time to inventory, in some way, our situation and then tell ourselves: we wish or do not wish to remain what we are, and therefore, here is how it seems appropriate to act?[211]

Two significant anniversaries will come to Franco-America in 2026. First, the United States will celebrate the 250th anniversary of the Declaration of Independence. This matters as we understand Franco-America to be the meeting of French heritage and U.S. institutions and culture. More than that, weeks before representatives in Philadelphia resolved on independence, in 1776, the Continental Army abandoned its occupation of the Province of Quebec. In tow, in its retreat, were hundreds of French Canadians who had cast their lot with the insurgents. After the war, some of these exiled Canadians settled with their families in upstate New York. They formed the first Little Canada on U.S. soil.[212]

Second, in 2026, two centuries will have elapsed since the first report of outmigration from Lower Canada as a mass movement rather than as isolated cases. Writing from Montreal in 1826, Romuald Trudeau deplored the growing tendency of French-Canadian youths to run to the United States to escape strict parents or in search of an easy life.[213] Though outmigration was, in the 1820s, a trickle when compared to the torrent that would later come, it no longer suffices to locate the beginnings of Quebec's significant demographic hemorrhage, *la grande saignée*, in the era of the U.S. Civil War.

Our way of honoring historical anniversaries says much more about the present than about the events we commemorate. Through a

---

[211] Morfit, 1949.
[212] Lacroix, 2019.
[213] Trudeau, 1826.

conscious act of remembrance, anniversaries help us contextualize our current experiences and find a usable past that gives meaning to our lives. They enable us to say explicitly something about ourselves. All of that rests on memory, *some* memory, of the past. In the Franco-American world, that memory has become shallower. This lapse mirrors concerns of a thinning identity: not a year goes by without a public declamation about the loss of the culture. The anniversaries of 2026 provide an opportunity to anchor *what is* in *what was*—not to compare or to assess losses merely, but to assert the relevance of the past to the present and to think creatively and deliberately about the future.

The last large-scale, region-wide anniversary, celebrated in 1949, marked the "centenaire franco-américain." It was a product of its time: an expression of traditional French-Canadian *survivance*. This event and other anniversaries helped cement Franco-Americans' stories about themselves. Despite the profound changes of the last seventy-five years and the erosion of myths through historical research, some of those stories subsist today. However, they do not always speak to the present-day realities of Franco-Americans. Looming anniversaries provide an opportunity to rescue a past that speaks to the early twenty-first century. This work may help us inform and inspire a Franco-American identity in 2026 and beyond.

By and large, Franco-Americans have few pedestals, real or metaphorical. A statue honoring prominent journalist Ferdinand Gagnon (1849-1886) on Manchester's West Side stands out as an exception. In the U.S. Northeast, the few other monuments to Franco-Americans are confined to historic Little Canadas in mill cities. Such limited *physical* representation is reflected in a larger historical consciousness. We may legitimately wonder how many Americans of French-Canadian or Acadian descent could today draw four figures from their history to consecrate on an imagined Mount Rushmore. Name recognition falls dramatically after Jack Kerouac—though Franco-Americans have achieved success, even prominence, in every conceivable field. In short, there is an asymmetry between history and historical consciousness.

The same "memory gap" appears in the dearth of historical anniversaries. Granted, community organizations continue to honor *la*

Saint-Jean-Baptiste (and, in Maine, Acadian Day) in June. Franco-Americans join in celebrations of Francophonie Month every March. Yet, these annual rendezvous—sometimes perfunctory—are quite different from historical anniversaries. Organizers can afford to copy and paste from one year to the next: traditional meals, flag raising, several family-friendly cultural activities, short public addresses, and perhaps a ceremony to honor this or that person. There is considerable merit in this ritual assertion of a distinct identity—in rising to say, in not so many words, "We are still here." On the other hand, the routine nature of these annual celebrations deters engagement with the past. They do not involve real people doing things in past times and places, which are the heart of history. They do not help us close the "memory gap."

Landmark anniversaries of historical events—a centennial, for instance—force a reckoning with the words and deeds of those who came before and who ushered the world we inhabit. What did they achieve? What values did they espouse? What did they leave behind? How do these historical figures still speak to us? These questions must be addressed consciously; they beget an answer beyond "We are still here." The basic idea is not to raise new pedestals or to worship heroes who embody a perfect, essential *Franco-Americanness*, as some sought to do with Ferdinand Gagnon, but to foster a conversation about a historically anchored identity. Such work is vital in communities that lack "institutional completeness," that is, "the extent to which a minority group can establish a network of social institutions (daycare, schools, universities, churches, workplaces, businesses, etc.) that sustain the minority language and culture."[214] In the absence of just such a system, which existed in many Little Canadas well into the postwar period, it becomes necessary to contrive forums in which to discuss identity—and landmark anniversaries supply the tools.

Specific organizations and communities have had their own anniversaries, but not since 1949 have Franco-Americans in the Northeast celebrated something more encompassing. The "centenaire franco-américain" of 1949 was imagined to celebrate one hundred years

---

[214] Larocque, 2024.

of organized Franco-American life. Although Little Canadas across the region might have very different histories, the steps taken in the pre-Civil War era ultimately served the large number of expatriated French Canadians and their descendants in disparate locales. The centennial was many-fathered and -mothered. Writing in *L'Etoile* in early 1948, columnist Yvonne Le Maître drew attention to the arrival of the first French-Canadian families in Lowell a century earlier. Months later, Antoine Clément, the editor of *L'Etoile*, popularized the idea of a centennial but still felt the need to defend its "authenticity." Beyond Lowell, Clément stated that efforts to organize a national parish in Burlington dated from 1849 (this is disputable) and the Société historique franco-américaine would soon celebrate fifty years of existence. "The Swedes," he added, "have just had a brilliant celebration of their centennial in this country; why not us?"[215] Fr. Adrien Verrette, a prominent member of the Société historique, helped publicize the event in Quebec and the Comité d'orientation franco-américaine, a relatively new group, agreed to organize it.[216] Later, in a piece reproduced in *Le Travailleur*, Adolphe Robert, the president of the Association Canado-Américaine and a member of the Comité d'orientation, would concede that "the organizing committee chose the year 1949 for the celebration of the Franco-American centennial not so much for a specific anniversary, but to mark a century of our people's participation in American life."[217]

Most texts published in *Le Travailleur* in the spring of 1949 in connection with the anniversary focused on the centennial of Burlington's national parish, thus placing Catholic institutions at the center of the Franco-American story. Yet, the centennial activities were held not in Burlington—nor even Lowell—but in Worcester, supporting the notion that organizers searched for an anniversary as a pretext to come together and celebrate. As the basis for study and reflection, the past seemed generally neglected through the two-day affair. The celebrations resumed in New Hampshire in June to honor the centennial

---

[215] Clément, 1948.
[216] Désilets, 1949; *Centenaire franco-américain*, 1949.
[217] Robert, 1949.

of Ferdinand Gagnon's birth with the dedication of his statue. It was yet another paradox of the time that the tribute to Gagnon took place not in Worcester, where he had made his name, but in Manchester. At times, this tribute centered less on his context and the ideas he represented than on personal virtues that might belong to any person or ethnic group.[218] On the other hand, the ceremony at Lafayette Park launched Franco-American Press Week, which affirmed the historic role of newspapers as a pillar of *"l'Oeuvre de Préservation Nationale et Religieuse."*[219] On behalf of the Société historique franco-américaine, attorney Eugène L. Jalbert explained—perhaps more clearly than anyone—how Gagnon spoke to the present. The statue, Jalbert stated, symbolized the gratitude and admiration of a people for their most illustrious nineteenth-century figure and recognition of the "founder" (this is disputable) of the Franco-American press. The newspaper conveyed a program focused on naturalization and establishing distinct parishes, schools, and national societies. Gagnon had preached unity and the pursuit of a common goal: the maintenance of French Canadians' "national character." Jalbert added what he perceived to be the lesson of Gagnon's program: it was incumbent on parents to remind the next generation that "our nationality, like our very nature, is a gift of God and that remaining true to it is to be faithful to God."[220]

This fit impeccably with the program of the congress held in Worcester in May. The Comité d'orientation had drafted and adopted a manifesto before the event; it was offered to delegates as the basis of discussion during the lone "study session." The Comité touted the document as something fresh, stating that it "consists of a new doctrine for our people or if you will, a new course of action that we must follow if we are to remain who we are."[221] In reality, it consecrated the orthodoxy of traditional *survivance*. Members of the Comité were leaders and organizers of the institutions that had structured Franco-American life in industrial cities for more than fifty years. Many dimensions of the

---

[218] Verrette, 1949; Dion-Lévesque, 1949; Nolin, 1949.
[219] "Début [...]", 1949; Lacasse, 1949.
[220] Jalbert, 1949.
[221] *La vie franco-américaine*, 1950, 24.

manifesto could have been adopted two generations earlier—down to identity. "[I]n spiritual matters," it declared, "Franco-Americans are Roman Catholics; in temporal matters, they are American citizens; finally, they are French by tradition, language, and spirit."[222] The document insisted on the need to maintain distinct institutions—parishes, schools, households, social organizations, etc.—and live out a Catholic and francophone identity in each sphere. It had little to offer on the new cultural challenges awaiting in the wake of the Second World War. Community leaders did not envision a future substantially different from the past, though, admittedly, the congress marked a crucial step towards the creation of the Fédération féminine franco-américaine.[223]

The fundamental injunction to stay the course reflected in part power dynamics within the Franco-American community. Leaders of the "old" institutions wielded outsized influence; Franco-American families increasingly dropped out of these leaders' "imagined community" due to life experiences to which traditional *survivance* failed to speak. The celebrations in Worcester required a small army of volunteers; the banquet and Mass were well-attended, as were some of the sessions. On the other hand, the organizers borrowed a top-down template to plan what they saw as the first Franco-American convention since 1901.[224] Tellingly, the *session d'étude*, which Robert moderated, centered on a lengthy exchange between Wilfrid Dufault, Lucien Dufault, and Thomas M. Landry, all clergymen, over French as a language of instruction.[225] Most delegates seemed to have had little space to express their concerns or to contribute beyond the manifesto, which had come from above.

The integration of Franco-Americans into mainstream U.S. society and culture occurred gradually over the course of generations. However, a symbolic transition occurred precisely in the "centenaire franco-américain" era as noticeable institutional losses occurred. The

---

[222] Comité d'orientation franco-américain, 1949.
[223] Quintal, 1997, 179.
[224] La vie franco-américaine, 1950, 18.
[225] Désormeaux, 1949.

geographical mobility of Franco-Americans, anglicization, a failure to speak to readers' concerns, and economic competition got the better of the French-language press. Manchester's *L'Avenir National* and Biddeford's *La Justice* ended operations in 1949. Lowell, Fall River, and Holyoke newspapers closed in the late 1950s and early 1960s. Lewiston's *Le Messager* became a weekly in 1957 and died a decade later.[226] In the same years, Catholic institutions began to contract; many lost their ethnic vocation. The financial pressures that underlay these changes did not spell the end of a culture or its efforts to remain organized: the 1970s and 1980s witnessed heretofore unseen advocacy on university campuses, federally-funded cultural initiatives, the rise of new genealogical and historical societies, Franco-focused academic conferences, efforts to promote bilingualism, excitement driven by Quebec neo-nationalism—the list goes on.[227] Still, there is something to the idea that a world was lost in the 1950s and 1960s. The institutional system of traditional *survivance*, where the Catholic faith and the French language were to buttress one another, disappeared. So did the French-Canadian idea of the culture, that is, the notion that the identity of Quebec migrants could survive intact in the United States.

In our century, the process of decentralization of culture has continued unabated. Though many Franco-Americans remain deeply committed to their faith, cultural institutions are now untethered from the Catholic Church. Events occur in French and English. Lectures, musical and theatrical performances, food events, conversation tables, language education programs, historical tours, and exhibits occur independently, for the most part, with a variety of groups—some ad-hoc, some well-established—providing the organizing drive. Decentralization has accelerated due to new technologies, ensuring a representation of views that was impossible in the 1940s. Juliana L'Heureux, David Vermette, James Myall, and Melody Desjardins's blogs and Query the Past have fostered online conversations. The same holds for *Maple Stars and Stripes*, the *French-Canadian Legacy Podcast*, *Franco-American Pathways*, and the *North American Francophone Podcast*.

---

[226] Paré, 1979, 257-260; Perreault, 1996, 334-335.
[227] see, e.g., Gosnell, 2018, 61-66, 95-105, 216-231.

This is in addition to many Facebook pages and an ever-rising number of hybrid and virtual events. In keeping with the age, Franco-American culture now lives less within institutions than in networks of self-selected people with a shared commitment. More than ever, self-identifying Franco-Americans can feel empowered to engage creatively and deliberately with their culture without the mediation of "higher-ups."

All of this comes while heritage itself is transformed. In the era of the Little Canadas, heritage was transmitted through family, local institutions, and the social environment of a geographically identifiable ethnic community. Children bathed in that environment and absorbed the culture of their elders from birth. Today, most young Franco-Americans do not encounter the culture of their ancestors *as heritage*. It is not inherited *per se*, for often even their parents have a tenuous connection to Franco-American culture—and then typically only as historical memory rather than lived reality.[228] Young people thus have to search for the past and dig up *the heritage of prior generations* in hopes of restoring a relationship with a broader community. It is not precisely heritage if these self-selected individuals' siblings can lead lives entirely uninfluenced by a French-Canadian or Acadian past.

This reflection should not be taken as a lament; neither does it reduce the legitimacy of Franco-American culture in the twenty-first century. There is added power in people *choosing* to engage with it. When memory fosters creation, and those pillars become part of the common language of a community, no matter how big or small, then we may speak of a living, breathing culture. Digital tools have considerably helped connect those elements and inspired self-identification among people of all ages. Such self-identification now often derives from an ancestral connection rather than the cultural markers of prior generations, particularly the French language.[229] Some Franco-Americans as well as Quebec observers have spied in the erosion of these markers the demise of a culture.[230] In truth, the memory of the thing lost can be as powerful a binding agent and as much of a lingua franca as the

---

[228] Pinette, 2017, 183-184.
[229] Salmon, 2019, 401-402.
[230] e.g., Wong, 2021.

language itself.[231] We are more likely witnessing a generational shift in which Franco-Americans adapt that culture to their lived reality to maintain its relevance. A culture that does not change fossilizes and dies.

As cultures evolve, so does their members' historical memory. Consciously or not, we all draw from the past the historical figures and events that speak to us. We may thus wonder what history is likely to be honored in anniversaries held in our day. What people, places, and events will speak meaningfully to a "Franco" identity? Would Franco-Americans living in the Northeast today put any figure on a pedestal, and if so, who and why? Would they seek to honor the first family to settle in a Little Canada or the founding of a national parish? These questions raise deeper ones on how Franco-American memory is formed and the extent to which academic historians, family lore, literature, popular media, and imagination have the power to mold it.

One academic historian has had his say. Less than twenty years ago, Yves Roby hoped that researchers, and perhaps self-identifying Franco-Americans, would continue to look beyond the disappointed hopes of elite advocates of *survivance*. In his view, the story at the heart of Franco-Americanness was the lived experience of "ordinary" people who became rooted, integrated, and sought a better life for generations to come.[232] Undoubtedly, the focus on *survivance* has often eclipsed how a Franco-American identity might be lived out—culturally, materially, geographically, and so forth—and clouded from view people on the margins, those who did not meet or have not met the strict standard of cultural orthodoxy. The search for an inclusive, regenerated community no longer involves *survivance*, be it as a prescriptive identity, as the cement of a community, or as an institutional system. It is important to understand history, but we cannot surrender the present to the past. That is a common issue with historical anniversaries: we easily spend more time fretting over what the dead would think of us than contemplating how we feel about the dead.

Let us close the memory gap and open a conversation about those who came before—not to judge *them*, but to understand *ourselves*. The

---

[231] Lacroix, 2022.
[232] Roby, 2007, 7-12, 140-143.

historical anniversaries that will be upon us in 2026 can help us do this. Whether we celebrate 250 years of French-Canadian participation in the American experiment or 200 years since the beginning of the mass migration (as closely as we can date it), a great deal can speak to the present. By stretching the Franco-American story back either to 1826 or to 1776, rather than taking *survivance* as a beginning and an end, we broaden our historical, geographical, and social lens. *Survivance* suddenly becomes a *phase* rather than the essence of Franco-Americanness. The broader scope brings into view migrants who settled in borderland and outlying regions and who could not count on a vigorous system of ethnic institutions. It draws in the families who neither came nor stayed to work in mills, including the vast majority of Franco-Americans born in the last seventy years, whose occupational life has had little relation to textiles. Inspired by the refugees of 1776, the anniversaries should recognize the many ways by which people of French-Canadian descent molded—and were molded by—the host society. Inspired by the migrants of 1826, the anniversaries should, as Roby suggested, recognize the struggles and achievements involved in seeking the well-being of future generations. The anniversaries should highlight the breadth of experiences that we understand as Franco-Americanness. They should be celebrated everywhere Franco-Americans live and thrive: Worcester and Manchester, certainly, Lowell and Burlington too, but really all around the Northeast and beyond.

Ultimately, by their very nature, the looming anniversaries are likely to speak to a culture that has witnessed the decline of ethnic endogamy and Catholic belonging—and that finds the story of Americanizing Irish bishops much less compelling. Life in Little Canadas is foreign to recent generations; interest in Quebec is much less emotional and much less reliant on language than previously. These recent generations may have seen non-Franco-Americans scoff at the mention of Quebec or French heritage, but they have likely never experienced exclusion based on ancestry. A narrative of perseverance and adaptation may today speak more loudly than one of marginalization. Naturally, the point would not be to deny any part of the past, but to find echoes of the present in the past, to find strands that can help young people feel comfortable in their own culture and help foster self-identification in all areas where a seed of Franco-Americanness exists. "Franco-Americans are still making themselves," argues Jonathan Gosnell.[233] Let us restore to that process the rightful place of history and memory.

---

[233] Gosnell, 2018, 289.

20. Bridging the Francophone Archipelago: Past and Present[234]
Camden Martin

I had to cross an initial bridge of my own before I could understand the importance of connecting Francophone communities across North America. Growing up in an English-speaking household in Auburn, Maine—an area that, along with Lewiston, forms a vital foothold for the French language in Central Maine—I was largely unaware of my rich heritage. Despite having all 16 of my great-great-grandparents and two of my great-grandparents born in Québec or Acadie, I never learned to appreciate or understand the significance of this legacy. Living in Lewiston-Auburn, it was inevitable that I would develop some awareness of my Franco-American heritage. Like many Franco-Americans in New England, I referred to my grandparents as *mémère* and *pépère* and was told I was of French extraction from Canada. While I rarely heard my family speak French, a few words such as *arrête*, *crotte de nez*, and *bibitte* occasionally surfaced. Growing up, I did not realize these were French words; I assumed they were family slang. It wasn't until middle school that I learned their true origins. My father's family sometimes gathered around the table for card games, and when someone lost, they would sing, *"Tu t'en vas, pis tu nous laisses, tu t'en vas, quel bon débarras!"* At the time, I did not understand the lyrics and could not have spelled them even if I had tried.

Aside from language, aspects of French-Canadian culture permeated my childhood, mainly through food. My father shined in the kitchen on Sunday mornings, making *crêpes* and *ployes*, often

---

[234] The title of this chapter was inspired by the book *Du continent perdu à l'achipel retrouvé. Le Québec et l'Amérique française* by Dean Louder and Éric Waddell. I had the pleasure of reading this book while attending college in Canada, and it helped me better comprehend the francophone reality on this continent.

accompanied by *creton* to spread on our toast. It was a tradition I enjoyed, though I was unaware that millions of French-Canadian descendants across North America shared these culinary customs. I mistakenly thought such meals were unique to my family or perhaps some families in Northern Maine. My ignorance about my ethnic identity did not prevent me from enjoying my childhood or sharing interests with my peers. The foundations of my identity at that time were built on my love for wildlife, history, and the experience of growing up in the Lewiston-Auburn area. Still, I often felt out of place and longed for belonging. I dreamed of traveling and was curious about other cultures, making it a point to engage with people from different backgrounds. Until then, I had only been presented with one culture as my own—the North American Anglo-Saxon experience. Reflecting on this, I realize I never fully adhered to that culture; consciously or not, I felt unfulfilled by the mainstream American narrative surrounding me. Little did I know I came from a people with a distinct culture and language. This realization shifted when I chose French as my foreign language option in 8th grade. I admit I selected the class partly because my older sister Hannah had already taken it, and I thought it would be convenient should I need her help. I enjoyed the class but felt disconnected from the language—it seemed indeed foreign to me. We primarily learned about France and metropolitan French culture, and the idea that my grandparents spoke this language and that it was part of my ancestry felt nebulous.

However, one decision that year had a profound impact on my future. We were offered an accelerated program allowing students to skip directly to French II in high school if they passed. I chose to do it mainly to get ahead academically, not realizing how much I would eventually come to value learning French. In my freshman year, I felt special being one of only two freshmen in a traditional sophomore class. It was at 14 years old that I embarked on a journey that would deepen my pride in being of French-Canadian descent and allow me to speak the language of my ancestors, who had been alive for over 400 years. I decided to take French more seriously, and I began to excel in the subject as I did. My teacher, also a Franco-American, incorporated many aspects of French-Canadian history and culture into the curriculum.

Suddenly, I was presented with a different narrative about my heritage. I realized that the history of the American Revolution and the Founding Fathers wasn't my own; my ancestors were still in Canada. My North American history began with the formation of la Nouvelle-France, and I became captivated by this realization, researching it on my own time. I borrowed books from the library, watched documentaries, and scoured the Internet for materials that would enlighten me on the subject. My thirst for knowledge about French Canada was insatiable. I was fascinated by the French explorers and their achievements, enthralled by the lives of the *coureurs des Bois*, and shocked to learn about the stigma and discrimination faced by Franco-Americans, including involvement from groups like the Ku Klux Klan.

As I dug deeper, I felt deprived of my history. Why hadn't anyone explained where my ancestors came from? Why hadn't anyone told me that I belonged to a unique culture? To truly understand myself and my direction, I knew I needed to learn French fluently. In tandem with my burgeoning interest in the history of the French presence in North America, I pursued every opportunity to learn French outside the classroom. I listened to French radio, watched French films with subtitles, and practiced speaking with *mémère* Martin, applying the new grammatical concepts and vocabulary I was learning in class. As I began speaking to my grandmother in French, I discovered new facets of her personality and humor I had never encountered before. The fruits of my labor were about to pay off. In the spring of 2011, I learned of a scholarship opportunity to study in France for two months. It was a nationwide competition where participants had to write in French and English, detailing why they deserved the scholarship. Thinking I had nothing to lose, I quickly prepared my application, explaining how learning French was vital to reviving a part of my identity. To my surprise, a few months later, I was notified that I had won the competition and would attend school in Nîmes, France. What began as two months turned into two years as I completed my Baccalauréat in the *littéraire* section.

Living in France opened many doors for me and allowed me to grow as a young man. Until my departure at 16, I had never flown on a plane, and here I had to integrate into the French public school system.

Leaving my comfort zone proved to be the best decision I could make. In France, I learned to appreciate gastronomy, leisure, academic rigor, and, most importantly, made countless connections with locals. In southern France, the weather was sunny and warm most of the year, with constant cultural activities and festivals. At school, we were treated like university students and required to be independent. For a young man who longed for travel and new challenges, I was in my element. My life in France was entirely in French, except for English class. I often shared with students that I was of French-Canadian descent and worked hard to master French as it was a language that belonged to me. I became so comfortable speaking French that upon returning to Maine, people I had never met remarked on my slight French accent. I took this as a compliment.

After two years in France, I returned to Maine, uncertain whether I would go back to France or start college in the United States. My academic journey took an unexpected turn. After starting a semester at Unity College in Maine studying wildlife biology, I encountered another unique opportunity to study in Québec, Canada, at the Cégep de Saint-Félicien. It became clear that it would be wise to continue studying French at a reduced cost. The Ministry of Education in Québec accepted my experience in France as a French student, allowing me to study for only $280 CAD for an entire academic year. I spent the next three and a half years studying *Protection de l'environnement* in Saint-Félicien in the Lac-Saint-Jean region of Québec. I encountered a French dialect similar to the one spoken in Lewiston-Auburn there. Explaining who I was to my classmates was often amusing; my name, Camden, was challenging to pronounce. I spoke with a Southern French accent, yet I was an American citizen of French-Canadian descent. You can imagine the confused looks I received while sharing my story.

In the spring of 2018, I returned to Maine with hopes of working in the environmental field. While I faced challenges finding work and readjusting to a predominantly English-speaking environment after spending six of the previous seven years in French, I wanted to continue speaking French in Lewiston-Auburn. Meanwhile, both cities had become home to many new Sub-Saharan African Francophones, including Rwanda, Burundi, Djibouti, and the Democratic Republic of

Congo. During a sabbatical year between finishing school in France and starting in Québec, I worked at a call center in downtown Lewiston as a customer service agent for French-Canadian customers. Many of my colleagues were newly arrived political refugees from the countries I mentioned. Having maintained those friendships while in college, it felt natural to continue speaking French with my friends, who had become like family.

I also became involved with various French language and Franco-American organizations, such as the Alliance Française du Maine and the Franco-American Collection at the University of Southern Maine. While visiting my brother in Fort Kent, Maine, near the New Brunswick border, I often spoke with native speakers from the Saint John Valley. During one visit in the summer of 2019, my brother Taylor handed me an old French novel that had belonged to *mémère* Martin, who had passed away in 2015. I was deeply moved, as it represented a connection to my grandmother. Upon opening the book, I discovered a sheet of paper glued to the inside cover, reading, « *L'École Saint-Pierre Lewiston Maine, prix d'excellence en lecture anglaise et française, accordé à Mlle Muriel Marois, 1941.*» I was astonished; until that moment, I had never connected the dots that my grandmother, a second-generation American, had attended Catholic school in French. I had assumed French was merely a family language without structures in place for living it, such as schooling. As I continued to flip through the pages of *La Vengeance de Renaud*, I noticed the text was written in the formal literary tense, *le passé simple*. Mastering reading in *le passé simple* requires a deepened understanding of French grammar, and I was again confronted with information that shook my understanding of my history to the core. Did Franco-Americans in Lewiston-Auburn have access to education and services in French while living in Anglophone Maine? Did they receive a similar education to that of their francophone counterparts in Canada and France? Once again, I wondered why this history had never been explained. I had to answer these questions; my thirst became yet again insatiable.

I began to collect any books related to Franco-Americans from Lewiston-Auburn and across New England. The more I researched, the more I realized that French-Canadians and future Franco-Americans had created structures such as schools, churches, newspapers, hospitals, mutual aid societies, and cultural organizations that allowed them to maintain a francophone environment for nearly a century. I learned that plays by Molière, an author we commonly studied in France, were reenacted in downtown Lewiston. In fact, there were so many French cultural organizations and clubs that the Québec historian Robert Rumilly dubbed Lewiston "L'Athènes de l'Amérique Française." As a result, I had a newfound pride and respect for both my ancestors who came to settle in Maine and the history of the francophone populations who did the same across North America at different times throughout the last 400 years. Now that I was able to cross the bridge of appropriating my own cultural and linguistic heritage, I felt the need to connect to other francophone minority groups across the continent. I have since made it my mission to understand not only the francophone communities of New England but also those in the Midwest, along the Mississippi until Louisiana and elsewhere. I would ask myself how these communities evolved and how they fare today. It is only natural for a linguistic and cultural group to seek each other out. After all, it is essential to stimulate the retention of different francophone cultures to come together and exchange and create together. The Organisation Internationale de la Francophonie, which groups 88 member states worldwide, is a prime example of the desire to come together based on a shared language. Within North America, the Centre de la Francophonie des Amériques, located in Québec City, has been a key player and catalyst for stimulating Francophonie across the Western Hemisphere. I had the great fortune of participating in two events organized by the CFA. Notably, the Mobilisation Jeunesse brought together young professionals who promoted the French language across the Americas to attend the 2019 Congrès Mondial Acadien in Moncton, New Brunswick. This event allowed me to connect better with francophone activists from Louisiana, Ontario, Yukon, Mexico, and elsewhere. It had the effect of taking me out of my silo that my story was a story shared by many. I found this to be reassuring and motivating to continue the work.

Yet, if I were to conduct an informal survey of Franco-Americans in Maine, few would be aware, for example, of the historical and current

French-speaking pockets in Michigan, Missouri, Illinois, Minnesota, and even the communities in Western Canada. Some fellow Franco-Americans would be amazed to know how much certain New England cities were and continue to remain francophone. Simply knowing that our experience is not a singular story helps to add vitality. At first glance, the isolated populations of French speakers are only now able to connect thanks to modern technology and means of transportation. However, despite the recent revival of interest in the French language in the United States and beyond, the inclination to weave strong links amongst the Francophone fabric is not new.

The 19th century saw many waves of French-Canadians immigrating to the United States. Early on, several settled in areas that once were under the sphere of influence of France, such as the Great Lakes region, Illinois, and Missouri. They followed the steps of the *Coureurs des Bois* and those who came to make a fortune in the fur trade. Later, as the Midwest began to open to agriculture, it was a natural progression for French-Canadians to seek new farmlands. This is how communities such as Bourbonnais, Illinois, came to be. By the mid-19th century, Bourbonnais possessed its own higher education institution, le Collège St-Viateur, which offered a bilingual education until the 19th century. Simultaneously, the Champlain Valley in New York and Vermont, as well as the forest camps and brick factories of Maine, were equally seeing the number of French-Canadians swell. Furthermore, there remained a desire amongst the ever-growing diaspora to hold on fiercely to the Catholic faith and the French language, just as their compatriots had been doing in the Saint-Lawrence Valley since the end of the French regime. The notion of *la Survivance* was a driving force in maintaining strong links between the highly mobile pockets of francophone populations scattered below the 48th and 49th parallels. The Francophone elites in New England were well aware of the developments in other communities and kept regular contact by corresponding by letters. The correspondence was often reported in the local French-language press. It was not unheard of that *L'Abeille* newspaper in New Orleans would keep tabs on the developments further North or share a message addressed to the newspaper from a French-Canadian journalist.

The connection was also facilitated thanks to the existence of mutual aid societies that emulated the ones already existing in French Canada. L'Union Saint Jean-Baptiste d'Amérique (USBJA), headquartered in Woonsocket, Rhode Island, and L'Association Canado-Américaine (ACA), headquartered in Manchester, New Hampshire, played a crucial role in stimulating Francophone cultural life. The USJBA, at its height, regrouped more than 50,000 members, both women and men, from New England, Michigan, Illinois, and Indiana, and even had councils in California. The criteria for being a member consisted of being a practicing Catholic and of French descent. The language of meetings and conventions remained French into the second half of the 20th century. The USBJA and its homolog, the ACA, encouraged their members to subscribe to their local Franco-American newspapers and supported younger generations with scholarships to attend post-secondary bilingual schools such as the Collège de l'Assomption in Worcester, Massachusetts. The societies would receive foreign Francophone dignitaries, acting as official representatives of the Franco-American communities. In 1930, the French Ambassador, Paul Claudel, was invited to tour Woonsocket, Rhode Island, Worcester, Lowell, Massachusetts, Manchester, New Hampshire, and Lewiston, Maine. During his *séjour*, he met with different Franco-American leaders, schools, hospitals, religious communities, and press members, always accompanied by USJBA and ACA representatives. This tradition would continue well into the 20th century. La Société Historique Franco-Américaine played a large piece in weaving links between the scattered North American Francophone populations by organizing annual meetings and conferences, where guest speakers from varying intellectual backgrounds were invited to speak in Boston, Massachusetts. Some notable examples include Alcée Fortier of the literary society L'Athénée Louisianais and Télésphore Saint-Pierre, a journalist from Michigan. L'Alliance Française de Lowell, Massachusetts, had shared a hand in providing opportunities to hear from other Francophone counterparts by hosting conferences. The New Orleans lawyer and member of L'Athénée Louisianais, André Lafargue was no stranger to presenting to New England Francophones the history and evolution of the francophone communities in Louisiana. In the late winter of 1940, the USJBA and ACA organized a trip for members to visit Louisiana. In the monthly publication of the USJBA, *l'Union*, it is possible to follow the progress of the idea of the trip germinating to the *compte-rendu* afterward. It was first advertised to members as *La Mission des Franco-Américains auprès des Acadiens de la Louisiane*. The trip included four days of travel and five days of visiting New Orleans and Lafayette. Over thirty individuals, including priests, journalists, mutual aid representatives, doctors, and lawyers, made the voyage to better understand *l'état des francophones en Louisiane*. Having learned this information over the past few years, I felt even more inclined to attend the 2023 Universtité d'été in Lafayette, LA, after being presented with the opportunity. What better way to perpetuate the tradition of cross-state connections amongst francophones? This unique week-long event, filled with conferences and classes, regrouping over several dozen participants from across the Western Hemisphere, was organized by the Centre de la Francophone des Amériques. Much like my experience in 2019 in Moncton, New Brunswick, I was yet again immersed in a Francophone environment with like-minded individuals. This event was unique as it was the first time the *Universtité d'été* was held outside Canada. This experience catalyzed me to generate new ideas and aspirations regarding Maine and New England's francophone populations, such as exploring French-language media and festivals.

Since I returned to Maine from France in 2013, I am proud to say that many new developments, events, connections, and endeavors have contributed to the prosperity of the French language across New England and beyond. I have made friends and met family members along the way. Without having had the fortune to cross my bridge to understand my French-Canadian heritage, I would have never had the opportunity to connect with the different Francophone communities across North America. This journey enriches my life daily. It is rare for a day to go by without speaking French, whether speaking French with a New Mainer from Rwanda or conversing with friends from Louisiana; being aware, connected, and collaborating with the North American Francophone archipelago will ensure that French will live all around us for generations.

21. Le Rêve
Jesse Martineau and Monique Martineau Cairns

My name is Jesse Martineau, and it was an absolute honor to be involved in the first French All Around Us book. I am from Manchester, New Hampshire, and I wrote that chapter early in my six-month stay in Québec City, where I went in hopes of learning as much French as possible. It has been a wild few years since writing that initial chapter, and I am writing this chapter in Montréal. I am in the city because a film crew interviewed me for a documentary film called Notre Rêve Américain, and a viewing took place for those involved in the film before it aired on Télé-Québec in a few weeks. As with the initial chapter, I think how I ended up in this situation is pretty interesting.

Those who know me well are probably sick of calling the six months I spent in Québec City the best six months of my life. However, it was the best six months of my life, and I have frequently been asked to outline a typical day. Each weekday followed a similar schedule. I would get up in the morning and walk from my Airbnb to the school. My Airbnb lay within Old Québec's walls, diagonal from the Kent Gate. I walked about forty-five minutes, a straight shot down the Grand Allée. I enjoy getting up early, so if the weather were nice, I would detour and walk through the Plains of Abraham. It was never lost on me that I was walking on the ground sometimes stated to be the site of one of the most significant battles in world history, though I understand historians disagree wildly on that. I do have a personal connection to the space. Albert Riezbos, whom I met because he listened to my podcast, the French-Canadian Legacy, reached out to me and told me that I was a direct descendant of Abraham Martin, the person for whom the plains are named. I have subsequently joked that I was strolling down land belonging to Pépère Abraham and figured the direct lineage should probably entitle me to at least set up a tent on the property.

I always got to school super early so that I would go to a small café near the school almost daily. I would get a coffee and a pastry and read through some of the materials we had covered the day before to prepare for the upcoming lesson. By the end of my time in Québec, the people in the café felt like friends. When I walked in, the cash register manager would greet me with a "Bonjour Monsieur Martineau!" He once told me how familiar the last name Martineau was in Québec. He seemed legitimately amused to have an American customer with that last name. I miss that café.

Usually, about 15–20 minutes after arriving at the café, my friend Claudia Föllmi would join me. Claudia comes from Switzerland but from the German section of the country, so she does not speak French. She works in the hospitality industry and spent a few years learning French and English in Canada. By the time she had arrived in Québec, she had already spent over a year in Western Canada. My very first conversation with Claudia came during the lunch break of my first day of class. During the conversation, Claudia told me, in her trademark frankness, that my accent "was terrible." She was not wrong. It still is terrible. But that initial conversation made me laugh and helped with the butterflies of meeting all new people in this new setting. We have been friends since.

The school I went to was BLI/Edu-Inter. I honestly don't know what I am supposed to call it. BLI and Edu-Inter are two separate language schools for adult learners. During the pandemic, the two temporarily merged. I worked with three teachers in Québec, two from Edu-Inter and one from BLI. When I started, the school was in a building that housed a law firm. However, by the end of my time in Québec, the school had moved back to the regular school building used by Edu-Inter. Classes were always pretty small. From memory, my largest class boasted about twelve; the smallest was around five or six.

Class make-up changed all the time. Students would move up once they had been at a certain level for a specific time. Additionally, we always experienced students entering and leaving the school. Some students only came for a week or two. Others were there before I started and were still there when I left. Constantly having new students in class made things fun, mainly because I was studying with students worldwide. In addition to classmates from a couple of other American states and a few Canadian provinces, I sat beside students from Switzerland, Belgium, China, Australia, the Bahamas, England, Mexico, Ecuador, and many from Columbia. The number of students from Columbia surprised me a lot. Some classes had as many students from Columbia as there were students from everywhere else combined. Additionally, unlike most other students I met at the school, all the students from Columbia hoped to immigrate to Québec permanently. Most other students, like me, intended to return to their home country after their time at the school was over.

Each school day followed a similar schedule. Nine o'clock to about noon was the grammar section of the day. Here, we would practice the four language skills—listening, speaking, reading, and writing. Then we broke up for lunch. After that, an afternoon session focused on communication lasted until about 2:00. We discussed different themes and projects. For example, one week, we learned about how board games are a big deal in Québec City, and then we broke off into groups and had to create a board game for the class to play. Another week, we covered media and had to create a live version of a TV news show.

I had intended to go up to Québec in 2020, which had to be canceled when the border closed due to COVID-19. However, I had paid in full for the Super Intensive program before the pandemic started. By the time I got to the school in 2021, they still were not offering the Super Intensive program, as they did not have enough participants. Therefore, the school provided one-on-one tutoring several times a week after classes. We spent much of this time working on that terrible accent. I have discovered that I think a significant problem I have is my hearing. I could not even hear the difference between what I was saying and what my instructor was trying to get me to say. Frequently, he would try to highlight it for me by repeating what I was saying and then contrasting it by stating what it should sound like. Often, I failed to hear any difference at all between these.

The school offered an activity every day after classes. These were frequently incredibly fun. In addition to giving more practice to use the language (they were offered only in French), they provided gratifying experiences. We went on a bunch of historic tours and visited several museums. We even toured a brewery. The best trip was the rare weekend trip to Tadoussac for whale watching. I am not kidding; I think we saw at least 20 whales. I may be way underselling this.

I did not do the optional activity daily because I had to pay for it. However, even on days when I did not have an optional activity or one-on-one tutoring, I still usually had a fantastic time just experiencing life in one of the coolest towns on the planet. I would usually go out with a group from school, and we would head to a cool place in the city. Because I was there for so long, the group I hung out with over time frequently changed as people came in and out of the program. Our group typically switched to English after school—especially in those early days. I vividly remember our excursion to an Escape Room in the city. We all agreed to speak to each other only in French. However, we eventually gave in after getting nowhere for half an hour. We switched to English, realizing there was no chance we would get out of that room unless we could communicate more easily. Later in the program, when my language skills improved, I spent more time hanging out with students from Spanish-speaking countries, as the better we all got at French, the more we could communicate without getting frustrated.

A significant benefit of this time in Québec was making friends with people who lived in the city. Through these interactions, I started to consider how we viewed cultural identity differently in the United States than in Québec. In the United States, a person's cultural identity refers to what shows up on a DNA test. I call myself "French" because all my great-great-grandparents were from Québec, and my test on Ancestry DNA shows that my ancestral region is almost all of France. However, many Québécois I met did not view it that way. It was all about what language a person spoke. And it always seemed like an either-or situation. Everyone was either an Anglophone or Francophone. Every once in a while, I would hear people talk about a third category of "everyone else," though usually, people were labeled either Francophone or Anglophone. It seemed people were labeled by what their first language was. Essentially, I got the impression that for many I met in Québec, it would not matter if I attained an expert level of French. Because my first language was English, I would always fall in the "Anglophone" category.

I also came across several Québécois who seemed confused by the idea of "Franco-Americans." Many could not understand at all how someone could call themselves a "Franco-American" if they could not speak French. I had someone ask me directly, right to my face, how I could call myself a Franco-American if I were an Anglophone. They were not trying to be a jerk but were sincerely confused. When I mentioned there was more to culture than just language, the person looked right at me and asked, as a genuine question, "What else is there?" For this person, cultural identity and language represented the same thing. You could not have an identity without the language. When I started talking about food and traditions, I think they began to understand better. However, I still left that conversation with the feeling that they would never be comfortable with me calling myself a "Franco-American."

I sincerely miss Québec. I want to spend another six months in the city. The perfect situation would be finding a way to move there permanently. I have started trying to get permanent resident status, but it would be hard with my job and family here. Of course, in my dreams, I somehow convinced everyone to move up to Québec with me, and we all found jobs, and life was perfect. I realize this is not likely.

I get asked from time to time if I could be a citizen. I can't. I am one generation too far removed. My dad recently obtained his proof of Canadian citizenship, which is a multi-year process. I spent much time getting all the documents needed. I could not find my grandfather's birth certificate anywhere. My dad and I went to city hall in Saint-Apollinaire, the town where my grandfather was born, but the clerk told us that all the records from the period we needed were sent to Québec City. We then attempted to track them down in the city but had no success. Fortunately, there is a terrific French-Canadian genealogy society here in Manchester, and they have tons of baptism records from all over the province. I could track down my grandfather's baptism record through these resources, which was sufficient. I compiled all these documents, mailed them to the processing location, and waited. About nine months later, we got everything back in the mail, which let us know we had submitted an incomplete application. When I checked what I had missed, I realized I had just neglected to check a box that confirmed the picture of my dad I submitted was an accurate likeness of him. Despite thirty pages of documents and nine months of waiting, we had to start again because I missed checking a box. But I got all the documents together again, checked that box, and resubmitted the application. About six or seven months later, my dad received a letter confirming he was a Canadian citizen. It was amusing to see that the rear of this certificate contained an oath to King Charles III of Canada. I am not sure whether my dad has taken that oath. I doubt it.

 I have been very fortunate that the fantastic experiences and opportunities have not ended since I returned from Québec. One of the most fun evenings of my life was a direct result of the first book. We had a book launch event at the Organisation Internationale de la Francophonie office in New York City. It was a bit overwhelming to be in that office and participate in a discussion with other outstanding contributors. Honestly, the real highlight of that night unfolded after the official event had wrapped up. Several of us chapter authors had flown into New York City for the occasion, and for many, it was the first time we finally met in person. Coinciding with Cinco de Mayo, our group roamed Manhattan in search of a venue spacious enough for all of us. We eventually gathered around one enormous table at a cozy restaurant, where we enjoyed drinks, savored great food, and swapped hilarious stories. It was simply incredible to realize that we had all come together, united by our shared passion for our French identity—and, of course, a generous dose of adult beverages didn't hurt one bit. Nights like that are truly rare.

 I have also had the terrific opportunity to be part of some fantastic projects. A significant highlight for me was being interviewed in French on Radio Canada. I recall the pre-interview conversation I had with the show host. They wanted to ensure I could have a conversation in French. I stated that I could chat in French but requested that I be given the questions beforehand. I felt nervous about being asked a question and having no idea what I was asked. I remember getting ready for work the morning the interview aired, and I got a call from my friend Jean-Philippe L'Etoile. He was in Drummondville, on his way to the school where he worked as a teacher, when my voice came on the radio. The thought of that still amazes me. Five years ago, when Mike

Campbell and I started the French-Canadian Legacy Podcast, I could not speak any French, I did not know Québec very well at all, I did not have any friends at all in Québec, and indeed, nobody at Radio Canada had ever heard of me. Thinking how much life has changed in half a decade is wild.

In 2023, I was honored to be named the Franco-American of the Year. When I look at the list of prior award winners, it is still wild to me that my name is included. What I find particularly astonishing is that my name will forever appear on the list of winners between two friends of mine. Tim Beaulieu, the brilliant individual who created New Hampshire and Maine PoutineFest, won the award in 2022. In 2024, the winner is the incredible producer of the French-Canadian Legacy Podcast, Mike Campbell. Without Mike, the French-Canadian Legacy Podcast doesn't exist, the New England Franco-Route GeoTour doesn't exist, and this chapter doesn't exist. I will forever feel privileged to see my name appear on any list of Franco-Americans between Tim Beaulieu and Mike Campbell.

Since writing the French All Around Us chapter, I have also had amusing interactions with podcast listeners. One listener approached Mike and me at New Hampshire PoutineFest and noted that she had been working at a business job when she stumbled upon our podcast. Listening reignited her passion for French heritage, so she left her job and became a French teacher. Mike and I met another podcast fan at the first-ever Maine PoutineFest. A woman approached the French Canadian Legacy table, pushing a baby in a stroller. The woman was from Montréal and had listened to all of our episodes. She had recently been on a tour with a former podcast guest and approached the individual because she recognized his voice from the show. My highlight of this conversation was when the woman informed Mike and me that she plays the podcast to get her baby to sleep, which seems to work every time. Never mind that the baby doesn't even speak English. While this is hilarious, I hope I don't cause the same reaction in most listeners.

Since the first book, Mike and I have also decided to take on additional projects. We started a YouTube video series called "Franco-American Voyages." We aim to introduce people to some of the important locations associated with the story of the Franco-

American experience in New England. Every episode is shot twice, once in English and once in French. We were fortunate to get Camden Martin to host. Camden is perfect for the job. Camden hails from Lewiston, Maine, and is considerably younger than I am. Not only does he switch effortlessly between French and English, but very few know the Franco-American story in New England as well as he does. In fact, without question, he understands the history of my hometown even better than I do. When we filmed, he presented without any notes at all. He just knew everything off the top of his head. Mike and I were also super fortunate to get my girlfriend Heather Howell to film, Mike's friend Mike Johnson to edit everything, and my high school friend Mike Liberty to make a substantial donation to cover the project's initial costs. We are very proud of what we have produced so far.

Of course, I began this chapter by discussing the documentary *Notre Rêve Américain*, which provided another incredible opportunity to share the Manchester Franco-American story. What was incredibly motivating to me was that a major theme of this documentary was that there is more to culture than just the language, something I have been trying to promote for some time. When my dad and I met with the production staff, they repeatedly told us the line in the film that many of them thought was the most impactful was when I recounted how my family would eat *tourtière* during the holidays, how I recall celebrating a réveillon after Midnight Mass, and how just the previous day my parents had beat me pretty bad in a game of *pichenotte*. I even noted that I would regularly go to school with *gorton* sandwiches, and I even specified that for us growing up, it was spelled *gorton*, not *creton*, as it usually appears in Québec. For those not from Québec, *gorton* (or *creton*) is a meat spread usually served on plain white bread or toast and topped with simple yellow mustard. One of the production staff told me this segment gave her chills every time she heard it because it reminded her of things she used to experience as a child. It never occurred to her that there would be English speakers in the United States who shared the same experiences.

I really could write much more about my experience in Québec. I distinctly remember that during my drive back home to Manchester at the end of my stay, I started to think about how I wish others could have that same experience. I genuinely believe anyone who could study French in Québec for six months would return with a strong desire to continue being involved in Franco-American activities. With this in mind, I formed a non-profit organization called Héritage Corp.

Héritage Corp exists to provide others with the same opportunity to study in Québec that I had. We are now raising money to send others to Québec for six months. We are an official non-profit organization whose board of directors includes Mike, Tim Beaulieu, Melody Dejardin, and Mark Belluardo; all fantastic people I spoke about in the first book have contributed their time to our story. I am very much looking forward to the day when, every year, I can be confident that there will be motivated Franco-Americans up in Québec who are learning the language and culture of their ancestors.

I currently work as a prosecutor at the Superior Court in Manchester and love my job. It is an absolute honor every time I get to stand behind the counsel table and say, "Jesse Martineau for the State, your honor." However, it would be an absolute dream to work on Héritage full-time. *C'est mon rêve*.

As I did in the first book, I want to turn this over to my sister, Monique Cairns.

Where has the time gone? Since our previous book, I have "grown" in many ways. In 2021 and again in 2024, I welcomed two more babies. This past year, I led a workshop at Southern NH University, my place of employment, on the importance of French culture and its impact on diversity, equity, and inclusion practices at the school. I have also exposed my dance students to opportunities to perform at Poutinefest in New Hampshire and Maine and planned a trip to Québec City to tour and perform a show.

As I mentioned in my previous chapter, growing up with the name Monique Martineau, it was evident that I came from a French family. When I married my husband, I felt some of that identity would be missing for my children. It was essential to me that I ensure they still felt that same identity I had for so long. When we were discussing our first daughter's name, it was a struggle. Naming a child is so hard! It is such pressure. We agreed on the name Aimée. My husband's aunt is named Amy, so it felt like a nice way to honor his relationship with her and still honor my wishes for a French name. It is a unique name, but I will never forget the first day I brought her to daycare. I had her daycare bag embroidered with her name on it. One of the moms dropping off their child at the school stopped me. She was so excited. Her name was Aimée, and she was even more excited when she saw that we had kept the accent! It reinforced how important it was to keep that French identity and how these experiences will be something our little girl will have to remember how special she is.

We welcomed our last baby in March of 2024. We were excited when we found out we were having another little girl. Then the pressure came back. NAMES! My husband and I went back and forth. He is so supportive of my wishes to keep French first names. He knows it means so much to me. We chose Eloise for our baby. We also picked Irene as her middle name. Irene was my Mémère's name, which I wrote about in the last book. She played such an essential role in my upbringing that I wanted to honor her legacy. We love the name Eloise, and I was so glad to be able to have another unique French name, or so I thought. In the second week, I brought Eloise to daycare, and another family was dropping off their daughter for the first time. What was this baby's name, you ask? ELOISE! What are the odds?!?! Two baby girls named Eloise, born about a month apart, are in the same class! I thought that was so cool, and it shows a strong tie to French culture and names. The connection is alive and strong! So, from now on, our baby is Eloise C. There is also an Eloise L. in her class!

While my family is my main priority, as well as my sense of focus and connection to French culture/heritage, since the last book, I have had a couple of other opportunities to share my experiences with others. Southern New Hampshire University is committed to Diversity, Equity, and Inclusion (DEI) education and training. I was asked to lead a workshop for a group of leaders on what it meant to be Franco-American. I met with a group of about 10 leaders to discuss my background and the impact being Franco-American might have on our learners. It opened lots of great dialogue about language experiences and ensured that we strive to be culturally fluent for all learners at the school. The best takeaway from the workshop was when one of the leaders spoke about his experience. He grew up somewhat unsure of his culture/identity. He then mentioned that someone referred him to my brother Jesse's podcast (The French Canadian Legacy) as something that might interest him. He said that listening to that podcast was so self-affirming to him. It showed him that he came from a strong culture and interested him in learning more. The legacy is strong!

Outside of work and my family, my other passion is my dance studio. I am the proud owner of Northern Explosion Dance Studio in Sanford, ME. We offer all types of dance classes but primarily focus on clogging. Clogging is mainly associated with Appalachian folk dancing but incorporates Irish and Canadian step dancing. For several years now, I have had the opportunity to have my students perform at the Poutinefest in New Hampshire and this past year in Maine. It allows my students to show their skills and learn more about French culture/heritage. I am also very excited because I am taking a group of students to perform in Québec City this June! What an experience! They will be able to show off their talents to the people of Canada while also taking in the sights and history of the city. We have lined up our performances and tours to show the students about Québec. I am so excited to be able to share this with my dance students.

The last three years have flown by so fast. Watching my kids grow and become little people has been a blessing and the greatest joy of my life. I am glad to continue to share our history's importance with them and its culture's beauty. We have taken the older two to Québec City, and I look forward to taking all three to Canada in the upcoming year. I think it is essential for them to see their history and appreciate where their family is from. Spreading joy and sharing history are my ways of keeping that legacy alive!

I will now hand it back to Jesse to add the final paragraph.

Our parents have given some interviews in which they blame themselves for our not speaking French. But, when you think about it, my sister and I are the grandchildren of an immigrant who grew up on a farm in rural Québec. We are also the grandchildren of a couple who met while working in a textile mill in Manchester. In two generations, our family has gone from working on farms and in mills to where my sister and I are now. I am a prosecutor and have started a non-profit organization. Monique has a Master's degree and owns her own business. She has three amazing kids, and my parents and I visit them in Maine frequently. Her oldest, my best bud Ben, named after my father, always asks to go "to New Hampshire" to my parents' house. His strong connection to our family and heritage is possible because our terrific parents and grandparents sacrificed significantly for us. When I think about it, if I could go back in time and show my grandparents when they were young adults the lives their grandchildren would one day be living, they would have viewed it as a dream. *Un rêve*. It really is *Notre Rêve Américain*.

22. The value of the French cross-cultural synergy
Franck Mounier

"Pardon my French!" This was one of the first expressions that surprised me when I arrived in the USA as a native French speaker. This simple phrase revealed how cultural perceptions can be distorted and highlighted the challenges of cross-cultural communication. That was twenty-two years ago when I first came to America.

The Cross-Cultural Encounter Challenge

When someone has done the same thing over and over in their own life and seen their close ones do the same, not only does that thing become natural when you think about it, but it also becomes the way to go, the norm, which quickly transforms into "this is the only way," and any deviation is thought of with a negative connotation, creating discomfort.

For example, someone coming from a "high-contact" cultural country who will naturally come in physical contact with someone in a "low-contact" country will be considered aggressive, intrusive, or maybe violent, even if the intention is excellent. A person from a "low-contact" country who would avoid physical contact with others in a "high-contact" country will isolate themselves and be considered cold, almost anti-social, or misanthropic. These are prominent examples that are easily spotted. However, countless other subtle cultural differences will create a gap that, most of the time, can be a blind spot to a newcomer in a foreign country, creating a challenge when trying to mingle in the local community.

In most cases, this is not a matter of right or wrong but of doing something differently, which produces reactions that can go from a tolerant smile to physical aggression. As a foreigner, it is very easy to get rejected, which is often a dual responsibility: the newcomer's lack of observation and openness to cultural differences and the host country's local people's lack of tolerance of openness.

How This Could Work: The Necessary Exchange and Openness

So then, how can we make it work? I have lived in five countries on four continents and visited many other countries, and I have realized how much people see the same things with different eyes. All these different approaches have their own merits, and they all work well in their own way. Any country could not stand to fail systematically on something, so each approach works well!

Witnessing these approaches made me feel richer and more fulfilled. They provided me with various options to achieve the same goals while enhancing my creativity by exposing me to different ways of thinking and approaching new ideas with an open mind. This diversity of perspectives is the type of richness that foreigners can bring to a country: offering a different point of view.

But this requires a critical "I make the first step" approach. When one moves to a foreign country, the first duty is to adapt, understand the codes and rules, and be open to a different way of living. Then, what could a French person bring to a country like the USA? Two words encapsulate French people: how they behave, what they aspire to, and how they are perceived: the "French Spirit."

The French Spirit – Definition

The French Spirit could be described as a triangle with summits almost stirring in their directions, making that triangle move in shape, showing some contradictions:

- Critical thinking: this is the country of Descartes. So, the French love to discuss. Can you guess what is the most enjoyable thing for French people to do? It is having a conversation with friends and family! As a consequence (or as a cause?), there are many French philosophers, and the French like to organize their thoughts and explore abstract concepts. Because of it, they are very good at developing strategies. They also love to count, measure, and classify: Binet was the first person in the world to create a metric and then measure the IQ; Escoffier was the first in the world to define how a professional kitchen must be

organized; and Michelin was the first to assess the quality of the restaurants. And since they like to count, they are happy to be at the top and don't dislike bragging about it!
- Hedonism: the French tend to search for pleasure, enjoyment, and refinement; they are very open and seek culture, art, poetry, and food, all with high quality, diversity, and distinctiveness; it is called *art de vivre*, and there is almost a permanent contest at who will find the most surprising and elaborate new thing to share with friends.
- Rebellious: This is the most challenging to understand since it is simultaneously a building and destructive process. The French navigate between order and disorder, play with opposite ideas, protest quickly and massively when disagreeing, and seek unity at the same time. Not even the French understand this, but they live by it and name it after their ancestors, the Gallic spirit.

Of course, this definition can be criticized as not correctly describing the French Spirit, and this criticism is part of it!

Let me raise a very telling and relatively recent example of the French spirit: the opening ceremony of the Olympic Games in Paris in July 2024. Their rebellious mind could not let the French have an opening ceremony like the others; it had to be different and better. And this is where the hedonism part plays a significant role. The ceremony's creative director used Paris, the city of romance, as a stage. Instead of having the athletes walk in a stadium like they always do, they had them stand on boats, sailing down the Seine River across the beauty of the city of light, with the Eiffel Tower, Place de la Concorde, beautiful bridges, and many historical monuments as backdrops. Critical thinking could not stand making it simple or linear, and it had to mix history and modernism, tradition and innovation, past heroes, and current societal realities. Fast forward to the magnificent final act, where the last relay of the Olympic torch lit a cauldron that was slowly lifted in the air by a *mongolfière*, a hot air balloon invented by French aviation pioneers the Mongolfier brothers, while listening to a stunning performance from Celine Dion, Edith Piaf's *L'hymne à l'amour* (hymn to love). It was unparalleled, and the French want to believe it will stay unparalleled!

With this understanding of the French mentality and its numerous distinctive cultural characteristics, it is easy to picture a French person's significant challenges in adapting to a leading country like the United States of America. And then, besides adapting, how could a French person bring any value?

The French Added Value:
My Experience of Building on Strengths in a Synergistic Mindset

Let's review three different aspects of it through some examples: history, adding knowledge, and complementarity.

- History: examples of the French influence

French King Louis XVI gave his name, Bourbon, to a county and ultimately to the most famous American whiskey that can only be produced in the United States. Bourbon is part of American culture. So, anytime someone pronounces the name of this iconic American beverage, they speak French! Have you ever enjoyed a Sazerac cocktail? A French pharmacist invented it in New Orleans, Louisiana, and the liquor in the recipe was initially cognac, coming from the Sazerac house in France. The name of Emile Coué is no longer known. Still, his method of positive thinking, which was very popular in the 1920s in the US, has undoubtedly contributed significantly to the fantastic American positive mindset.

- Adding knowledge: The example of my spirit education

I have an activity of spirit education across the United States. Of course, I teach and introduce American palates to French spirits: calvados, cognac, armagnac, and even French rum (rhum Agricole) and French whisky. I take immense pleasure in transmitting that knowledge and showing my passion to the thousands of participants who attended my classes. Most of the people in my sessions are drinkers of bourbon, American whiskey, and Scotch or Irish whiskey, but very few are familiar with the French spirits despite their high quality.

My mission is to educate their noses and palates and engage them in analyzing their sensory stimuli to appreciate better what is offered. Through my guidance and with the different expressions we experience together, they develop their tasting senses little by little and become more open and appreciative of different styles. Having a French origin, I take great pride in offering the opportunity to taste these precious French liquids, which come directly from the local terroirs, and I am so pleased when I see the students enjoy them. To make the experience more enjoyable, I ensure that the atmosphere is very relaxed, and I always make fun of my accent, which is a cool way to share a laugh and engage them in a journey of French style!

- Complementarity: The example of my leadership at Mensa

The two cultures can benefit from each other. The American mindset is very action-forward oriented, one major component explaining why I came here. The first thing that my American cross-cultural teacher told me before arriving was that example: "Are you ready? 3, 2, 1, fire! Oops, wrong target; charge again." It is funny and so different from the French mindset, but it works pretty well, following the path of trial and error.

French people are very good at strategy, prioritizing the most impactful actions to focus the resources and efforts on the most profitable return on investment. We can also make fun of this aspect: sometimes people want to make the strategy "so perfect" that they spend all their time on it, and there is no more time for action.

Imagine a context where a French person provides the strategic framework while an American person focuses on action-oriented execution. This combination would create a highly effective collaboration, likely driving outstanding results. This is the power of complementarity, and it is incredibly impactful. Let me illustrate this with another personal experience.

The Mensa Northern New Jersey:
The Example of Leadership and Complementarity

You might have heard about Mensa, the high-IQ society. There are only two requirements to be part of it: have an intellectual quotient (IQ) at least in the 98th percentile (the 2% highest in the population) and pay the dues. I was admitted to Mensa a long time ago and became a member, but I only started to be more involved in my local group in Northern New Jersey in 2017. I became a proctor in a chapter that was completely asleep, and one day, the president of our group passed away unexpectedly. At that time, our group, one of the 130 groups in American Mensa, was completely dormant for at least the last ten years. There were no events besides a modestly attended yearly picnic, no activity, and no energy. Nobody was to blame necessarily; it was just the natural evolution of a chapter once vibrant in the 80s that slowly faded away.

To my surprise, since I was the newest team member, the two remaining officers designated me to take over. I had not planned on leading our chapter, but there was no one else, so I accepted the challenge. The moment I stepped into this role was at the end of June 2020. Does that date ring a bell? Yes, it was just three months after the start of the stay-at-home order due to the pandemic. In addition, one of the two remaining officers decided to resign, and the last, the treasurer, accepted to stay but was so involved with his job that he could only complete the administrative task of preparing the quarterly reports, which was quite simple since we were not doing anything. Well, it was not exactly the best possible start.

Less than four years later, this chapter was cited as one of the most vibrant nationwide! We won three diamond awards in a row, a national prize recognizing the best group in a given size category based on 30 parameters; our third award was even better since we were the best chapter in any size category, surpassing chapters with as many as three times more members than us.

Not only did we succeed locally, but also many achievements were visible at the national level: we created the first ever Young Mensans weekend-long gathering in the history of American Mensa, hosting almost 180 gifted children and their parents coming from everywhere nationwide; we reinstated a yearly regional gathering that hadn't happened in the chapter in the last 30 years; we brought our finances from a yearly loss to substantial benefits; we hosted many events; partnered with local towns on some projects; built an admission testing powerhouse with proctors, a testing coordinator, and monthly sessions that is yet unmatched; and much more. How could this French guy spearhead such a significant shift so quickly?

The answer lies in how cultural differences, when used synergistically, can create a powerful impact. I combined all the different strengths around me in a collaborative manner. My trumps? Of course, my professional experience in leading teams played a role, but the cultural aspect was the most impactful. I had the seeds of a vision, a strategy, a plan all in my mind, and a strong will to achieve. I took advantage of the complete lack of recent history in our group to rebuild it from scratch with a start-up mindset, limiting the constraints of the existing framework as much as possible—that is the French spirit!

The first thing is to keep and cherish my assets. They were meager, but without them, I would have been in an even more difficult situation: the treasurer was utterly overwhelmed, but without him, I could no longer officially sustain our group; the editor of our newsletter had moved to Florida and was very busy with her studies: without a newsletter, a group is considered for closure. Seeing my enthusiasm, energy, and determination, they both agreed to do the bare minimum, which was enough for me, and I showed them a lot of recognition and patience.

The second thing was to find people to help administer our group. I wanted to find people who were keenly interested in rebuilding our chapter. Where to find them? Well, I targeted the only group I thought could meet that requirement: the parents of Mensa children. Having gifted kids at home is not easy; they are demanding and sometimes frustrated by the gaps they see in others, including the teachers, and their frustration would sometimes show not in the best ways. The parents have to nurture their needs somehow to meet other kids like them or be exposed to like-minded people. Three parents were listed as having been involved at some point, and I reached out. Two did not reply, and one agreed. We started just the two of us, and of course, we targeted children first in terms of activities.

The third thing was to signal the members and shake the chapter up through mass emailing and the newsletter. Our newsletter was short and dull, with no relevant information. I started writing a column to show what was going on, like a wake-up call and advertised anything we were doing boldly. And people started to get interested, one at a time.

I wanted to kick-off the restart of the chapter, and, in the pandemic, the only option was to do an online gathering. On Saturday, August 22, 2020, barely two months after my first day in the position, we had a virtual regional gathering with a complete program and three tracks! A four-hour track for kids, starting with a lunch together led by a Young Mensan and then speakers (origami teacher, science expert, video tech expert, and so on), followed by the "picnic" track, open to all kids and adults, where I presented the vision for the chapter, had a few volunteers to speak, and exchanged with all the participants. The rest was for adults, with games, happy hours, and other sessions. By the way, what was the vision? Well, it was not a vision but a direction or an inspiration; it had to be very simple, and I embedded it in only one word: connection. Build connections, develop connections, and create opportunities for connections. That was enough for the time being, and people got it.

The gathering was a huge success, and it was everyone's success. Maybe 6 or 7 people contributed to it, and they all were proud of the accomplishment. They all had a keen interest in making it happen: three parents, one teen, and a few adults. We brainstormed about the name of our gathering, and we came up with BLAST!, expressing the idea of a new big bang for our chapter. It was interesting to witness that the energy level rose and never went down as soon as the name was agreed upon. We all needed a common goal, and we wanted BLAST! be a blast! One of the parents asked her husband, an art designer, to create a poster; it was terrific, and we still use it! Another volunteer asked someone in another chapter to be a game master, and so on. We were all building that gathering together, and everybody was enjoying it.

How can I know if the people were motivated or not? It is straightforward: inspiring and not pushing the people. They decide what they want to do and what they do not want to do. We have a specific project, and we define the shape and its content together. Since it is a collaborative effort, everybody owns the project. Since everybody owns the project, everyone wants it to succeed and will decide to go the extra mile to make it work.

Let's pause here: the cultural synergy worked beautifully. I could not have achieved anything without the people acting their way—ways that were obvious to them and quite effective but that I could not fathom. They could not have done it without me. I was like the catalyst or enzyme, making it happen happily. We all were complementary, and we felt like we were all different, matching puzzle parts. OK, that was great; everyone was happy, so what was next?

Focusing people on a project like this regional gathering was short-term, and this matched the aspirations of the members. But in the long run, we could not hop from one project to another; people would fade away quite quickly. So, we needed a more profound aspiration, a collective vision that could pull us into the future. What were the dearest things that our small team of officers wanted?

I organized a team brainstorming exercise. We were in September 2020, and I asked only one question: "Imagine that we are one year from now, December 31, 2021; describe what has happened that has made you proud." I called it "paint the ideal picture." Everyone freely wrote a few short sentences about the accomplishments they thought would make them proud. We gathered about 15 of them scattered on the screen. Then, each participant was given 10 tokens to allocate to the accomplishments they felt were most important to them, and they could put more than one token on one accomplishment. We selected the topics that received the most votes and bundled them by categories. We had four categories that became the four strategic pillars or key directions. For each pillar, we developed a simple action plan to help achieve what we had decided. In total, this took less than four hours! Volunteers' time is a precious currency that should be allocated wisely.

Of all the plans I have ever worked on, this first plan was the smallest and most primitive. But it turned out to be very satisfying. Everyone knew what to do, how to contribute, why we were doing it, and what we aimed at. It was everyone's plan, so everyone wanted to succeed. We have since improved the quality of our plans, and as a result, our outcomes have also improved.

This progress marked the next step in our cultural synergy. The success of our first project built mutual trust and confidence. My team members saw me as a leader and appreciated my cultural differences positively, viewing them as an asset to our team's success. At the same time, they operated naturally in ways I would have found challenging to replicate myself. With that dynamic, many people wanted to join our efforts.

We decided to revamp our website, and 10 members applied to help, including four young Mensans. We renovated the organization of our picnic, and 90 people attended. Our newsletter frequently surpassed 30 pages, and we increased the content while decreasing costs. People show appreciation for me in various ways, but the most touching is when we meet and they say a few words in French to me. They are happy to say "bonjour," "au revoir," or "merci," and some even go further. It is charming because it seems to say: "I appreciate your difference in a positive way."

The Quest for Legacy

And what if it was just a tiny hiccup in the Mensa history? What if the natural course of life and behavior of all that was coming back and slowly driving the chapter into another dormancy mode? I have been working on that precisely: passing the torch, not keeping it. In December, I expressed to our Executive Committee that I wanted to withdraw from my position on July 1st, 2024. I explained that my influence and work would mean little if the chapter declined after my departure, and I felt the group was ready to take over. In the meantime, I announced my candidacy for the position of Director on the American Mensa Board of Directors, along with the role of Regional Vice Chair for the Northeast region. Both are elected positions, and I was running against the incumbent, who traditionally holds a decisive advantage and almost always wins.

So, it meant that on July 1st, 2024, I would either be part of the Board of Directors or a simple member. I created a small task force with a few officers to engineer my succession, and it took us about six months to have a plan in place and my successor ready to roll. It is too early to tell, but what I see after three months seems promising. I will feel that my mission will be accomplished after we see that the chapter continues to strive. I am now a member of the American Mensa Board of Directors, in charge of the Northeast region, and discovering its 12 groups and 5,000 members. I can see many opportunities and good people. Besides the size of this region, one of the main differences is that officers are already in place and follow their process, which is quite different from the chapter I rebuilt from scratch. This will be a longer journey to make a difference. Still, opening a new opportunity to make a bigger difference through my cultural synergistic approach is very exciting.

Conclusion: The Exchange; The Ties

To conclude, cultural diversity is a richness we should cherish and use to be better, more open, and more successful. French culture is peculiar and like no other, and its appropriate and synergistic use can make a significant positive difference. I have experienced it with the people around me, which created an additional value from which we all benefited.

When I heard the expression "pardon my French," I learned that it meant pretending to be sorry for using a word that may be considered offensive, not necessarily valorizing the French. But I chose to use it to my advantage. Each time I heard it, I took my strongest French accent and said, "But it is not French!". Guaranteed laugh each time! It is OK to show a difference if this creates a better environment. But, knowing all the positive influence French people have had on the USA, why not create a new expression highlighting these benefits? So, from now on, when someone refers to their useful French cultural knowledge, why not punctuate their reference with "Bless my French!"?

23. The "Mindset of Possibility": The Role of External Funding in Building and Preserving College and University French Programs in the United States
Steven J. Sacco and Megan Diercks

World language programs face unprecedented challenges in our history as we approach the end of the first quarter of the 21st century. Hundreds of K-16 French programs have been eliminated. The University of West Virginia is perhaps the most visible example. To complicate matters, world-renowned linguist and former French major John McWhorter published a piece in the New Republic where he sardonically suggested that they "stop pretending that French is an important language."[235]

We cannot control the circumstances or the conditions around us, but we can control our response. Controlling our response cements our "mindset of possibility." Controlling our response gives us a chance to save our French programs, and when we have a "mindset of possibility," our options become limitless. External funding is one of those limitless options. External funding, such as grants, gifts, and contracts, has preserved many programs; external funding has made other programs untouchable. Our solution is not 100% certainty for preserving and safeguarding French programs, but the odds are that it will. Before sharing how to secure external funding, possessing the "mindset of possibility" is a prerequisite to pursuing limitless options. *Impossible n'est pas français* must become our mantra, as the Emperor pronounced it numerous times during the *Premier Empire*.[236]

External funders are eager to support "disruptive innovation," a term coined by Clayton M. Christensen. In an educational context, disruptive innovation refers to:

---

[235] McWhorter, 2014, para. 1
[236] laculturegenerale.com/impossible-est-pas-francais-origin

> An innovative approach to learning that challenges traditional educational models and seeks to create new and more effective ways of educating individuals. It breaks from conventional methods and embraces new technologies and personalized learning experiences to enhance student engagement and improve learning outcomes.[237]

Despite the negative connotation of "disruptive" for classroom teachers such as ourselves, it is "a positive force" in this context.[238]

For us French-language educators, a relevant example of disruptive innovation" can be traced back to Bonaparte and his Army of Italy in 1797. Bonaparte's foe, the massive Austrian army, practiced traditional, conservative battle strategy and tactics. The Austrian army was slow, plodding, and unimaginative. Conversely, Bonaparte's undersized Army of Italy won battle after battle through speed, versatility, and flexibility. Military historian Hidayat Rizvi[239] condenses Napoleon's "disruptive" leadership in one paragraph:

> Strategic agility was a cornerstone of Napoleon's leadership style, allowing him to adapt to changing circumstances and seize opportunities. He consistently outmaneuvered larger and more established armies through rapid movements and surprise tactics, a willingness to take risks, and thinking outside conventional warfare norms. His qualities of clear vision, the ability to inspire, courage, and decisiveness were integral to his success.[240]

We need not attempt to emulate Napoleon, but we can adopt some of his strategies and tactics that respond to our current situation. Deb Reisinger's introduction of virtual learning across continents is one example;[241] the University of Rhode Island's (URI) interdisciplinary Engineering/French major is another. Under the senior author's

---

[237] smowl.net/en/blog/disruptive-education para. 3,4.
[238] Ibid, p. 11.
[239] Rizvi, 2024.
[240] para. 13, 25.
[241] Reisinger, 2022.

leadership, San Diego State University's (SDSU) interdisciplinary, international business program boasted 745 majors, among them 209 courses away from a French major. Reisinger, URI, SDSU, and many others we do not mention here demonstrated surprise tactics, clear vision, and a willingness to take risks; they challenged conventional norms and were eager to inspire. They continue to show courage and decisiveness. They all possess a mindset of possibility.

Despite crushing programmatic cuts to French programs, URI's and SDSU's programs have never been concerned about enrollments and may never worry. Their national stature protects them from meddlesome politicians and administrators. URI and SDSU created security, in large part, due to external funding, which is the same funding opportunity we will share with you in the following few pages. Neither university is a member of the Ivy League nor resides among the pantheon of elite universities. If URI and SDSU can attain national status because of their disruptive programs, your program can, too.

À la Recherche des Sous Cachés

- Conducting a department-wide needs assessment.

The first step in establishing an external funding system is to conduct a needs assessment. A needs assessment is a systematic process for identifying and describing the current conditions within a French program or a world language department. We like using SWOT analysis, the business world's needs assessment method, because it systematically categorizes four key conditions: a company's STRENGTHS, WEAKNESSES, OPPORTUNITIES, and THREATS. Like any company or corporation, a French program or world language department faces the same four conditions, especially threats in this era of "West Virginization." The better a program knows itself, the more effective it will be in designing "disruptive" activities or a "disruptive" program.

In an educational context, the SWOT analysis identifies a French program's:

- *Strengths*: characteristics of the program that give it an advantage over others,

- *Weaknesses*: characteristics that place the program at a disadvantage relative to others,
- *Opportunities*: elements in the environment that the program could exploit to its advantage,
- *Threats*: elements in the environment that could cripple or destroy a French program.[242]

The program's or department's faculty can conduct a SWOT analysis on a timetable desirable to the faculty or at a weekend retreat. We recommend bringing in a consultant to direct the SWOT analysis in person or via Zoom. The senior author, for example, has conducted needs assessments for several decades. His clients include 80 business schools, world language departments, and the U.S. Navy SEALs. His consulting for French programs is done *pro bono*.

Let us select OPPORTUNITIES as an example. Does the program or department possess a working relationship with faculty from the professional schools or the humanities? A working relationship with a global-minded business colleague, a women's studies colleague, or an environmental sciences colleague could develop a "disruptive" interdisciplinary major that combines French, Women's Studies, and Sustainability. By the way, all three are much needed and highly sought after in Francophone Africa, the "continent of the future," according to French President Emmanuel Macron.[243] As we mentioned earlier, URI and SDSU have triple-digit enrollments due to the popularity of their interdisciplinary majors.

Second, within the category of OPPORTUNITIES, has the French program considered partnerships with external constituencies such as small businesses, corporations, or business organizations such as a state local chamber of commerce, a department of commerce, or a World Trade Center? The local French American Chamber of Commerce or the *Alliance Française*? Are there small businesses that hope to become more global? Are there companies or corporations that would like to enhance their global profile via language or intercultural training? Examples include sponsoring a workshop entitled *Doing Business in*

---

[242] Wikipedia: SWOT analysis.
[243] O'Mahony, 2019, para. 1.

Francophone Africa or teaching languages on the company's premises. Has the French program partnered with business organizations in your grant proposals? Has the French program sought their advice in designing globally oriented majors or minors? Has the French program provided interns to small businesses and business organizations? This cooperation could make your French program a "global think tank" for external constituencies interested in the Francophone World. One example is Boise State University's close and profitable ties with these external constituencies.[244]

Third, has the French program taken full advantage of the services of the American Association of Teachers of French (AATF)? The AATF and its partner organizations support French programs at all levels. The French for Specific Purposes (FSP) Commission can assist in developing innovative courses that fit within a university's specialties and areas of focus. The French Embassy's 'French in Higher Education' grant program allows college and university faculty to apply for funds to innovate, be it creating an FSP or other new course, an OER, or redesigning existing courses around a theme (DEI, sustainability). These initiatives can be modeled and replicated in other institutions. The College and Universities Commission is actively increasing student (undergraduate and graduate) participation in the AATF. Mentored students are encouraged to submit articles for publication to the *National Bulletin*, a stepping-stone towards publication in *The French Review*. The AATF is also building a dedicated time for student poster sessions to take place during future conferences and offers reduced-rate student registration.

Is the institution showcasing its innovative or interdisciplinary courses or collaborations? Publishing an article about these novel innovations in a course catalog in The French Review or National Bulletin can draw more positive attention to the program and serve as an example for other institutions. Cross-departmental collaborative classes can be featured in an FSP Commission or Colleges and Universities Commission webinar. Working with other departments not

---

[244] Loughrin-Sacco, 1996

only reinforces the importance of French in other disciplines but can also help ensure the retention of the French department.

Has the institution applied for AATF Exemplary Program status? This designation by an outside national entity (the AATF) elevates a program's status and gives it 'bragging rights,' allowing the institution's successes to be highlighted and celebrated. To the best of the AATF's knowledge, no program earning the Exemplary Program status has ever been cut.

Engagement with students is key. Is the institution taking advantage of vertical alignment possibilities? Has the university's Pi Delta Phi chapter invited local *Société Honoraire de Français* chapters to a joint event, or vice-versa? The AATF has email templates that can facilitate communication between schools and encourage combined events. Hosting AATF events on a college or university campus is a great way to expose middle and high school students to the higher education institution, allow them to experience the campus, and showcase the French program.

Does the French program need some financial support? The AATF Small Grant is the perfect opportunity to bring a creative idea to life! Funding up to $500 is possible, and since an AATF Small Grant requires matching funds from the local chapter, the potential budget for the project can be more significant. In addition, instructors, especially those who have never attended an AATF convention before, can apply for the AATF Convention Travel Award. This award offers funds to offset the costs of traveling to the AATF convention and includes free registration.

Is the institution looking for additional funds for student scholarships? The AATF and its partner organizations, such as the American Society of French Academic Palms (ASFAP) and the National Federation of Modern Language Teacher Associations (NFMLTA), offer student scholarships and grants. These funds can be used for study abroad, dissertation research, dissertation writing, conference presentations, and more.

The AATF seeks to increase the number and types of scholarships it offers. A larger membership can help make this a reality.

- Cataloguing and selecting potential external funders

There are dozens of funding sources that support disruptive education. The major categories are Federal, state, corporations, individuals, and organizations. The U.S. Department of Education tops the list of federal funding sources. The two best programs, what we call "low-hanging fruit" because of their availability and high success rate, are the Undergraduate International Studies and Foreign Language Program (UISFL) and the Fulbright-Hays Group Projects Abroad (GPA) Program. The UISFL Program is designed to support interdisciplinary proposals like the French, Women's Studies, and Environmental Sciences joint degrees mentioned earlier. The UISFL Program will assist you in "planning, developing, carrying out programs to strengthen & improve undergraduate instruction in international studies & foreign languages."[245]

The GPA Program funds thematic month-long seminars in Francophone African countries such as Morocco, Senegal, Côte d'Ivoire, and Cameroon. The program provides faculty, teachers, and undergraduate and graduate students with opportunities to conduct individual and group projects overseas. Projects may include short-term seminars, curriculum development, group research or study, or long-term advanced intensive language programs.[246] It is the perfect program to strengthen ties with K-12 French educators who will become recruiters for your French program. The senior author will help you design a proposal and walk you through each step until its submission.

- Discovering the strategies of a successful grant proposal

Regardless of the funding source, an applicant must answer these four questions as they compose their proposal:

1. What's the problem?
2. What's the solution?

---

[245] U.S. Department of Education, 2024.
[246] United States Department of Education, 2024.

3. How will you execute the project?
4. Why you? Why should the funding source fund you?

The applicant's problem must be compelling. It must address the French program's weaknesses, which you want to transform into its strengths. Your problem might be low enrollments, threats from an administration, or a new need for a curriculum to understand Francophone Africa better. The program's solution should be "disruptive" and make reviewers say, "Wow!" Question three makes or breaks proposals. You need to show reviewers that you can complete the proposed project. The applicant can accomplish this with timelines, arguments of cost-effectiveness, the selection of the program's key personnel, a mistake-free budget, and a demonstration of the adequacy of resources. Finally, the French program must persuade reviewers that the program or the institution merits funding. For example, the institution is one of the leading liberal arts colleges in the U.S., and its faculty are recognized experts in their field. The institution is a community college or a Hispanic-serving institution. The Coca-Cola Foundation, for example, thrives in supporting underserved student bodies. The Koch Foundation loves student-centered education, a self-paced, mastery-based program.

World language educators hold one significant advantage as grant-getters. Why? Because all funding sources have a culture with its norms and taboos. Who better to analyze an unknown culture than us? To analyze the UISFL Program, for example, let us use the senior author's Diamond Model of Information Collection:

1. Study the Request for Proposal (RFP), watch the UISFL webinar several times, and read successful abstracts listed on the UISFL website;
2. Contact past recipients and ask for their proposals. Their names are listed in their abstracts.
3. Contact past reviewers to get insights into the review process and
4. Develop a relationship with the program officer.

Again, a consultant can help the French program in every step, from the needs assessment to the proposal submission.

Program Overview—Selection Criteria[247]

Criteria	Points
Plan of Operation	20
Quality of Key Personnel	10
Budget and Cost Effectiveness	10
Evaluation	20
Adequacy of Resources	5
Impact	15
Relevance to Institutional Development	10
Need for Overseas Experience	10
TOTAL	100
Short-Term Program Priorities (additional points)	9

As you write your proposal, it is wise to use their organizational pattern. Start your proposal with a "plan of operation" and finish with a "need for overseas experience." Reviewers often score one category at a time instead of reading the whole proposal and returning to score. Again, this is part of the culture of this funding source.

Conclusion

"Persistence, drive, determination, dedication, and patience, patience, patience" comprise the unique talents of the grant getter.[248] We mention "patience" three times because funders often take months to review your proposal. We mention "patience" three times because, sometimes, reviewer comments make no sense. We mention "patience" three times because grant writing is more like hitting in baseball than shooting free throws. Rejection is a normal part of grant writing. You will fail more than you will succeed, but your program and students are worth it. In baseball, even Hall of Fame hitters fail about 70% of the time. Roger Federer, one of tennis' all-time greats, lost 46% of the hundreds of

---

[247] Webinar, 2024, 15:18.
[248] Sacco, 2024.

thousands of points he played. We get stymied and frustrated with proposal writing and dealing with shortsighted administrators and politicians.

As we conclude, we would like to recommend an excellent book to guide your efforts as it has guided our efforts. Ryan Holiday's *The Obstacle is the Way: The Timeless Art of Turning Trials into Triumphs* reveals a success formula, citing the Stoics of Ancient Greece and Rome. Holiday's stories reveal how the greats throughout history turned obstacles into opportunities and adversity into victories[249] by using Marcus Aurelius and other stoics as a guide.

> Faced with impossible situations, they found the astounding triumphs we all seek. These men and women were not exceptionally brilliant, lucky, or gifted. Their success came from timeless philosophical principles laid down by a Roman emperor who struggled to articulate a method for excellence in any and all situations.[250]

Let us work together to protect and advance our programs using our powerful tools of the "mindset of opportunity," seeking external funding, creating visionary programs, and focusing on the wisdom of the stoics.[251]

---

[249] Holiday, 2014.
[250] Goodreads, 2024, para. 1,2.
[251] For those interested in Louisiana's musical landscape, here are key works that inspired this chapter, along with upcoming titles on the French Opera House from LSU Press and other local university presses. *Louis Armstrong's New Orleans*; *Creole New Orleans: Race and Americanization*; *Africans in Colonial Louisiana: The Development of Afro-Creole Culture in the 18th century*; *White by Definition: Social Classification in Creole Louisiana*. See Reference section.
Digital Collections of the American Folklife Center at the Library of Congress, which houses field research collections on Louisiana music going back decades.

24. Just a Francophile from New Jersey
Jennifer Schwester

Writing this chapter has led me to reflect deeply on how the French language, France, and other Francophone areas have influenced my life and how I have embraced and integrated French into my daily routine. Growing up in a small yet densely populated state, I have always had an insatiable desire to be elsewhere and experience life beyond my hometown's familiar confines. While I often return home—after all, I live within easy reach of the beach and am equidistant from the vibrant cultural hubs of New York City and Philadelphia—I am constantly yearning for more. Some people eat to live, some work to live, but I work so that I can travel, explore, and, most importantly, eat.

Food is one of my greatest passions. I am a true omnivore and self-proclaimed "foodie," always seeking new flavors and culinary experiences. If I have never tried a dish, that's the first thing I will order. In my section of town, which spans a mere two square miles, there are seven pizzerias, three Italian fine dining establishments, a variety of breakfast joints, American and European delis, two Mexican restaurants, a fish taco chain, a Japanese restaurant, two fast-food outlets, a salad bar, a health-conscious eatery, two sports bars, and two bakeries—all within walking distance. While this may seem like a large and diverse range of options, many of these places offer variations on the same theme, with "American Cuisine" dominating the landscape, punctuated occasionally by some homemade pastries, cured meats, or a dash of umami.

But I genuinely crave meals where I can sit down, savor each bite, and enjoy the moment without feeling rushed or interrupted. This, however, is a rare occurrence, both in the limited restaurant options I have and in the whirlwind of my daily schedule. My life is busy, and finding the time to slow down and enjoy a meal—genuinely enjoy it without distraction—is a challenge. Nevertheless, I strive to create those moments, carving out time to relish the company of family and friends unhurried by work demands or the constant buzz of electronic devices.

When I travel, I am far more conscientious about how I eat and when I eat, even if it is during a hectic student group tour. One of my coworkers has a phrase for our leisurely European lunches: "civilized meals." These are the meals where we take our time, try new dishes, and savor the experience— freshly made food, thoughtful service, and a palpable appreciation for our surroundings. Water is plentiful, and a glass of wine or an adult beverage enhances the experience, though not merely as a coping mechanism for dealing with the hormone-driven chaos of students exploring a foreign country for the first time.

Back home, I try to maintain that same sense of mindfulness around food, though the constraints of a busy schedule often interfere. Some nights, I eat early; others, I sit down for dinner closer to the European standard of 7 or 8 pm, though this still feels a bit early compared to other countries. I always make a point to turn off the TV, put my phone away, and focus on the food in front of me. I prefer a heavier lunch and a lighter dinner— partly because my school day starts before 7 am and my lunch period is at 10 am. For teachers, school schedules wreak havoc on our digestive systems, not to mention the bizarre and often frustrating challenge of being restricted to bathroom breaks at predetermined times. This is a concept utterly foreign to our students, who have far fewer bodily constraints.

I was not always this way. Like many Americans, I grew up on quick, easy-to-prepare meals— flavored gelatin, fast food, and a time when the concept of "blue food" did not exist. But my first real encounter with French cuisine came when I was fifteen, during a spring break trip to Paris with my high school French teacher, a woman I still regard as *amazing*. This trip was my first time out of the country, and I was utterly *boulversée*—completely overwhelmed—by the magic of Paris. Everything from the sights and sounds to the food and people left a lasting impression on me. I still remember the two-scoop ice cream cones designed to prevent the ice cream from toppling over—such a clever idea! That trip planted the seed in me, and from then on, I knew that French culture would play a central role in my life.

After returning from Paris, I tried convincing my family to travel to Québec City, my next French-speaking destination. This was long before the Internet, so I researched everything at the library, wrote letters, and made phone calls to reserve our hotel rooms. Looking back, it seems absurd that my family believed my three years of high school French would make me fluent enough to navigate everything seamlessly, but it was an adventure. I distinctly remember the thrill of trying ketchup-flavored potato chips for the first time and the frustrating search for a "Coke diète" because I could not figure out how to say it correctly in French. Then, there was the time I accidentally locked myself in a gas station bathroom. Those moments taught me that travel, with all its highs and lows, is about embracing the unexpected and learning to "go with the flow." Despite any mishaps, I always feel grateful for the opportunity to explore new places and cultures.

Right before college, I returned to Québec for a week as part of a study-abroad program hosted by a local university. I was still a high school student then, but there I was, hanging out with college kids, attending lectures at Université Laval, and soaking up everything there was to learn about *la culture québécoise*. I loved the freedom to explore the city independently, and this experience only deepened my connection to French-speaking communities. Québec felt familiar and foreign—nature and food were not too different from home, but the accents and vocabulary challenged me. Despite the cold (which I still do not love), Québec has remained one of my favorite places, and I feel at home whenever I return.

During my college years, I had the good fortune of returning to l'Université Laval for a summer study program, which cemented my love for Québec and its people. The more I visited, the more at ease I felt— whether in the cities, towns, or countryside.

Upon graduating, I began my teaching career at the tender age of twenty-two, full of energy and excitement but somewhat puzzled by my students' lack of enthusiasm for my travels. This was, after all, before the days of the Internet and smartphones, when travel still felt like a big deal. Back then, researching a trip involved a lot of legwork—library visits, phone calls, and meticulous planning. Early on, I realized that, as a teacher, it was my responsibility to find ways to bring the French language to life for my students, even if they could not see its immediate value.

In those pre-digital days, I did what I could to stay connected to the French-speaking world. I joined local French-speaking groups, scoured libraries for books and movies, and made frequent trips to larger cities to visit museums, see plays, and try new foods. Field trips with students were a special treat— opportunities to expose them to new cultures, cuisines, and perspectives, even for only a few hours.

I sought out every possible resource and community where French was spoken. In New Jersey, this is not as challenging as it might be elsewhere, but it still requires effort. I found language groups at local libraries, conversed with French speakers whenever I could, and even took advantage of the "sympathetic listeners" at Epcot's French and Moroccan pavilions during family trips to Disney. It was all part of my effort to keep the language alive and build bridges between my experiences and my students.

Fast forward to today, and the landscape of language learning has changed dramatically. The Internet has opened up a world of possibilities for teachers and students. With streaming services offering films and series from France and other Francophone countries and with access to online communities and language exchanges, the resources available are nearly endless. Students can now experience real-time glimpses of daily life in Francophone countries, listen to music, watch live performances, and even "visit" museums through virtual tours. I love sharing tools such as Google Earth with my students, allowing them to explore the world without leaving the classroom.

But even with all the modern tools at my disposal, there is something irreplaceable about actual travel. As I navigate my life as a French teacher, it is clear that travel has been one of the most significant ways that the French language and culture have impacted me. Every trip, every meal, and every conversation with a heritage speaker has enriched my understanding of the language and the world, and I strive to pass that on to my students.

As my career progressed and I continued to explore different parts of the Francophone world, I became increasingly passionate about the role of advocacy in promoting French language learning. While I fell in love with French culture and the language through personal experiences, I also realized that it was not just about the language itself but about opening up students to a wider world filled with diverse people, places, and perspectives.

Communication is essential for everyone; the more people we can connect with, the better our world and future may be. I am constantly on social media to spread the news of activities, French and Francophone groups, and community events and to share knowledge and joy. It has been a long-fought, unfinished battle to explain the relevance of French in the United States today. I tend to discuss the CONNECTIONS we all have through shared language. There are a large number of children and adolescents in our country who are already bilingual (home language and English). While encouraging them to use those languages, becoming tri-literate or more is essential. Students can strengthen and build on their current language skills, and by being able to communicate and connect with more people, they are solidifying a strong future for themselves and their families and hopefully helping to aid peace and understanding with others worldwide.

In the United States, foreign language programs, particularly those involving languages other than Spanish, often face cuts due to budgetary constraints, declining enrollment, or shifts in educational priorities. French tends to be considered "a language of privilege" and "a language of the past"—an outdated relic that, in the eyes of some, no longer holds relevance in an increasingly globalized and English-dominated world. However, this could not be further from the truth.

French remains a global language spoken across multiple continents, with deep ties to international diplomacy, business, culture, and education. France and the broader Francophone world contribute enormously to global culture, literature, art, and thought. But beyond France itself, countries in Africa, the Caribbean, and North America have their rich traditions of Francophone culture that are often overlooked.

The Francophone world is vast and varied, including more than 300 million speakers across Africa, Europe, North America, the Caribbean, and Asia. French is not just the language of Parisian cafés and high fashion; it is the language of many African countries where multilingualism flourishes, of Creole cultures in the Caribbean, of the French-Canadian heritage in Québec, and even of island communities in the South Pacific. Each of these regions brings something unique to the global Francophone community. Through French, students access an immense tapestry of human experiences beyond what they learn in the classroom.

That is why I believe it is crucial to advocate for language learning, not just as an educational tool but as a means to develop empathy, cultural understanding, and global awareness. In my classroom, I try to emphasize to my students that learning French isn't just about conjugating verbs or memorizing vocabulary—it is about opening doors to new opportunities, both personal and professional. I want them to see that learning French gives them access to a diverse and rich world beyond their immediate environment.

One of the things I strive to teach my students is the idea that "Francophone" doesn't just mean "from France." Many students come into the French classroom with images of the Eiffel Tower, croissants, and berets as their only reference points for the language. While these symbols of French culture are undoubtedly iconic, the Francophone world is much more expansive, encompassing regions and countries with distinct identities, histories, and ways of speaking French.

For instance, many students are surprised that French is spoken in Senegal, Morocco, and Haiti. These countries have their own cultures, traditions, and dialects of French, which are just as vital to the global Francophone community as Parisian French. By studying French, students are not just learning a language— they are gaining the tools to understand and appreciate how language and culture intersect in different parts of the world.

Through discussions on topics like *la Négritude, la Francophonie,* and the historical role of French colonialism, I introduce my students to the complex and often painful histories of many Francophone regions. But alongside these histories, I also highlight the beauty and resilience of these cultures— their music, literature, art, and cuisine. These lessons go beyond traditional grammar and vocabulary instruction; they broaden students' worldviews and foster a deeper appreciation for the diversity of human experiences.

For example, when we study French-speaking countries in Africa, we not only learn about the languages spoken there but also discuss contemporary issues such as the role of French in post-colonial societies, the rise of African cinema and music in the Francophone world, and the contributions of writers like Léopold Sédar Senghor. Similarly, when we explore Québec, we talk about the unique political and cultural dynamics of being a French-speaking region in a predominantly English-speaking country.

Each of these regions adds something unique to the larger Francophone community, and my goal as a teacher is to help students appreciate those nuances. I want them to understand that French isn't a monolith; it is a living, evolving language that exists in many forms across the globe. When they learn French, they are not just learning how to speak to people in France—they are gaining the ability to connect with people in Cameroon, Belgium, Switzerland, Martinique, and beyond.

One of my proudest moments as a teacher has been seeing students apply what they have learned in my classroom to real-world experiences. Some have traveled to France or Québec, while others have pursued study abroad programs in Francophone countries. A few have even gone on to careers where they use French daily—working in international relations, translation, hospitality, or global business.

I firmly believe that learning a language opens up pathways to understanding people and cultures that would otherwise remain closed off. Whether my students go on to use French in their professional lives or simply as a means of personal enrichment, the cultural exchange that comes with language learning is invaluable. They may begin their French studies to fulfill a school requirement, but by the end, many realize they have gained something much more profound: a sense of connection to a global community.

Language advocacy is about ensuring that students can access this global community. It is about fighting for the survival of French programs, emphasizing the importance of multilingualism, and showing students that by learning another language, they are expanding their horizons and helping build bridges between cultures and countries.

By the end of their time in my classroom, I want my students to understand that French is more than just a subject they study in school. It is a key that unlocks doors to different parts of the world, fosters empathy and understanding, and is a tool for navigating an increasingly interconnected global society. Through French, they gain access to the Francophone world—a vast, diverse, and ever-evolving tapestry of cultures that stretches far beyond the borders of France itself.

The work is challenging at times and thrilling, and I could not imagine my life any other way due to the influences of excellent teachers, professors, and patient strangers. So, how have the language and cultures impacted me? It has given me the inquisitiveness and openness to explore, speak with people I do not know, and continue to learn. It has affected my tastes, both nutritionally and culturally, and helped me appreciate other traditions, understand their historical and cultural significance, and make me feel more connected in the world since I can communicate with more people.

I am grateful and blessed for the opportunities afforded me since I am aware that not everyone has similar situations. I believe my job at this point in life is to be an advocate, share my joy, and help others to connect with humankind through language, food, customs, shared experiences, learning about each other, and overall, how to be a good human. That is my wish for all: to be a good human, no matter what language you speak or what you believe.

25. La Francophonie des Amériques: Conversation and Community
Joëlle Vitiello and Sophie Kerman

In Spring 2022, Joëlle Vitiello, Professor at Macalester College, and Sophie Kerman, Upper School Teacher at St. Paul Academy and Summit School, joined forces to co-create a course on Francophone North America from a decolonial perspective. Our collaboration with each other, as well as with local members of the Francophone community and with high school and college students in both 2022 and 2024, was the source of many rich and fruitful explorations of what it means to speak French in North America today. Enhanced by our respective connections to the French language, this approach offers possibilities for building partnerships with community leaders and organizations at both a local and a national/international level, empowering younger generations to expand their horizons and engage in thoughtful citizenship and making a strong argument for the continued relevance of French programs in the face of declining enrollments. Because our complementary backgrounds and perspectives have enriched our curriculum development process, we are sharing our experiences below as a dialogue.

Why and How Did You Decide to Become a French Teacher?

SK: As an American learning French in middle and high school, I grew up with a rose-colored view of French culture, and I use French culture in the singular here because most of my memories of my early French education involve the tried-and-true classics of high school French class - "Le Petit Prince," memorizing "La Cigale et la Fourmi," etc. I appreciated the beauty of the language and the literature, but my college major was sociology & anthropology. I loved my college French courses, but somehow, I did not see French as a topic I could sink my teeth into in a way that could energize an entire career, and I also did not feel like my spoken French was good enough to teach it to others.

That changed during the year after college when I worked as an *assistante d'anglais* through the TAPIF program, which was both the immersion experience I needed to gain confidence in speaking and a formative experience for my future career. This was in 2008, during the election of President Barack Obama, so I was a witness to my students' excitement at seeing a Black President of the United States and also their disheartening certainty that a Black or Arab president would never get elected in France in their lifetimes. Seeing the diversity of faces in my classroom and how my students reflected my culture at me through their variety of lenses was all the proof I needed that there was much more about French and Francophone identities (this time, in the plural) that I needed to explore. It shaped my career professionally because my first real teaching experience focused more on culture than language acquisition. Taking a more sociocultural approach has made language teaching an incredibly enriching experience for me and my students.

JV: It was different for me; I wanted to teach for as long as I can remember. When I studied literature in school, it was clear that I would be engaged with literature, reading, and writing. During my studies in France, I also learned different languages: Greek and Latin, English and German at school, and Spanish and Esperanto at the Cultural Center. As a child, my first pen pal was from Holland, so I was also trying to learn Dutch. Languages and translation have always been part of my history. I trained to become a teacher in France. I tutored as a student and studied different pedagogies in the School of Education.

Then, I came to the United States as an Amity Aid. The program provided teaching assistants in various languages to U.S. schools. I was posted first in a suburb of Minneapolis and then in a small town in Wisconsin, in a junior and then a senior high school. I loved this experience. I also lived a year in Japan, where I trained as a technical translator between English and French. When I came back to the United States, I did some tutoring and teaching as an instructor while also doing translations, and when I went back to school, we had to take classes on how to teach French, observe classes, and teach ourselves. It was fascinating because I kept learning about the English and French languages through teaching. I genuinely enjoy teaching and sharing knowledge at all levels, whether the course is about language, stories, or advanced research. When I was in France, I wanted to teach French linguistics and literature, and in the United States, that is also what I did, even though teaching French as a foreign language requires different tools and techniques. When I completed my French and Comparative Literature graduate degree, it was almost natural that I would continue teaching. I do teach in French and English, and I have always thought that it is not because I am French that I can teach French but that it derives from both the desire to understand language in depth and from the desire to share the richness of the different literatures and cultures that derive from French through different themes be it immigration, human rights, or the environment.

How Has the Role of French Changed Your Professional and Personal Lives Since the Start of Your Career?

SK: As a learner of French in middle and high school, I loved the process of learning the language, but my classes were mainly skills-based. I remember learning verb conjugation charts and doing fill-in-the-blank exercises in my AP workbook. Most of our forays into the Francophone culture were via those two-page textbook inserts about the Carnaval de Québec or what a *pagne* looks like. It wasn't until college and graduate school that culture became a regular part of French coursework (and even then, it was more centered around literature than lived practices).

JV: This was true in my experience as well. When I started as a young professor, the literature written in French outside of France was rarely taught, or it was taught as a "culture course," and African texts were taught along Québécois or Swiss texts. My department was the French Department. Today, the department's name is French and Francophone Studies, and we were considering something even more inclusive, such as Global French Studies. We now have specialized courses and even full-time professors teaching literature and cinema from Africa. We teach specialized courses on Caribbean literature and cultures, Francophone Indigenous literature and films, Francophone islands, the environment, food from France and the Francophone

World. So, the role of French has tremendously expanded and, as we have heritage speakers from various parts of the globe, we emphasize communication over perfect grammar, we have opened up the notion of the standard French language to include varieties of French, we face the colonial heritage as well that comes with the richness of the literature, cultures, and music expressed in French or Creolized French.

SK: This is truer and truer in the middle and high school teaching community. Technology has had a considerable role in highlighting the limits of the old approach because it is becoming less necessary to know French (or even leave your couch) if all you want to do is visit the Louvre. Students are looking for a purpose to their learning that Google Translate, virtual visits, and AI can't give them, so it is our role as teachers to show them the kind of deeper learning that becomes available to them in another language. It is more challenging since we can't just teach from a textbook. I know countless teachers (of multiple languages) who are essentially writing their own textbooks to connect better with their student populations and incorporate more global citizenship in their courses. However, there is an excellent payoff to all that work regarding student motivation when they can see the intrinsic value in their language classes.

JV: Yes. This shift has enriched me a lot personally, intellectually, and spiritually, but it is also significant in transmitting the great diversity of Francophone cultures to younger generations. Soon, more people will communicate in French on the African continent than in France. The creativity that is deployed in the use of the French language is remarkable.

How do You Balance Teaching the France of Baguettes, Berets, and The Tour Eiffel with a Decolonial Approach to France and the Francophone World?

SK: We constantly balance the clichés that many students expect when entering French class and what I know to be true about the world. In the private school where I teach, international travel is accessible to much of the student body, and there are many students for whom French is a gateway to an incredible vacation of shopping at designer boutiques or skiing in the Alps. However, even within a relatively privileged population, the "baguettes, bérets, Tour Eiffel" vision of France doesn't reflect the diversity of students in my classroom. Not only are some of them financially unable to see France as a travel destination, but at various political moments in the last decade, I have had multiple students of different identities (Muslim, Jewish, gender non-conforming) ask me if France is a safe place for them to travel. We all know that in order to be effective educators, students need to see themselves reflected in the curriculum. A decolonial approach to the Francophone world allows more students to see themselves as possible French speakers and to see some of their personal and family experiences reflected through another cultural lens.

JV: I agree with you, Sophie. We constantly balance the romantic clichés of France with its colonial histories. I have students of diverse backgrounds as well. Some are of French heritage or have studied French in various places around the world, and they come to my courses with diverse experiences and points of view. A decolonial, inclusive approach allows students to find their place in the language, experiment, change lenses, and take the parts of French they want to explore further. Some are apprehensive about experiencing racism in France; others go for a semester abroad in Senegal or Morocco, where they are also out of their comfort zone. A great gift is a course that can leave the students with new perspectives and more confidence in their abilities to navigate the Francophone world, be it linguistic, social, or cultural. As we want to be inclusive and reflect the great diversity of our students' identities, in my department, we design our courses, from French 101 on, on themes of interest to students. We try to create meaningful entry points to the realities of Francophone cultures, whether in France or the Francophone world in general.

SK: Exactly. Students don't need to imagine themselves as tourists at the foot of the Eiffel Tower to find a valuable reason to learn French; expanding the scope of our French programs allows more students to find their place. If that same approach can also teach our more privileged students how to respectfully engage with identities other than their own, it has also done them a service.

How does Teaching in French help students tackle broader global issues such as Climate Change, Social Justice, or Other Issues that Interest them?

JV: First, learning another language dramatically expands one's horizon and place in the world. The languages themselves reflect cultural differences, small and large. As an example, reading about how Haitians are affected by man-made environmental disasters such as plastic washing on their shores in a French newspaper article and then discussing this in class can help students develop empathy. They can understand the impact of such disasters on a personal level, which may lead them to reflect on how environmental issues are connected globally.

SK: Even further than that, having access to another language allows students to gain multiple perspectives on a single issue. They can go beyond the headlines and dive into social justice issues from different angles within the target culture. Thinking about climate change, for instance, there are often cases where environmental and economic interests are at odds and where those conflicts have ripples across other spheres, such as Indigenous land rights or gender roles. With the ability to take a deep dive, students aren't walking away from a lesson thinking that French (or Canadian, or Haitian, etc.) culture is a monolith; they're seeing the variations *within* any given culture as well.

JV: Absolutely. Understanding an issue from many angles, whether a global event, climate change, or anything else, equips students with critical thinking tools to develop their opinions, educate themselves and others, and reflect on their cultures. This understanding empowers them to participate in global citizenship, fostering a sense of engagement and motivation.

SK: This is why we have worked so well together! It is so energizing for both me and, hopefully, my students to have a shared purpose that is truly global in scope. Teaching language and culture is also teaching a habit of mind. For many students, it is easier to analyze other cultures from an outsider's perspective because the emotional stakes are lower, and they're less likely to get defensive or feel like their values are under attack. But suppose they build the habit of looking at issues from multiple angles, seeking out local perspectives, and recognizing nuance and gray areas. In that case, they're primed to make that leap when thinking about their own communities.

How do you establish connections with local and international members of the Francophone community in a non-extractive way, and how do these connections enrich the students' perspectives?

JV: This is a tricky question in teaching courses with multi-year rotations. I would say that since I arrived in Minnesota many years ago, I have been able to develop long-term, sustainable relationships with several diverse cultural organizations, from the Alliance Française to the Twin Cities Film Society and other organizations. Internationally, I have also been privileged to develop deep relationships with individuals and organizations in Haiti and the Haitian diaspora. I tend to remain in touch regularly with most of them. So, when I open up these professional and personal relationships to my classes, I think there must be mutual respectful understanding on the part of the students and of my institution that these connections are precious. These connections enrich the students' perspectives, fostering a sense of open-mindedness and appreciation.

Every such exchange is a fabulous opportunity for students to be in touch with the real world. In turn, because it demands labor, we must cultivate an ethos of recognizing labor through equitable compensation, even though these opportunities are also real gifts. I was very grateful to have obtained a national Pericles grant to fund, at least partially, our guest speakers the first time we taught the course and the second time our institutions partnered effectively. It also requires one to be clear about one's position and to be able to enter a reciprocal relationship. In any case, we need to be able to enter and maintain long-term sustainable relationships with the communities we engage with. One way we have thought about how we can contribute to educating our teaching communities has been through open-access research by the students in our paired course, showcasing resources that can help change the narrative or make the heritage or the issues of the Francophone world in the Americas visible. We do value the connections between the K-12 educational system and higher education so that when we work in synergy, students at all levels can be exposed to at least an introduction to viewing the world in a decolonial way, finding authentic resources, acknowledging the power and limits of engaging with cultures different from theirs, and creating possibilities for others to continue their explorations.

SK: Knowing that so many of the speakers you have invited into our course have been your personal friends, I feel fortunate that my students and I have benefitted from those relationships, and I don't take that for granted. Hearkening back to the discussion of global issues above, there's such power in conversing with a real-life human being, whether virtually or in person. They bring the world into the classroom, both in the content they present, the cultures they represent, and how they model different ways that French can be spoken. My students have gotten so much out of these encounters that it has motivated me to try and seek out more community connections on my own. But on top of the compensation piece, which is so important on an individual level, the idea of non-extractive community connections also means giving of ourselves, which you are particularly good at, Joëlle. Many students must be taught how to do it and allowed to practice with thought and intention.

How Will the Teaching of French Stay Relevant In the Face of Declining Enrollments?

SK: I am lucky to be one of the minority who can say the French enrollments in my school are staying strong. However, the greatest argument for the relevance of French is when we can find and cultivate local and global connections. Depending on the community, that might take a little digging. Still, here in Minnesota, there is a fairly straightforward case to make: French has local relevance based on our history, proximity to Canada, and immigrant communities from various countries in Francophone Africa and Southeast Asia. I wonder how that shakes out for you, Joëlle because your students come from various contexts. Do you find French to be a harder sell at the post-secondary level?

JV: Certainly, over the years, we have noticed a decline in enrollments, which is a bit uncanny given that, especially in Minnesota and the Twin Cities and suburbs of the Twin Cities, there have been an increasing number of French immersion programs that have flourished. A few years ago, we had the first generation of students who had received a French immersion school education their entire lives. One of the students had no connection whatsoever with France. Still, the parents knew that learning another foreign language early had a positive effect on the brain so that we could welcome the student at a reasonably advanced level.

SK: Now that I have a child attending one of our local French immersion elementary schools, I can echo that gratitude for them! Apart from the benefits of the language, my 1st grader doesn't bat an eyelash that he has teachers from Laos, Cameroon, and the Democratic Republic of the Congo, that his kindergarten teacher was from France, and that he learns to dance a few weeks a year from a Haitian dance troupe. Students from there don't have any questions about whether French is relevant and global.

JV: Yes! We are also fortunate that a number of our students come from Francophone countries and work in our department, modeling a diversity that is unique on our campus as they serve as tutors and model the diversity we strive to achieve, a diversity reflected, as you note, in the educational system itself. We are also fortunate to have a few students every year coming from your school who enter our program at an advanced level.

We have adjusted to student interests over the years, so we cover the Francophone world in its entirety, and this course on the Francophonie des Amériques that we are co-teaching was born because students were interested in learning about Louisiana and the connections between Québec and Acadia and the local migrant groups from various Francophone countries. We also found fantastic connections with Francophone Indigenous communities, including a local scholar whose family had both Francophone African and Indigenous roots, some Metis communities still using their language, Michif, and various Francophone Indigenous communities in Canada.

We are also aware of the students' interest in the environment and economics, so we partner with other concentrations and teach about food, the environment, animals and humans, humanitarianism and human rights, immigration, and translation. A recent event on women and sports (in the wake of the Olympic Games) in France and the Francophone world has also sparked in me the desire to explore a course with the athletic department on that topic (I did not know that at the end of the 19th century, France was the oldest basketball playing country in Europe! – I learned this in Lindsay Sarah Krasnoff's book on *France and the Making of a Global NBA and WNBA*! Bloomsbury Academic, 2023). And next semester, I am teaching a course focused on French for the Professions. So, I would not say it is a harder sell; I would say that students are aware that the world is more significant than France and that through our language sequences, they pick up different interests that we respond to. I am optimistic that French will continue to be relevant. It is a global language in many areas and an American heritage language. However, I would add that it is essential that post-secondary academics connect with K-12 teachers, and the American Association of Teachers of French is one of our survival links.

SK: Those connections are equally important to us in the K-12 world! My students benefit so much from studying alongside college students. Our collaborative course demystified the idea of college language study, and knowing that we were covering the same content and presenting it together at the Alliance Française with your students was a huge confidence boost to my students. So many of them plan to continue French as a major, double major, or minor, and many more plan to study abroad.

JV: And I look forward to our next course co-teaching again.

SK: As do I! In the meantime, readers can explore our students' work at the link: bit.ly/MacSPAFrancophonie. They have created lesson plans and other resources on French in North America, which we, and they, are excited to share with the teaching community! Community is at the heart of this endeavor and all that we do as language teachers, and we hope that this work can enrich others' teaching as it has our own.

26. French Education from One Generation to the Next
Rebecca Fortgang and Jasmine Grace St. Pierre

Personal Impact

RF: During our three weeks of French and Spanish classes in middle school, we covered more French vocabulary, so I selected to learn French in high school. Little did I know that decision would impact the rest of my life. Where I grew up on Lake Winnipesaukee, many local businesses, including the ice cream shop I worked at, would bring foreigners to work in the summer. I loved meeting students from all over the world and learning bits of their language. When students from France stopped to buy ice cream, I knew I had to connect with them. After chasing them down the street to give them my number, my friend and I waited patiently for a day before a call came. We befriended the French students through our French skills and were thrilled to use our language to form new connections. This started with hanging out on the beach but turned into sending emails and keeping in touch for many years after they returned home.

I was impressed that after taking French III in high school, I could have conversations and meaningful relationships with native French speakers. I did not realize at the time how much culture I was learning through my new friends. Since they did not have cars, we would all go to the mall together to buy jeans because they were cheaper in the U.S. The students told me their sizes, and I was initially very confused, not realizing this was based on the metric system and required conversion. We had to do some trial and error to be successful.

Due to having a small school, I could only take up level IV French classes. However, I was committed to furthering my French education after my experiences with my summer friends. When I started attending Keene State College, I wanted to be a math teacher but asked about

French when signing up for courses. Having taken through French IV in high school, I was signed up for French 315, which was a conversation class. I took two more French classes in the second semester.

After being misplaced in math, I realized I wouldn't continue with math and switched my major to French, where I made friends both in class and in the French Club. As a student, making friends in French class is easier because you are always talking and learning to share your life just in another language. French Club in college led to multiple trips to Québec, where I grew closer to my fellow travelers through shared experiences. I learned how to ride public transportation, found out that everyone moves on July first, and how to make poutine.

French Club wasn't my only opportunity to go to Québec. In 2009, I chose to do my semester abroad at the University of Sherbrooke to have a different experience than most other French teachers who studied in France. This made certain aspects of becoming a teacher challenging because the standardized tests were designed for Parisian French and not my Québecois dialect. However, I knew I had made the right choice when I landed my first job. My experiences in Québec enabled me to help with the school's upcoming field trip.

Teaching French isn't like teaching other subjects. Since I have been the only French teacher at most of the schools I worked at, I see the students year after year. I have been able to build deeper bonds with my students as a result of this. These students have also wanted to continue their studies in French and have done so by becoming student teachers in my high school French classroom as students. The other advantage is the need to collaborate with others. I did this with other French teachers and the local Francophone community. I have been working with these colleagues to help create the best classroom learning environments.

Advancing The Cause

RF: I believe the future of French in New Hampshire is for students learning French as a second language. I have worked in public middle schools and high schools across New Hampshire in both urban and rural areas. I have also been able to teach university-credited classes to high school students through the Dual Enrollment program. I have worked in a private school in Massachusetts with preschoolers through eighth grade, teaching French as a second language using a Montessori style. As an educator in various environments, I have developed French for many student populations. My experience being so diverse is an indicator that there is a diverse group of students learning French as a second language. To meet this diverse group of learners where they are, I have worked to provide my students with a variety of opportunities to suit their interests. With this experience, I have created a program that has led to future French educators and more Francophones.

The French Program at Fall Mountain Regional High School has been recognized by the American Association of Teachers of French (AATF) as an exemplary program. Some of our program's highlights include a full sequence of French courses (French I through V), dual enrollment options that offer college credit while in high school, an Extended Learning Opportunity through which students gain teaching experience, an active French Club for cultural enrichment, a French Honor Society for high-achieving students, and the opportunity to earn the Seal of Biliteracy for demonstrating advanced language proficiency.

The French Honor Society students organize and run the French Club. We have created the foremost list of French Club activities, and the Honor Society students choose an activity from this list and then plan and execute the activity with the club. This has been wildly successful. As a result, the students have been annually putting together a slideshow for French teachers on how to do every activity in a mini-lesson plan style format. The students have taken this presentation on the road and presented at AATF's annual conferences twice, at the Northeast Council for Teachers of Foreign Languages and the New Hampshire Association of World Language Teachers conference thrice. We believe it is essential for teachers to hear from students about what they love about learning French and share how others can make that happen for their students. One of the other important things we do in the French Club is create systems that allow one generation to pass on leadership knowledge and skills to the next. Juniors are the students presenting at these conferences so that seniors can support them and will be there to support the next generation.

The French Club and Honor Society members conduct "The Middle School Invasion" to recruit the next generation of students. This is where they take over the cultural studies class for a day or two and share all the fun we have in both French Club and French Class with students. The members do a crêpe making demonstration and play Cognate Frenzy with the students – think Apples to Apples but with cognates! This shows students they already know so much French. The students also explained the French program, including the opportunities they can take advantage of if they work hard.

As part of the program's more traditional academics, students have the opportunity to earn the prestigious Seal of Biliteracy (SoBL). This is now available in every state and has an international version. To achieve this, students need to pass a standardized test with a score of intermediate high in all four areas of language: reading, writing, speaking, and listening. What we love about the SoBL is that it benefits all students. It tells colleges that students have the language skills to be successful, and it tells employers of students who are going into the workforce that they have the skills needed to communicate with customers, coworkers, etc. The Seal of Biliteracy continues to grow and is seeking to gain traction in the House of Representatives through the Biliteracy Education Seal and Teaching Act, otherwise known as the BEST Act. Earning the SoBL is a significant achievement that students can be proud of, and it serves as a strong motivator for their language learning journey.

Another way to support students' academics is the Dual Enrollment program. This is where high schools partner with local community colleges so that courses taught in the high school can count towards college credit. These credits earned at the community college can be used by students who study there or can be easily transferred with about a 90% success rate. Students in French can earn Elementary French I & II credit and a Sociology credit for the course Contemporary Social Issues. In addition, students can take the Advanced Placement French exam and graduate with four credits from their college classes.

One of the students' favorite opportunities has been participating in cultural events. My French students have volunteered at the New Hampshire PoutineFest for three years. They help check people in, stamp passport cards, sell raffle tickets, and even help cook the food! The Franco-American Centre of Manchester, NH (FAC) organizes all the volunteers, and my students always feel very appreciated for their contribution. Since this has been such a success, we partnered with the FAC to host a table at the Keene International Festival in Keene, NH. The French students choose an arts and crafts project that attendees can do for free to help promote the French language. In the past, we did an activity based on works by artist Henri Matisse where students cut and pasted colorful shapes in a collage style similar to his. We plan to try a new activity where students build the Eiffel Towers from dry spaghetti and marshmallows for the next fair. These cultural events not only promote the French language but also foster a sense of community and connection among the students, making them feel included and engaged.

We also travel to Francophone countries as part of our school program and as a part of extracurriculars. Students enjoyed an extended stay in Québec for the Winter Carnival in 2022, where they visited the carnival and could dance at the sugar shack and go dog sledding. They explored Vieux Québec, saw the old city walls, le Château Frontenac, and walked la Grande Allée. That summer, two students and I traveled to New Orleans to present at the AATF national conference, sharing a student perspective with teachers. While we weren't attending conference sessions, we could explore the city and see the historic Vieux Carré. We even left the city to tour the bayous and saw many alligators in the swamps. But the most meaningful part of our trip was the connections we built because of our French language use. We met with friends we had made during one of the virtual French conversations I attended with students and attended a Bastille Day party hosted by a branch of Alliance Française. There were connections to be made even where we did not expect: We had a lovely conversation in French with a woman from Sénégal selling dresses and skirts at a market stall in the Vieux Carré. These travel experiences provide students with a deeper understanding of French culture and ignite a sense of adventure and discovery, making them feel excited and inspired.

In 2024, students visited Paris and Provence, enjoying local cuisine, sights, and train travel. Since this was a combined trip with the Spanish students, the French students had to help the Spanish students with all aspects of the trip. They encouraged and helped students with ordering at restaurants, navigating the metro, and ensuring no one got stuck in the self-cleaning restrooms! While students loved the classic views of Paris, many commented on how much they enjoyed the south of France because the way of life reminded them of home. With that feeling in their hearts, many also mentioned wanting to study abroad in college.

Students also enjoy local francophone field trips such as the Franco Route Tour to learn about French-Canadian workers who immigrated to New England to work in the Mills. We also traveled to the Clark Art Museum in Massachusetts, which has a wonderful collection of impressionist art. Tours are also available in French if requested ahead of time. I went on one such tour with a group of students, and the guide was thrilled to tell us all about the paintings and the artists behind them, giving us new vocabulary relating to art and history.

Another particularly successful aspect of our program is the Extended Learning Opportunity for student teaching, developed for those students who have already finished the French program and want to continue their studies. As a student teacher, students can try out teaching before committing to a career in education. They do this by teaching the lower levels of French. They can plan lessons and units for students and execute them with feedback from the students and the veteran teacher (me). So far, 100% of the students who have done this program with me are continuing their education to become French teachers, such as Jasmine Grace St. Pierre.

Future Perspectives

JSP: The COVID-19 pandemic hit during my first year of high school, and during that time, French class was the only social connection I had. French was one of the few courses that continued to be engaging, partly because we were learning language, and there was a social element to the class that is not found in a math or science class. Language learners must practice speaking, and we did. Our conversations were limited at first by our small but growing vocabulary.

Nearly halfway through my first year of French, our teacher invited us to a virtual French conversation hosted by the FAC to practice our new language skills. A close friend and I attended with all of one month's study of French. The conversation was held between native and fluent speakers, so we understood next to none of the words exchanged. But we understood the laughter and the smiles we saw on the cameras and knew this was a fun group of people. We returned the following month for the next meeting, this time with a short script we'd use to introduce ourselves. We kept coming back, even over the summer, and by the fall, we understood more and more of each conversation.

By sophomore year, nearing the end of French II, we were invited to intern at this organization because the directors had noticed our perseverance and passion for French. We delightfully accepted the position and were soon charged with breathing new life into the blog. We began immediately with a whole new schedule, with weekly articles on a rotating variety of topics, from current events to historical French-speaking figures. We wrote about Lafayette's contributions to the American War for Independence and how that shaped the modern world. Another article discussed French idioms such as *comme trois pommes* (three apples tall) and *tomber dans les pommes* (to fall into the apples; to faint) and their origins. The thread that links all topics together is the promotion of the French language and francophone culture around the globe. Yes, everyone knows French is spoken in France, and many know some French is spoken in Québec, but a great number of people fail to realize that a variety of places in the world speak French. It is a truly global language, learned and spoken by people on every continent. Right from the start, we wanted to teach the global nature of this language.

As time passed, another goal we shared was reaching a broader audience with which to share our articles. We began to track how many reads each article received and tried to use that information to find how best to improve future pieces. For the first few months, that was our whole job: writing the articles and monitoring their popularity to see what the following articles should be. Over time, we took on more and more responsibility. Today, four years later, we write, manage, and edit the project. We continue to create the schedule, publish articles, and edit articles written by other interns.

This experience working with the Franco-American Centre has shown me how valuable this language is as a connection between people. Even though the articles we write are in English, and the vast majority of the people I interact with speak English, our passion for promoting French brings us together.

Even then, near the beginning of high school, I knew I wanted to continue studying language. I loved French class. I loved the connection the language gave me to so many other people, even though this was a language I was learning, not one I'd been raised with. I quickly decided I wanted to be a language teacher. My French teacher had a significant impact on my high school experience and my life thereafter, and I wanted to be able to share those sorts of opportunities with the next generation. However, I also had a passion for English for Speakers of Other Languages (ESOL) teaching.

Such teachers are essential in our schools. I worked at a summer school with a student who spoke exclusively Spanish. Since I was one of the few staff members who spoke even a little bit of Spanish, I was tasked with using my limited knowledge of Spanish to teach her math and some English. Working with that student and seeing the extra challenges she faced, yet how brilliant she was when given the opportunity and tools to express herself, showed me the importance of ESOL teachers.

I was torn between my love of French and my new passion for ESOL. Ultimately, I found a program that allowed me to study ESOL and French teaching. I am currently in my second year of college, studying those fields. Whichever subject I teach, I want to connect people through language.

The future of French lies in the hands of native speakers and second-language learners alike. As a student of French, I gained many connections through the language and was put in contact with many wonderful people I otherwise would never have met. I hope to connect my future students similarly and prepare them to navigate a multilingual, multicultural world better.

To better prepare myself to lead students in this multicultural world, I plan to study abroad in the coming semesters to understand Francophone cultures better. Like many other students, I am limited in my choices. I can go to France or, with some difficulty, Québec. However, the future of French lies not just in France and Québec; various African nations are home to more than half of all Francophones. Yet I, and many others who share this language, cannot study there. We cannot better understand the cultures of many Francophones with whom we share this language.

Language belongs to all those who speak it, learners and native speakers. French, in New Hampshire in this day and age, is not spoken at home by as many as learn it in classrooms. The future of our language relies on the importance of education and second language learning, in addition to keeping French speakers engaged with their language.

Conclusion: The Ongoing Journey of French in America
Kathleen Stein-Smith and Fabrice Jaumont

After the inspirational journey through the narratives of our authors, emotions lead to thoughts and questions about the future of French and our role in this constantly evolving story. Even as individuals, we can ensure that the French language remains an active part of our daily lives by engaging in activities and interactions in French—through reading, listening, speaking, and seeking opportunities to use it with family, friends, and community members. In our increasingly multilingual society, there have never been so many ways to integrate French into daily routines, whether through social media, streaming services, or local cultural events.

Two interwoven concepts—*Franco-responsabilité* and *Franco-activisme*—are critical to the continued vibrancy and growth of the French language and Francophone culture in the United States. Franco-responsabilité calls on those who believe in the language's role and value to use French as much as possible and to encourage its use in day-to-day life. Building on this individual responsibility, *Franco-activisme* extends the commitment more broadly, supporting French language learning, championing Francophone media, and promoting cultural initiatives in local communities and throughout society. Taken together, these principles underscore the necessity of widespread—and ideally universal—engagement to protect French as a genuinely American language.

Building upon these two concepts, it is helpful to revisit *Franco-responsabilité* and *Franco-activisme* as guiding principles for anyone who values the continued vitality of the language. At its most personal level, *Franco-responsabilité* encourages each speaker, learner, or enthusiast to take genuine care of French—whether by reading, writing, speaking, or engaging with it in daily settings such as family gatherings, online discussions, or cultural events. Beyond mere usage, this principle also implies a dedication to preserving and celebrating French culture. By exploring French-language literature, music, and historical narratives—and transmitting them to new generations—we deepen our collective understanding of a heritage that has taken root in America for centuries.

While *Franco-responsabilité* begins at an individual level, *Franco-activisme* carries that dedication into communal spaces. It urges proactive efforts to organize cultural events, advocate for language policies, support bilingual education, and create environments that celebrate French. This activism can take many forms: hosting festivals, sponsoring conversation groups at local libraries, partnering with community centers, or using social media to connect with Francophones worldwide. By participating in or promoting these initiatives, community members ensure that French is not only preserved but actively shared, forging stronger cultural bonds that span regions and generations.

In addition, it is essential to reflect on the place of French within an increasingly multilingual world. Those of us with roles in communities and institutions have both the opportunity and responsibility to foster an environment where heritage and additional languages—including French—are available from an early age. Seeing these languages used in educational, healthcare, workplace, and public settings demonstrates their ongoing relevance. When children learn to value different languages and cultures from their earliest years, the foundations of linguistic and cultural diversity become stronger, benefiting society as a whole.

Language learning and preserving heritage languages are responsibilities we all share. This collective effort can be realized by ensuring the availability of French instruction from the earliest grades in public schools, whether through immersion programs or traditional classes. Partnerships between K–16 institutions can integrate French across curricula, enabling students to see its applicability in disciplines such as engineering, sustainability, and the arts. Beyond formal education, community-based language learning through public libraries and cultural organizations can reach adult, nontraditional, and intergenerational learners in both in-person and virtual settings. The more inclusive and accessible these opportunities, the more likely French will thrive.

Language advocacy is both values- and data-driven, rooted in the belief that languages carry intrinsic worth and supported by evidence showing broad benefits—from cultural enrichment to economic opportunity. The key is a willingness to act: whether by engaging in direct conversation, using social media to champion bilingualism, volunteering in community language programs, or even pursuing policy reform. In this way, all of us can become language advocates, defending multilingualism and the use of additional languages in the United States and beyond. Educators, in particular, have a crucial role—promoting their programs within schools, campuses, and wider communities to sustain and grow the presence of French.

The most important thing to remember is that we can all practice language advocacy daily. Teachers advocate by guiding and inspiring learners in the classroom; parents and community members can champion French when talking with local school boards or cultural institutions; and scholars and writers shine a light on the language's history and ongoing relevance. This shared commitment recognizes that the future of French—indeed, of all languages—relies on each of us to keep it alive in our words, actions, and outreach.

Turning back to the broader tapestry of Francophonie in America, readers have traveled through diverse regions, from the Franco-American enclaves of New England and the Midwest to emerging communities in the Rust Belt and the South. These accounts reveal how language and culture adapt, forming a complex mosaic of American life. Through historical legacies and innovative responses, we see that French—and its variants—continues to influence everything from local customs and educational models to artistic expression, demonstrating remarkable resilience in the face of changing social landscapes.

At the core of these collected perspectives is an understanding that Francophonie is a dynamic phenomenon shaped by countless voices. It is not merely an echo of colonial ambitions but a living, adaptive resource that resonates with speakers of diverse backgrounds. Whether in Franco-Americans rediscovering their heritage or in Haitian and Senegalese communities bridging transatlantic experiences, each narrative reaffirms that language remains a transformative force capable of forging new identities and connections in the United States.

One of the most compelling insights emerging from these explorations is the need to challenge narrow definitions of Francophonie. The French language in America transcends a single tradition or region, instead revealing itself as a mosaic that combines historical foundations with contemporary realities. For example, enduring enclaves in New England and the Midwest preserve language through family traditions, architecture, and communal practices. Far from static, however, these communities continuously reinterpret and revitalize their cultural heritage—merging ancestral French with new linguistic encounters to form hybrid identities that reflect both past and future.

This same adaptability appears in diasporic communities whose members have brought French—and often Creole—to new destinations. Haitian and Senegalese enclaves exemplify resilience and ingenuity, using French as a vital means of communication, cultural expression, and identity building. In these settings, French and its variants serve not just as linguistic tools but also as repositories of memory and anchors of belonging. By capturing the interplay between remembrance and forward-thinking innovation, these stories show that Francophonie is very much alive, continually redefined by each new generation.

Throughout these accounts, education stands out as a key axis of renewal. Innovative bilingual and immersion programs, from early childhood settings to university-level curricula, give learners the chance to engage with French in ways that intersect with other fields, including engineering, sustainability, and the arts. By emphasizing practical connections to real-world endeavors, these initiatives ensure French remains relevant and exciting to new generations. They also underscore the possibility of bridging heritage and modernity, blending local cultural practices with forward-looking methodologies.

Yet, as many contributors remind us, education does not stop at classroom doors. Cultural centers, festivals, and community gatherings also play a vital role in sustaining Francophonie. They highlight the importance of creativity in nurturing a language, bringing traditions such as Cajun and Creole music into conversation with global audiences. These cultural expressions connect longstanding heritages to contemporary moments, preserving the past while inviting new forms of artistic experimentation.

Of course, no candid discussion of Francophonie can ignore challenges: linguistic assimilation, declining enrollments in heritage programs, and sociopolitical marginalization are formidable hurdles. Yet, the optimism woven through these stories is powerful. Through resilience, inventive cultural traditions, grassroots advocacy, and new educational models, communities are illuminating pathways to ensure that French does not merely endure but evolves. Despite pressures, Francophonie continues to inspire and unite across generations and regions.

Another prominent theme is the power of community engagement. Leaders and cultural practitioners across neighborhoods—from historic districts in New England to post-industrial Rust Belt towns—form alliances that transcend linguistic and cultural divides. Community centers host conversation groups, bilingual storytelling events, and open-mic nights, aligning tradition with contemporary issues. These grassroots projects make clear that language thrives where there is creative energy, mutual support, and a collective desire to build inclusive spaces.

Looking ahead, several key questions arise: What does it mean to be a French speaker in a predominantly English-speaking society? How can heritage language programs remain relevant and accessible to increasingly diverse populations? And what long-term strategies will protect the cultural legacies bound to French for future generations? While there are no easy answers, a call for broader definitions of Francophonie rings loud. Such an inclusive approach avoids lamenting assimilation as inevitable and instead embraces the infinite possibilities that arise when French is recognized as a living, continually transforming language in the United States.

Education, artistic expression, and community engagement form a system of renewal—one capable of reversing linguistic marginalization through cross-pollination of ideas and resources. Integrating local cultural practices into educational models energizes students' language learning, making it more immediate and compelling. Meanwhile, festivals and cultural events that juxtapose historical narratives with new forms of artistic expression create continuity between tradition and innovation, ensuring that French culture remains both rooted and relevant.

External support through public policy, funding, and international partnerships can also strengthen Francophonie's standing in the United States. Many contributors call for strategic investments in heritage language programs, highlighting the social, economic, and diplomatic benefits of a robust French-speaking population. Recognizing French as a valuable cultural and economic resource shifts it from being viewed solely as a relic of the past to a catalyst for global engagement, entrepreneurial ventures, and cross-cultural collaborations.

Scholars, educators, artists, and community leaders unite in these pages to offer personal perspectives, often rooted in family histories, diasporic experiences, and innovative pedagogical practices. Their voices show how every generation refashions Francophonie, weaving new layers into a centuries-old story. Far from static, French remains in dialogue with contemporary realities, global contexts, and the creative minds that embrace it.

Although historical legacies loom large, the message for tomorrow is equally vital: sustaining and expanding Francophonie is both a cultural imperative and a forward-thinking strategy. Demographic changes, new waves of migration, and evolving social contexts call for an approach that is flexible and inclusive. By celebrating the full spectrum of French expression—from traditional church choirs in small towns to the linguistic kaleidoscope of urban classrooms—we see that the language adapts continually, remaining a source of renewal and inspiration.

Ultimately, the future of French in the United States hinges on conscious decisions made by communities, institutions, and individuals. Our shared efforts to speak, teach, and innovate in French maintain and reshape its cultural significance. The notion of an "ongoing conversation" is central here: by actively choosing French in our homes, schools, workplaces, and social spaces, we confirm its enduring relevance and power to unite.

The narratives presented in these pages serve as a call to action, highlighting the combination of collaboration, creativity, and dedication necessary to revitalize Francophonie. Educators can build more inclusive, forward-thinking curricula; community organizers can sustain cultural traditions while embracing new influences; policymakers can enact measures that bolster language access; and artists can imagine fresh expressions of French culture. Each effort helps ensure that French remains a living force, shaping our collective future.

This journey through Francophonie is at once challenging and inspiring. It reveals how communities adapt, confront obstacles, and draw on cultural strengths to stay vibrant. By engaging a wide spectrum of voices—from historic Franco-American enclaves to newly arrived diasporas—we see that language is more than communication; it is an embodiment of identity, memory, and aspiration. Today, as we stand at the crossroads of past legacy and future possibility, the diverse threads of Francophonie weave together resilience, imagination, and solidarity.

May these reflections serve as both catalyst and prompt for all who appreciate the unifying power of linguistic and cultural diversity. The story of Francophonie in America remains open-ended—renewed each time we choose to speak, create, and connect in French. By carrying it forward collaboratively, we celebrate an inheritance that continues to evolve, full of potential to shape and enrich our shared tomorrow. In short, the future of French all around us truly depends on us—on our commitment, engagement, and activism in support of this enduring heritage and its ever-unfolding promise.

Appendix

Table 1: Number of French speakers at home by state and year between 2015 and 2023.

The states are listed in descending order of their respective number of French speakers at home in 2023.

State	2015	2016	2017	2018	2019	2020	2021	2022	2023
New York	134,768	143,251	126,476	145,979	112,415	129,735 *	132,797	142,480	134,108
California	130,605	131,901	132,930	123,226	123,607	129,503 *	126,371	129,585	127,674
Florida	121,635	105,816	110,117	102,143	101,296	105,110 *	103,125	104,481	106,907
Texas	72,224	74,430	63,666	77,739	76,884	74,893 *	71,795	92,675	75,976
Maryland	52,702	51,994	57,705	60,237	56,182	69,974 *	57,606	52,848	69,974
Louisiana	98,270	87,771	87,004	77,066	72,567	58,157 *	60,593	64,302	58,157
Massachusetts	58,206	50,585	56,693	52,086	49,442	76,909 *	42,251	44,129	41,957
Georgia	46,974	40,635	35,488	36,825	37,861	36,777 *	33,248	45,029	36,777
New Jersey	37,179	33,001	34,879	42,857	36,615	35,687 *	32,944	29,201	35,741
Illinois	39,313	36,612	34,441	32,783	34,281	35,390 *	38,133	34,573	34,463
Virginia	28,867	34,265	35,823	35,316	33,050	34,352 *	35,106	30,101	34,079
Pennsylvania	39,239	40,993	37,441	35,229	35,769	36,571 *	35,008	34,984	33,349
North Carolina	25,287	28,212	30,182	27,652	30,004	29,939 *	35,604	32,522	32,501
Maine	41,664	38,695	37,126	35,752	34,473	31,675 *	33,580	32,665	31,675
Ohio	24,900	24,012	24,785	27,702	27,884	26,457 *	27,200	30,013	27,399
Connecticut	24,269	24,959	19,420	26,330	21,757	23,056 *	18,990	20,545	24,269
Arizona	18,818	16,405	15,109	17,414	15,432	16,567 *	16,691	18,573	22,884
Washington	22,700	20,083	24,532	23,834	24,466	24,141 *	27,556	27,400	20,845
Michigan	19,343	21,895	22,397	21,009	20,066	21,522 *	17,894	24,852	19,053
Colorado	16,507	19,423	16,844	19,690	18,294	18,965 *	17,409	24,969	18,818
Indiana	8,171	10,728	10,970	12,801	14,199	18,120 *	19,989	19,818	18,120
New Hampshire	20,070	17,985	17,658	17,102	18,153	17,619 *	16,958	15,231	14,250
Minnesota	16,108	14,075	14,665	16,672	14,760	16,288 *	17,960	16,229	13,702
South Carolina	11,484	11,482	10,609	10,772	10,946	10,970 *	10,948	10,143	12,007
Missouri	10,932	11,814	10,008	12,330	10,474	11,836 *	14,217	10,769	11,690
Tennessee	14,280	10,870	8,331	9,806	11,182	10,625 *	10,258	12,798	11,629
Kentucky	6,027	6,065	9,921	6,627	9,855	9,006 *	9,790	8,158	11,182

Continued on next page

State	2015	2016	2017	2018	2019	2020	2021	2022	2023
D.C.	9,527	8,841	7,273	9,079	8,516	8,372 *	7,779	8,505*	11,0
Wisconsin	9,562	11,566	7,260	8,974	7,730	8,926 *	7,297	8,546	9,10
Utah	8,684	6,228	6,980	7,827	9,323	7,380 *	7,790	7,570	9,08
Nevada	9,117	7,934	7,897	9,726	8,713	8,661 *	7,205	7,769	8,72
Oregon	10,941	8,263	12,399	10,656	11,924	12,250 *	10,471	12,163	8,50
Iowa	6,182	4,976	6,908	9,773	9,157	8,256 *	7,025	7,263	8,50
Rhode Island	9,818	8,530	9,325	10,732	9,406*	9,545 *	7,244	6,896	8,35
Vermont	8,855	8,508	8,558	8,371	8,385	8,338 *	8,356	8,196	8,11
Nebraska	3,704	4,145	4,147	3,623	3,673	4,660 *	5,668	3,663	6,08
Alabama	6,307	6,110	7,873	8,255	5,805	6,543 *	5,673	5,203	5,50
Oklahoma	4,098	4,244	5,970	4,886	5,846	5,467 *	4,879	3,867	4,63
Kansas	4,971	4,487	3,695	3,961	4,716	3,976 *	3,254	4,884	4,5
New Mexico	5,427	5,118 *	5,041 *	4,580	4,030	4,040 *	4,014 *	2,066	4,2
Mississippi	3,889 *	3,983	3,758 *	3,452 *	3,876 *	3,969 *	3,771 *	3,585 *	3,84
Delaware	3,625	1,655	2,591	2,529 *	4,463	3,257 *	2,471	4,560	3,3
Hawaii	2,048	3,377 *	3,434 *	3,285 *	3,307 *	3,827 *	3,944 *	3,774 *	3,27
Arkansas	2,999	2,308	2,890 *	4,260	3,438 *	3,127 *	3,603 *	3,170 *	3,0
Idaho	3249 *	3,111 *	3,054 *	2,972 *	2,675 *	3,135 *	3,057 *	2,755	2,9
Alaska	1,402	2,365 *	2,034 *	1,969 *	1,664 *	2,100 *	2,115 *	2,114 *	2,10
North Dakota	1,165	1,471 *	1,709 *	2,122 *	2,012 *	2,087 *	2,039 *	2,248 *	1,94
Montana	1,764	1,770 *	1,797 *	1,983 *	1,955 *	1,763 *	1,880 *	1,920 *	1,90
West Virginia	2,768 *	2,389 *	2,300 *	2,194 *	2,538 *	2,367 *	2,225 *	2,032 *	1,87
Puerto Rico	1,320 *	1,186 *	1,178 *	1,224 *	1,131 *	1,067 *	1,193 *	1,509 *	1,29
Wyoming	1,007 *	1,159 *	1,292 *	1,328 *	1,131 *	1,072 *	1,155 *	976 *	1,17
South Dakota	928 *	846 *	906 *	900 *	1,140 *	1,174 *	955 *	904 *	1,02
Total USA	1,263,899	1,222,527	1,205,489	1,235,640	1,178,468	1,235,203	1,179,084	1,225,211	1,203

Table 1. Number of French speakers at home by state and year between 2015 and 2023. Source: American Community Survey, Languages Spoken at Home for the Population 5 Years and Over, 2015-2023. Jaumont, F. and Tabusse, M. Francophonie in the United States: Historical Roots, Cultural Diversity, and Future Perspectives.

The estimates marked with an asterisk are 5-year estimates. The others are 1-year estimates. 5-year estimates are displayed in this table when 1-year estimates are not available for the corresponding state and year in the American Community Survey.

Table 2: Number of French speakers at home in major US cities for 2015, 2019, and 2023.

Ville	2015	2019	2023
New York City, New York	84,762	71,783	88,631
Los Angeles City, California	25,378	20,969	21,845
Houston City, Texas	13,722	13,581	14,360
Washington City, DC	9,527	9,079	11,081
San Francisco City, California	10,555	7,608	10,460
Chicago City, Illinois	13,188	12,530	10,179
Philadelphia City, Pennsylvania	8,008	8,449	8,342
Dallas City, Texas	3,633	5,952	5,602
Phoenix City, Arizona	4,193	2,195	5,369
Austin City, Texas	4,070	5,195	5,203
Seattle City, Washington	3,498	4,370	4,195
Baltimore City, Maryland	4,163 *		
New Orleans City, Louisiana	3,963 *		
Jacksonville City, Miami	2,916 *		

Table 2. Number of French speakers at home in major US cities for 2015, 2019, and 2023. Source: American Community Survey, Languages Spoken at Home for the Population 5 Years and Over, 1-year estimates, 2015, 2019, 2023. Jaumont, F. and Tabusse, M. Francophonie in the United States: Historical Roots, Cultural Diversity, and Future Perspectives.

The estimates for Baltimore, New Orleans, and Jacksonville are only available for years prior to 2015, with 5-year estimates in the American Community Survey.

Table 3: Number of people with a French or French-Canadian ancestry: top 10 states in 2023.

State	French ancestry	French-Canadian ancestry
California	492,485	68,468
Massachusets	309,937	197,187
Florida	397,759	104,173
Louisiana	423,868	71,889
Texas	417,355	57,557
Michigan	295,679	116,743
New York	313,257	87,242
New Hampshire	132,567	100,347
Maine	143,318	81,764
Connecticut	133,400	82,162

Table 3. Number of people with a French or French-Canadian ancestry: top 10 states in 2023. Source: American Community Survey, People reporting ancestry, 5-year estimates, 2023. Jaumont, F. and Tabusse, M. Francophonie in the United States: Historical Roots, Cultural Diversity, and Future Perspectives.

Table 4: People reporting French or French-Canadian ancestry for each state of the USA, 2023.

State	French Ancestry	French-Canadian Ancestry
Alabama	55,143	7,408
Alaska	13,371	4,842
Arizona	132,793	28,067
Arkansas	35,844	4,267
California	492,485	68,468
Colorado	131,984	23,463
Connecticut	133,400	82,162
Delaware	12,220	3,034
District of Columbia	12,502	2,779
Florida	397,759	104,173
Georgia	112,967	21,532
Hawaii	18,510	2,441
Idaho	37,084	8,985
Illinois	170,052	27,065
Indiana	109,820	14,186
Iowa	48,140	6,125
Kansas	55,034	6,885
Kentucky	59,238	7,855
Louisiana	423,868	71,889
Maine	143,318	81,764
Maryland	73,144	14,788
Massachusetts	309,937	197,187
Michigan	295,679	116,743
Minnesota	142,443	42,491
Mississippi	48,504	5,847
Missouri	137,016	12,774
Montana	29,438	6,659
Nebraska	33,618	4,407

Continued on next page

State	French Ancestry	French-Canadian Ancestry
Nevada	49,207	10,917
New Hampshire	132,567	100,347
New Jersey	81,319	16,937
New Mexico	27,259	4,842
New York	313,257	87,242
North Carolina	142,501	30,185
North Dakota	19,069	5,375
Ohio	186,357	20,482
Oklahoma	51,113	5,766
Oregon	93,856	21,625
Pennsylvania	157,163	25,048
Puerto Rico	2,077	193
Rhode Island	76,199	37,400
South Carolina	82,685	16,350
South Dakota	16,378	3,074
Tennessee	92,841	14,380
Texas	417,355	57,557
Utah	46,429	7,060
Vermont	58,487	46,459
Virginia	118,898	28,529
Washington	170,907	32,049
West Virginia	20,461	2,257
Wisconsin	144,991	38,810
Wyoming	13,859	2,348
Total USA	**6,180,546**	**1,593,548**

Table 4. People reporting French or French-Canadian ancestry for each state of the USA, 2023. Source: American Community Survey, People reporting ancestry, 5-year estimates, 2023. Jaumont, F. and Tabusse, M. Francophonie in the United States: Historical Roots, Cultural Diversity, and Future Perspectives.

Table 5: Number of United States residents born in French-speaking countries, 2023.

Country	Residing in the USA[1]	% F.S. people[2]	F.S. people US[3]
Benin		34%	
Burkina Faso		24%	
Burundi		9%	
Cape Verde	31,441	11%	3,459
Cameroon	90,749	41%	37,207
Central African Republic		29%	
Comoros		26%	
Congo	43,066	61%	26,270
Ivory Coast	25,426	34%	8,644
Djibouti		50%	
Dem. Rep. of Congo	62,547	50%	31,274
Gabon		65%	
Gambia		20%	
Ghana	241,477	1%	2,415
Guinea		27%	
Guinea Bissau		15%	
Equatorial Guinea		29%	
Madagascar		26%	
Mali		17%	
Maurice		73%	
Mauritania		13%	
Mozambique		0.3%	
Niger		13%	
Rwanda		6%	
Sao Tome and Principe		20%	
Senegal	28,581	26%	7,431
Togo	36,951	41%	15,149
Chad		13%	

Continued on following page

Country	Residing in the USA[1]	% French-speaking[2]	F.S. people USA[3]
Andorra		70%	
Albania	106,957	1%	1,070
Armenia	104,153	0,3%	312
Austria	37,929	13%	4,931
Belgium	32,883	76%	24,991
Bosnia and Herzegovina	104,381	1%	1,044
Bulgaria	70,801	2%	1,416
Cyprus		7%	
Croatia	36,087	2%	722
Estonia		1%	
France	187,003	97%	181,392
Georgia	32,353	0,4%	129
Greece	113,433	7%	7,940
Hungary	62,703	1%	627
Ireland	117,219	13%	15,238
Kosovo		1%	
Latvia	20,081	1%	201
Luxembourg		92%	
North Macedonia	29,314	2%	586
Moldova	47,498	1%	475
Montenegro		2%	
Poland	382,844	3%	11,485
Czech Republic		2%	
Romania	152,470	12%	18,296
Serbia	39,571	4%	1,582
Slovakia		2%	
Slovenia		2%	
Switzerland	40,589	67%	27,194
Ukraine	468,780	0,1%	469

Continued on following page

1. The second column displays the number of residents of the USA born in the corresponding country in column 1. *Source: American Community Survey, Place of Birth of the Foreign-Born Population in the USA in 2023, 1-year estimates, 2023.*

Country	Residing in the USA[1]	% French-speaking[2]	F.S. people USA[3]
Egypt	225,665	3%	6,770
United Arab Emirates	26,444	3%	793
Lebanon	146,143	38%	55,534
Morocco	109,370	36%	39,373
Tunisia		52%	
Haiti	777,845	42%	326,695
Canada	828,396	29%	240,235
Cambodia	151,167	3%	4,535
Laos	161,116	3%	4,833
Thailand	252,628	1%	2,526
Vietnam	1,365,841	1%	1,366
Algeria	42,129	33%	13,903
Germany	520,418	15%	78,063
Colombia	1,049,821	0.01%	105
Denmark	25,005	8%	2,000
Spain	126,067	12%	15,128
Finland		8%	
Israel	133,393	6%	8,004
Italy	295,000	20%	59,000
Norway	21,321	3%	640
The Netherlands	82,469	19%	15,669
Portugal	160,729	25%	40,182
The U.K.	693,465	16%	110,954
Russia	415,809	0.4%	1,663
Sweden	43,413	8%	3,473

Table 5. Number of United States residents born in French-speaking countries, 2023. Jaumont, F. and Tabusse, M. Francophonie in the United States: Historical Roots, Cultural Diversity, and Future Perspectives.

2. Percent of French-speaking people in a given country. Source: Marcoux, R.; Richard, L.; & Wolff, A. *Estimation des populations francophones dans le monde en 2022. Sources et démarches méthodologiques.* Québec, 2022, Observatoire démographique et statistique de l'espace francophone, Université Laval.

3. The authors' calculations are based on the strong assumption that the percentage of French speakers among US residents born in a given country is approximately the same as the percentage of French speakers in that country.

Table 6: List of Alliances Françaises in the United States in alphabetical order

Alliance Française of Aiken	*South Carolina*
Alliance Française of Albuquerque	*New Mexico*
Alliance Française of Annapolis	*Maryland*
Alliance Française of Atlanta	*Georgia*
Alliance Française of Austin	*Texas*
Alliance Française of Baltimore	*Maryland*
Alliance Française of Berkeley	*California*
Alliance Française of Birmingham	*Alabama*
Alliance Française of Boise	*Idaho*
Alliance Française of Bonita Springs	*Florida*
French Library Alliance Française of Boston & Cambridge	*Massachusetts*
Alliance Française of Buffalo	*New York*
Alliance Française of Central Iowa	*Iowa*
Alliance Française of Charleston	*South Carolina*
Alliance Française of Charlotte	*North Carolina*
Alliance Française of Charlottesville	*Virginia*
Alliance Française of Chicago	*Illinois*
Alliance Française of Cincinnati	*Ohio*
Alliance Française of Columbia	*South Carolina*
Alliance Française of Columbus	*Ohio*
Alliance Française of Dallas	*Texas*
Alliance Française of Denver	*Colorado*

Alliance Française of Detroit (French Institute of Michigan)	*Michigan*
Alliance Française of Doylestown & Bucks County	*Pennsylvania*
Alliance Française of DuPage	*Illinois*
Alliance Française of El Paso	*Texas*
Alliance Française of Frederick	*Maryland*
Alliance Française of Fresno	*California*
Alliance Française of Gainesville	*Florida*
Alliance Française of Grand Rapids	*Michigan*
Alliance Française of Greater Orlando	*Florida*
Alliance Française of Greater Phoenix	*Arizona*
Alliance Française of Greenwich	*Connecticut*
Alliance Française of Grosse Pointe	*Michigan*
Alliance Française of Hartford	*Connecticut*
Alliance Française of Hawai'i	*Hawaii*
Alliance Française of Houston	*Texas*
Alliance Française of Indianapolis	*Indiana*
Alliance Française of Jackson	*Mississippi*
Alliance Française of Jacksonville	*Florida*
Alliance Française of Kalamazoo	*Michigan*
Alliance Française of Kansas City	*Kansas*
Alliance Française of Knoxville	*Tennessee*
Alliance Française of Lafayette	*Louisiana*
Alliance Française of Lake Champlain Region	*Vermont*
Alliance Française of Las Vegas	*Nevada*
Alliance Française of Lansing (Michigan Capital Area)	*Michigan*
Alliance Française of Los Angeles	*California*
Alliance Française of Louisville	*Kentucky*

Alliance Française of Lynchburg	*Virginia*
Alliance Française of Maine	*Maine*
Alliance Française of Manchester (Franco-American Center)	*New Hampshire*
Alliance Française of Memphis	*Tennessee*
Alliance Française of Miami Metro	*Florida*
Alliance Française of Milwaukee	*Wisconsin*
Alliance Française of Minneapolis	*Minnesota*
Alliance Française of Mobile	*Alabama*
Alliance Française of Montclair	*New Jersey*
Alliance Française of Monterey	*California*
Alliance Française of Napa Valley	*California*
Alliance Française of Naples	*Florida*
Alliance Française of Nashville	*Tennessee*
Alliance Française of New Haven	*Connecticut*
Alliance Française of New Orleans	*Louisiana*
Alliance Française of New York (L'Alliance New York)	*New York*
Alliance Française of Newport	*Rhode Island*
Alliance Française of Norfolk (Hampton Roads)	*Virginia*
Alliance Française of North Shore	*Illinois*
Alliance Française of Northwestern Connecticut	*Connecticut*
Alliance Française of Oklahoma City	*Oklahoma*
Alliance Française of Omaha	*Nebraska*
Alliance Française of Pasadena	*California*
Alliance Française of Philadelphia	*Pennsylvania*
Alliance Française of Piedmont	*South Carolina*
Alliance Française of Pittsburgh	*Pennsylvania*
Alliance Française of Portland	*Oregon*

Alliance Française of Princeton	*New Jersey*
Alliance Française of Providence	*Rhode Island*
Alliance Française of Raleigh-Durham-Chapel Hill	*North Carolina*
Alliance Française of Reno	*Nevada*
Alliance Française of Richmond	*Virginia*
Alliance Française of Riviera Californienne	*California*
Alliance Française of Rochester	*New York*
Alliance Française of Sacramento	*California*
Alliance Française of Saint Joseph (Missouri Western State College)	*Missouri*
Alliance Française of Saint Louis	*Missouri*
Alliance Française of Salt Lake City	*Utah*
Alliance Française of San Antonio	*Texas*
Alliance Française of San Diego	*California*
Alliance Française of San Francisco	*California*
Alliance Française of San Juan	*Puerto Rico*
Alliance Française of Santa Rosa	*California*
Alliance Française of Sarasota	*Florida*
Alliance Française of Seattle	*Washington*
Alliance Française of Silicon Valley	*California*
Alliance Française of Tallahassee	*Florida*
Alliance Française of Toledo	*Ohio*
Alliance Française of Topeka	*Kansas*
Alliance Française of Tucson	*Arizona*
Alliance Française of Tulsa	*Oklahoma*
Alliance Française of Washington DC	*District of Columbia*
Alliance Française of Westchester	*New York*

Total: 102 as of 03/11/2025

References

Adichie, C. N. (2009). *The danger of a single story* [Video]. TED Conferences.
Adichie, C. N. (2016). *Le danger d'une histoire unique*. Facing History & Ourselves.
American Community Survey (ACS). (2010). *Language use in the United States: American Community Survey reports*. U.S. Census Bureau.
American Community Survey (ACS). (2012). *Statistical abstract of the United States: Higher education enrollment in languages other than English (1970 to 2009)*. U.S. Census Bureau.
American Community Survey (ACS). (2019). *Demographic data on ancestry origins and languages spoken at home*. U.S. Census Bureau.
American Community Survey (ACS). (2023a). *1-year estimates: Detailed languages spoken at home by English-speaking ability for the population 5 years and over*. U.S. Census Bureau.
American Community Survey (ACS). (2023b). *People reporting ancestry*. U.S. Census Bureau.
American Community Survey (ACS). (2023c). *Place of birth of the foreign-born population in the United States: France*. U.S. Census Bureau.
American Community Survey (ACS). (2023d). *1-year estimates: People reporting ancestry*. U.S. Census Bureau.
American Community Survey (ACS). (2023e). *2023 American Community Survey, 1-year estimates, people reporting ancestry*. U.S. Census Bureau.
Ancelet, B. (1988). A perspective on teaching the "problem language" in Louisiana. *The French Review, 61*(3), 345–356.
Ancelet, B. J. (2007). Negotiating the mainstream: The Creoles and Cajuns in Louisiana. *The French Review, 80*(6), 1235–1255.
AXIS International Academy. (2024). *History of AXIS – About – AXIS International Academy*. [Website at axiscolorado.org]
Bâ, M. (1981). *So long a letter*. Heinemann.
Baudry, R. (1998). *Graal et littérature d'aujourd'hui*. Terre de Brume.
Baudry, R. (2008). *Le mythe de Merlin*. Terre de Brume.

Bélanger, D. C. *Franco-Americans, the Sentinelle Affair and Quebec*. Quebec History, Marianopolis College.

Bélanger, D. C. *French Canadian emigration to the United States 1840–1930*. Quebec History, Marianopolis College.

Bishop O'Leary to officiate at Leominster dedication, Sunday Telegram (Worcester), September 9, 1934. (n.d.). [Newspaper article, no author listed]

Blanquer, J.-M. (n.d.). *Recommandations pédagogiques*. Ministère de l'Éducation Nationale, de l'Enseignement supérieur et de la Recherche.

Blyth, C. (1998). The sociolinguistic situation of Cajun French: The effects of language shift and language loss. In A. Valdman (Ed.), *French and Creole in Louisiana* (pp. 25–46). Plenum Press.

Bodanza, M. C. (2019). *Risk takers & history makers: The story of Leominster*. North Hill Press.

Bosman, J. (2007, August 22). French gains foothold on New York City's dual-language map. *The New York Times*.

Bourdieu, P. (1984). *Distinction: A social critique of the judgment of taste* (R. Nice, Trans.). Harvard University Press. (Original work published 1979)

Bourdieu, P., & Passeron, J.-C. (1964). *Les héritiers: Les étudiants et la culture*. Les Éditions de Minuit.

Boxberger, A. M., & Brasseaux, E. (2023). Overview of the FY 24 executive budget. Louisiana Legislative Fiscal Office.

Brasseaux, C. (2005). *French, Cajun, Creole, Houma: A primer on Francophone Louisiana*. Louisiana State University Press.

Brault, G. (1986). *The French-Canadian heritage in New England*. University Press of New England.

Brothers, T. (2006). *Louis Armstrong's New Orleans*. Norton.

Brunot, F. (1936). *La pensée et la langue: Méthode, principes et plan d'une théorie nouvelle du langage appliquée au français*. Masson et Cie.

Caldwell, W. (2007). Taking Spanish outside the box: A model for integrating service learning into foreign language study. *Foreign Language Annals, 40*(3), 463–471.

Camus, A. (1972). *La chute*. Gallimard. (Original work published 1956)

Candelier, M. (n.d.). « La didactique intégrée des langues – apprendre une langue avec d'autres langues ? ». Association pour le Développement de l'Enseignement Bi/plurilingue.

Cartier, A. (1999). *The Franco-American of New England: A history*. Assurance and Institut Français of Assumption College.

Centenaire franco-américain, le 28 et 29 mai, 1949 à Worcester: Programme-souvenir. (1949). Imprimerie du "Travailleur."

Clément, A. (1948, September 4). Un centenaire franco-américain. *Le Devoir*, p. 14.

Clerk, N., & Bergeron, C. (n.d.). Church architecture. *The Canadian Encyclopedia.* [No further details provided]

Clifford, J., & Reisinger, D. (2019). *Community-based language learning: A framework for educators*. Georgetown University Press.

Climax in Leominster: French Catholics omit offerings: Their first open act of rebellion, The Telegram (Leominster), December 25, 1899. (n.d.). [Newspaper article, no author listed]

Colorado QuickFacts from the US Census Bureau. (2023). *Quickfacts.census.gov.*

Comité d'orientation franco-américain. (1949). Notre vie franco-américaine. *Le Travailleur*, June 2, p. 1; June 9, pp. 1, 4; June 16, pp. 1, 3.

Conseil de l'Europe. (2021). *Cadre européen commun de référence pour les langues: Apprendre, enseigner, évaluer: Volume complémentaire.* Conseil de l'Europe.

Coppel, A. (2007). Les Français et la norme linguistique: une passion singulière. *Cosmopolitiques, 16*, 157–168.

Cormier, R. (2000). *Portrait of a parish: Saint Cecilia's Church of Leominster, MA*. [Blog Post].

Début de la semaine de la presse. (1949, June 28). *L'Impartial*, pp. 1, 6.

Dei, G. J. S. (2002). Learning culture, spirituality and local knowledge: Implications for African schooling. *International Review of Education, 48*(5), 335–360.

Désilets, A. (1949, May 26). Le fossé de ligne... *Le Travailleur*, pp. 1, 6.

Désormeaux. (1949, June 2). Echos de notre centenaire. *Le Travailleur*, pp. 1–2.

Dietrich, S., & Hernandez, E. (2022). *Language use in the United States: 2019. American Community Survey Reports* (pp. 1–37). U.S. Census Bureau.

Digital Collections, American Folklife Center, Library of Congress. (n.d.). [Website or resource]

Dion-Lévesque, R. (1949, June 28). A Ferdinand Gagnon. *L'Impartial*, p. 2.
Diop, C. A. (2000). *Les fondements économiques et culturels d'un État fédéral d'Afrique noire*. Présence Africaine. (Original work published 1974)
Dominguez, V. R. (1993). *White by definition: Social classification in Creole Louisiana*. Rutgers University Press.
Dunn, J. (2023). Job creation is essential to Louisiana francophone movement. *Le Louisianais*.
Désormeaux. (1949, June 2). Echos de notre centenaire. *Le Travailleur*, pp. 1–2.
Freeman, S. L., & Pelletier, R. J. (n.d.). *Manuel du professeur pour introduire les études franco-américaines. Initiating Franco-American studies: A handbook for teachers.* University of Maine.
French Culture. (2022). *French for all initiative, French for all – French Culture*. [Website]
French Heritage Language Program. Villa Albertine. (n.d.). [Website]
García, O. (2009). *Bilingual education in the 21st century: A global perspective*. Wiley-Blackwell.
Garza, R. T., & Herringer, L. G. (1987). Social identity: A multidimensional approach. *The Journal of Social Psychology, 127*(3), 299–308.
Gascoigne Lally, C. (2001). Service/community learning and foreign language teaching methods: An application. *Active Learning in Higher Education, 2*(1), 53–63.
Gide, A. (1967). *Les nourritures terrestres*. Le Livre de Poche.
Gide, A. (1972). *La symphonie pastorale*. Folio.
Ginn, V., & Tairov, J. (2024). *Louisiana's comeback: A tax plan for our brighter future*. Pelican Institute for Public Policy.
Goldberg, D. (1983). Ku Klux Klan in the Montachusett Area. [Pamphlet in Leominster Library Special Collections]
Goodreads. (2024). *The obstacle is the way: The timeless art of turning trials into triumphs*.
Gosnell, J. K. (2018). *Franco-America in the making: The Creole nation within*. University of Nebraska Press.
Grim, F. (2010). Giving authentic opportunities to second language learners: A look at a French service-learning project. *Foreign Language Annals, 43*(4), 605–623.

Grim, F. (2011a). J'apprends et j'enseigne le français: Etudiants de français dans leur communauté. *French Review, 85*(2), 1132–1140.

Grim, F. (2011b). Socio-cultural sensitivities and service-learning. *Modern Journal of Language Teaching Methods, 1*(1), 15–19.

Grim, F. (2017). Experiential learning for L2 students: Steps for a service-learning program in a local community. In M. Bloom & C. Gascoigne (Eds.), *Creating experiential learning opportunities for language learners: Acting locally while thinking globally*. Multilingual Matters.

Grim, F. (2022). Teaching pronunciation through community outreach. *Journal of Linguistics and Language Teaching (JLLT), 13*(1).

Grosjean, F. (n.d.). What is translanguaging? *Psychology Today*. [Blog post]

Hagège, C. (1996). *Le français: Histoire d'un combat*. Éditions Michel Hagège.

Hamayan, E., Genesee, F., & Cloud, N. (2013). *Dual language instruction from A to Z: Practical guidance for teachers and administrators*. Heinemann.

Hirsch, A. R., & Logsdon, J. (Eds.). (1992). *Creole New Orleans: Race and Americanization*. LSU Press.

Holiday, R. (2014). *The obstacle is the way: The timeless art of turning trials into triumphs*. Penguin Random House.

Hurt, E. (2023, June 19). Why Louisiana's economy keeps ranking so poorly. *Axios New Orleans*.

Intercultural Development Research Association. (2000, January). Why is it important to maintain the native language? *IDRA Newsletter*.

Irving, D. (2023). The economic returns of foreign language learning. RAND.

Iser, W. (1985). *L'acte de lecture: Théorie de l'effet esthétique* (2nd ed.). Mardaga.

Jalbert, E. L. (1949, July 1). A Ferdinand Gagnon. *L'Impartial*, p. 2.

Jaumont, F. (2017). *The bilingual revolution: The future of education is in two languages*. TBR Books.

Jaumont, F., & Ross, J. (2014). French heritage language communities in the United States. In T. Wiley, J. K. Peyton, D. Christian, S. C. Moore, & N. Liu (Eds.), *Handbook of heritage and community languages in the United States* (pp. 101–110). Routledge.

Jaumont, F., Ross, J., & Le Dévédec, B. (2017). Institutionalization of French heritage language education in U.S. school systems. In O. E.

Kagan, M. M. Carreira, & C. H. Chik (Eds.), *The Routledge handbook of heritage language education* (pp. xx–xx). Routledge.

Jaumont, F., Ross, J., Schulz, J., Dunn, J., & Ducrey, L. (2016). Sustainability of French heritage language education in the United States. In *Handbook of research and practice in heritage language education* (pp. 1–18). Springer International Handbooks of Education.

Kamkwamba, W., & Mealer, B. (2009). *The boy who harnessed the wind: Creating currents of electricity and hope.* HarperCollins.

Klinger, T. A. (2003). Language labels and language use among Cajuns and Creoles in Louisiana. *University of Pennsylvania Working Papers in Linguistics, 9*(2), 77–90.

Koch, C., & Hooks, B. (2020). *Believe in people: Bottom-up solutions for a top-down world.* St. Martin's Press.

Kramsch, C., & Whiteside, A. (2008). Language ecology in multilingual settings: Toward a theory of symbolic competence. *Applied Linguistics, 29*(4), 645–671.

La vie franco-américaine: Centenaire franco-américain 1849–1949. (1950). Manchester: Comité de la survivance française en Amérique.

Labrosse, C. (2021). *Pour une langue sans sexisme.* Fides.

Lacasse, A. (1949, July 1). Importance de la presse franco-américaine. *L'Impartial*, p. 2.

Lacroix, P. (2018) Franco-American Religious Controversies: The Flint Affair. Retrieved September 4, 2024, from querythepast.com

Lacroix, P. (2019). Promises to keep: French Canadians as revolutionaries and refugees, 1775–1800. *Journal of Early American History, 9*(1), 59–82.

Lacroix, P. (2022). The lost wor(l)ds of Franco-American. *Le Forum, 44*(2), 8–10.

Ladson-Billings, G. (1995). Toward a theory of culturally relevant pedagogy. *American Educational Research Journal, 32*, 465–491.

Lafayette Convention & Visitors Commission. (2012). *Essentials* [Brochure].

Lagrée, M.-C. (2016). Montaigne on self. In P. Desan (Ed.), *The Oxford handbook of Montaigne* (Oxford Handbooks). Oxford University Press.

Larocque, F. (2024, July 13). The grind: A Franco-Ontarian's perspective on minority language rights. *The Rover*.

Lave, J., & Wenger, E. (1991). *Situated learning: Legitimate peripheral participation.* Cambridge University Press.

Laye, C. (1954). *L'enfant noir (The dark child)*. Heinemann.
Levine, B. (Director). (2003). *Waking up French (Réveil): The repression and renaissance of the French of New England* [Documentary film].
Lindner, T. (2008). *Attitudes toward Cajun French and international French in South Louisiana: A study of high school students* [Doctoral dissertation, Louisiana State University]. ProQuest Dissertations & Theses.
Lindner, T. (2013). Access to French education and attitudes toward international French and Cajun French among South Louisiana high school students. *French Review, 86*(3), 458–472.
Lo Bianco, J., & Aliani, R. (2010). *Language learning from the inside: Learners' voices and public policy ambitions*. Multilingual Matters.
Loebe, A. Y. (2004). *Educational leadership for change—stories by six Latina elementary school principals* [Doctoral dissertation, University of Arizona]. ProQuest Dissertations & Theses.
Loughrin-Sacco, S. J. (1996). Redefining the role of the foreign language department chair: The chair as fundraiser, program developer, and entrepreneur. *ADFL Bulletin, 27*(2), 39–43.
Louisiana Budget Project. (2023). *The 2023 legislature: Missed opportunities*.
McLeod, W., & O'Rourke, B. (2015). 'New speakers' of Gaelic: Perceptions of linguistic authenticity and appropriateness. *Applied Linguistics Review, 6*(2), 151–172.
Maurer, Bruno, et Christian Puren. « Cinquième partie : Vers une méthodologie plurilingue intégrée (MPI) ». In CECR : Par ici la sortie ! Paris : Édition des archives contemporaines, 2019.
Meester, P. (de). (1982). *Notes inchoa tives pour une didactique du latin*. Presses Universitaires de Lubumbashi.
Midlo Hall, G. (1992). *Africans in colonial Louisiana: The development of Afro-Creole culture in the eighteenth century*. LSU Press.
Monénembo, T. (2008). *Le roi de Kahel (The king of Kahel)*. Éditions du Seuil.
Morfit, R. (1949, May 26). Fin ou commencement? *Le Travailleur*, p. 1.
Mudimbe, V. Y. (1988). *The invention of Africa*. Indiana University Press.
Mukasonga, S. (2012). *Notre-Dame du Nil (Our Lady of the Nile)*. Éditions du Seuil.
Nickerson, K. (1970). *150 years of education in Maine: Sesqui-centennial (1820–1970) history of Maine's educational system and the growth and*

development of the Maine State Department of Education. State of Maine Department of Education.

Nolin, L. A. (1949, July 1). Hommage à Ferdinand Gagnon. *L'Impartial*, p. 2.

Nsafou, L. (2017). *Comme un million de papillons*. Éditions Cambourakis.

O'Rourke, B., & Pujolar, J. (2013). From native speakers to "new speakers": Problematizing nativeness in language revitalization contexts. *Histoire Épistémologie Langage, 35*(2), 47–67.

O'Rourke, B., & Pujolar, J. (2015). New speakers and processes of new speakerness across time and space. *Applied Linguistics Review, 6*(2), 145–150.

O'Rourke, B., & Walsh, J. (2015). New speakers of Irish: Shifting boundaries across time and space. *International Journal of the Sociology of Language, 231*, 63–83.

O'Rourke, B., Pujolar, J., & Ramallo, F. (2015). New speakers of minority languages: The challenging opportunity—Foreword. *Applied Linguistics Review, 6*(2), 1–20.

Oyono, F. (1956). *Le vieux nègre et la médaille*. Julliard.

Paré, P. (1979). A history of Franco-American journalism. In R. S. Albert (Ed.), *A Franco-American overview* (Vol. I). National Assessment and Dissemination Center for Bilingual/Bicultural Education.

Pelican Institute for Public Policy. (2023). *Citizen's guide to the Louisiana budget*.

Pérochon, E. (1930). *Contes des cent un matins*. Delagrave.

Perreault, R. B. (1996). The Franco-American press: An historical overview. In C. Quintal (Ed.), *Steeples and smokestacks: A collection of essays on the Franco-American experience in New England*. Éditions de l'Institut français – Assumption College.

Pinar, W. F. (1991). Understanding curriculum as a racial text. *Scholars and Educator, 15*(1), 9–21.

Pinette, S. (2017). Un "étonnant mutisme": L'invisibilité des Franco-Américains aux Etats-Unis. In J. E. Price (Ed.), *La jeune francophonie américaine: Langue et culture chez les jeunes d'héritage francophone aux Etats-Unis d'Amérique*. L'Harmattan.

Poarch, G. J., & Bialystok, E. (2015). Bilingualism as a model for multitasking. *Developmental Review, 35*, 113–124.

Podea, I. (1950). Quebec to "Little Canada": The coming of the French Canadians to New England in the nineteenth century. *The New England Quarterly*.

Pottie-Sherman, Y. (2018). Rust Belt placemaking: Migrants and the transformation of declining towns. *Journal of Urban Affairs, 40*(4), 442–455.

Potvin, R. (2023). The Franco-American parishes of New England: Past, present and future. *American Catholic Studies*.

Public Affairs Research Council of Louisiana. (2017a). *New patterns on the spending side: As the state budget takes shape, a new look is needed for TOPS, the Medicaid expansion and appropriations policy*.

Public Affairs Research Council of Louisiana. (2017b). *The future is now: Improved tax policies, a better business climate and an answer to the fiscal cliff are still possible this session*.

Pujolar, J., & Puigdevall, M. (2015). Linguistic mudes: How to become a new speaker in Catalonia. *Applied Linguistics Review, 6*(2), 167–187.

Quintal, C. (1997). La Fédération féminine franco-américaine ou Comment les Franco-Américaines sont entrées de plain-pied dans le mouvement de la survivance. *Francophonies d'Amérique, 7*, 177–191.

Reed Marshall, T., & Rodick, W. H. (2023). The search for more complex racial and ethnic representation in grade school books. *EdTrust*.

Reisinger, D. (2022). Online intercultural exchanges in a French for the professions course. *Global Advances in Business Communication, 10*(1), Article 3.

Rhodes, N. C., & Pufahl, I. (2010). *Foreign language teaching in U.S. schools: Results of a national survey*. Center for Applied Linguistics.

Richard, Z. (n.d.). *Réveille* [Song/album].

Robert, A. (1949, June 23). La pénétration canadienne-française aux Etats-Unis. *Le Travailleur*, p. 4.

Roby, Y. (2007). *Histoire d'un rêve brisé? Les Canadiens français aux États-Unis*. Éditions du Septentrion.

Romaine, S. (2006). Planning for the survival of linguistic diversity. *Language Policy, 5*, 441–473.

Ross, J., & Jaumont, F. (2012). Building bilingual communities: New York's French bilingual revolution. In O. García, Z. Zakharia, & G. Bahar Otcu (Eds.), *Bilingual community education and multilingualism* (pp. 232–246). Multilingual Matters.

Ross, J., & Jaumont, F. (2013). French language vitality in the US. *Heritage Language Journal, 10*(3), 316–317.

Ross, J., & Jaumont, F. (2015). Maintien et transmission de l'héritage linguistique chez les francophones des États-Unis. *Québec français, 174*, 43–44.

Sacco, S. J. (2024, July 29). *Grant-getting: A strategy for world language departments to survive and thrive in the post-pandemic era of university program elimination* [Conference presentation]. AATF Annual Convention, San Diego, CA, United States.

Sacco, S. J., & Diercks, M. (2024). *Creating an interdisciplinary Francophone African curriculum for K–16 educators and students*. U.S. Department of Education's Fulbright-Hays Group Projects Abroad Program.

Salmon, C. (2019). Immigrations francophones d'hier et d'aujourd'hui en Franco-Américanie. *Revue de l'Université de Moncton, 50*(1–2), 379–412.

Sanchez, J., Thornton, B., & Usinger, J. (2009). Increasing the ranks of minority principals. *Educational Leadership, 67*(2).

Schecter, S. R. (2015). Identity and multilingualism. In J. Cenoz & D. Gorter (Eds.), *The Routledge handbook of bilingualism and multilingualism* (pp. 203–215). Routledge.

Schmidt, S. R. (2011). Theorizing place: Students' navigation of place outside the classroom. *The Journal of Curriculum Theorizing, 27*(1), 20–35.

Schulz, J. (2012). Innovative approaches for preventing and reversing heritage language decline and loss. In *Handbook of research and practice in heritage language education* (pp. 1–18). Springer International Handbooks of Education.

Semple, K. (2013, June 8). City's newest immigrant enclaves, from Little Guyana to Meokjagolmok. *The New York Times*.

Seneca. (2018). *Tragedies* (J. G. Fitch, Ed. & Trans.). Harvard University Press. (Original work written ca. 1st century CE)

Senghor, L. S. (1962). Le français, langue de culture. *Esprit, Novembre*, 837–844.

Silvia, P., Jr. (1979). The "Flint Affair": French-Canadian struggle for survivance. *The Catholic Historical Review*.

Smith, M. A. (2015). Who is a legitimate French speaker? The Senegalese in Paris and the crossing of linguistic and social borders. *French Cultural Studies, 26*(3).

Smith, M. A. (2017). French heritage language learning: A site of multilingual identity formation, cultural exploration, and creative expression in New York City. *Critical Multilingualism Studies, 5*(2), 10–38.

Smith, M. A. (2019). *Senegal abroad: Linguistic borders, racial formations, and diasporic imaginaries*. University of Wisconsin Press.

Smith, M. A. (2021). Enunciating power: Amanda Gorman and my battle to claim my voice. *Yes! Magazine*.

Smowl Tech. (2023, June 22). Disruptive education: Definition, features, benefits and disadvantages. [Blog post]

Soroosh, M., Chik, C. H., & Jaumont, F. (2022). French in Greater Los Angeles: Challenges and opportunities. In C. H. Chik & M. Carreira (Eds.), *Multilingual La La Land: Language use in sixteen Greater Los Angeles communities*. Routledge.

Stein-Smith, K., & Jaumont, F. (2023). *French all around us. French language and Francophone culture in the United States*. CALEC – TBR Books.

Tchoumi, B. (2020a). The leadership of the marginalized: A literature review. *Journal of Educational Leadership in Action, 7*(3).

Tchoumi, B. (2020b). *Why do you "talk" like that? The accented voices of Black African immigrants in school leadership* [Doctoral dissertation, Morgan State University]. ProQuest Dissertations & Theses.

Tchoumi, B. (2024a). Enseigner sous des angles multiples: Modèles d'adaptation et d'appropriation pédagogiques [Paper presentation]. AATF Annual Conference, San Diego, CA, United States.

Tchoumi, B. (2024b). *Regards sans complexe: Vingt-six mots pour célébrer l'enfant africain. Uniquely you: A celebration of the African child*. TBR Books.

Tétu, J.-F. (1997). *Qu'est-ce que la Francophonie ?* Hachette.

The Public Affairs Research Council of Louisiana. (2017a). *New patterns on the spending side: As the state budget takes shape, a new look is needed for TOPS, the Medicaid expansion and appropriations policy*.

The Public Affairs Research Council of Louisiana. (2017b). *The future is now: Improved tax policies, a better business climate and an answer to the fiscal cliff are still possible this session*.

The task force on structural changes in budget and tax policy. (2017, January 27). *Louisiana's opportunity: Comprehensive solutions for a sustainable tax and spending structure.*

Thiong'o, N. (1986). *Decolonising the mind: The politics of language in African literature.* Heinemann.

Tilton, S., & Bazenet, R. (n.d.). Documenting the Francophone contribution to American music. [Unpublished].

Trudeau, R. (1826). Expatriation. In *Mes tablettes: Mémoires de ce que je croirai assez intéressant pour en conserver le souvenir (1820–1848)* (Vol. II, pp. 223–224). Bibliothèque et Archives nationales du Québec.

Valdman, A. (2000). Standardization or laissez-faire in linguistic revitalization: The case of Cajun French. *Indiana University Working Papers in Linguistics, 2*, 127–138.

Valdman, A. (2010). French in the USA. In K. Potowski (Ed.), *Language diversity in the USA* (pp. 110–127). Cambridge University Press.

Vermette, D. (2019). When the influx of French-Canadian immigrants struck fear into Americans. *Smithsonian.*

Verrette, A. (1949, June 28). Pour honorer un précurseur. *L'Impartial*, pp. 1–2.

Vitiello, J., & Kerman, S. (2022/2024). *La Francophonie des Amériques: Conversation and community* [Dialogue chapter; publication details not provided].

Vogel, S., & García, O. (2017). Translanguaging and the bilingual brain: Implications for educational research. *Journal of Multilingual Education Research, 8*(1), 1–10.

Wade, M. (1950). The French parish and survivance in nineteenth-century New England. *The Catholic Historical Review.*

Walker, W. E. (2000). Policy analysis: A systematic approach to supporting policymaking in the public sector. *Journal of Multi-Criteria Decision Analysis, 9*, 11–27.

Ward, R. K. (1997). The French language in Louisiana law and legal education: A requiem. *Louisiana Law Review, 57.*

Watterson, K. (2011). *The attitudes of African American students towards the study of foreign languages and cultures* [Doctoral dissertation, Louisiana State University]. ProQuest Dissertations & Theses.

Webinar: Fulbright-Hays Group Projects Abroad technical assistance. (2023). [Online webinar].

Westerman, A. (2012, August 23). The future of French in Louisiana. *WRKF: All Things Considered.*
Williams, I., & Loeb, S. (2012). Race and the principal pipeline: The prevalence of minority principals in light of a primarily white teacher workforce. *Center for Education Policy Analysis.*
Wong, D. (2021, July 4). Les derniers Franco-Américains. *ICI Radio-Canada.*
Zeiger, S. *Entangling Alliances: Foreign War Brides and American Soldiers in the Twentieth Century,* 1996.
Zéphir, F. (2004). *The Haitian Americans.* Greenwood Press.

Legal References

Acts and contracts in French language; effect, 1 L.R.S. §51. (n.d.).
Advertisements to be in English; duplication in French permitted, 42 L.R.S. §204. (n.d.).
Amount of fees; credit or refund; duration of license; veteran designation; disabled veteran designation; university logo; "I'm a Cajun" designation; needs accommodation designation; autism spectrum disorder designation; disbursement of funds; renewal by mail or electronic commerce of Class "D" or "E" drivers' licenses; disposition of certain fees; exception, 32 L.R.S. §412. (n.d.).
Archivist, 44 L.R.S. §181.3. (n.d.).
Creation; domicile; purposes, 25 L.S. §651. (n.d.).
Department of Culture, Recreation and Tourism; program responsibilities; cooperation of departments, 25 L.R.S. §673. (n.d.).
Donations and grants, 25 L.R.S. §654. (n.d.).
Duties, powers, and functions, 25 L.R.S. §653. (n.d.).
École Pointe-au-Chien; creation; location; governance, 17 L.R.S. §1977.1. (n.d.).
Foreign language immersion programs; certification process; criteria, 17 L.R.S. §273.2. (n.d.).
French language and culture; teaching in public schools, 17 R.S. §272. (n.d.).
High school core curriculum requirements; Opportunity, Performance, and Honors Awards, 17 L.R.S. §5025. (n.d.).

High school core curriculum requirements; Opportunity, Performance, and Honors Awards for students graduating 2021–2022 through 2025–2026, 17 L.R.S. §5025.5. (n.d.).

High school core curriculum requirements; Opportunity, Performance, and Honors Awards for students graduating in the 2026–2027 school year, 17 L.R.S. §5025.6. (n.d.).

Louisiana Educational Television Authority; creation; domicile; membership; term; vacancies; quorum; staff, 17 L.R.S. §2503. (n.d.).

Louisiana French Language Services Program; purposes, 25 R.S. §672. (n.d.).

Membership; appointment; terms; vacancies; compensation, 25 L.R.S. §652. (n.d.).

Monies derived from taxes on petroleum products; distribution for entrepreneurial and employment enhancement, 47 L.R.S. §820.51. (n.d.).

Recommendations; Award of Excellence, 25 L.R.S. §674. (n.d.).

Special prestige license plate; "En français S.V.P.", 47 L.R.S. §463.211. (n.d.).

Special prestige license plates; "Chez nous autres", 47 R.S. §463.135. (n.d.).

Special prestige license plates; "I'm Cajun", 47 L.R.S. §463.163. (n.d.).

Special prestige license plates; "I'm Creole", 47 R.S. §463.164. (n.d.).

State identification cards; special identification cards; issuance; veteran designation; disabled veteran designation; university logo; "I'm a Cajun" designation; needs accommodation designation; autism spectrum disorder designation; fees; expiration and renewal; exceptions; promulgation of rules; promotion of use; persons less than twenty-one years of age; the Protect and Save Our Children Program; Selective Service Registration, 40 L.R.S. §1321. (n.d.).

Statement of purpose, 17 R.S. §2501. (n.d.).

Teacher certification programs in instruction of elementary school French, 17 L.R.S. §3382. (n.d.).

Uniform Highway Marking System, 32 L.R.S. §235. (n.d.).

About the Authors

Eileen M. Angelini, Ph.D. is a French professor and a Fulbright Scholar who has extensively researched Franco-American studies. She has published numerous articles on French language and culture, contributing significantly to understanding Francophone heritage in the United States. Her work has been recognized with various awards, highlighting her commitment to French education and cultural preservation. Dr. Angelini's scholarship continues to influence academic circles and the Franco-American community.

Valérie Barrau-Ogereau transitioned from a 15-year career in the aviation industry to education after moving from France. She pursued this path to support her children's plurilingual journey and meet the demand for French teaching in the area. She has taught at a FLAM (Français Langue Maternelle) association dedicated to providing French classes to children with French heritage while continuing her studies. She earned a Master's degree in French as a Foreign Language from the University of La Réunion, specializing in Digital Learning and Plurilingualism, and continues to advance her qualifications in education.

Timothy Beaulieu founded NH PoutineFest, New England's largest celebration of the famous Québécois dish. He was named to the 2019 New Hampshire Union Leader's 40 Under Forty class for his work on the event. Beaulieu holds a B.S. from the University of New Hampshire and an M.B.A. from Plymouth State University. He is actively involved in the Franco-American community, working on small business projects and spending time with his family.

Joseph Bolton is a researcher and writer focused on French-Canadian ancestry and genealogy. His work explores the intricate tapestry of French-Canadian migration, identity, and cultural preservation in North America. He has contributed to projects documenting French-speaking communities' historical and social impacts. Through his research, Bolton highlights the enduring legacy of French-Canadian families in shaping American society.

Claire-Marie Brisson, Ph.D. is a historian and educator specializing in Francophone identity in the United States at Harvard University. She has extensively researched and written about the presence of French culture in the Rust Belt. Her work focuses on language retention, cultural shifts, and the evolving identity of French-speaking communities. Brisson is also an active advocate for promoting the teaching and learning French as a heritage language.

Megan Diercks is an advocate for French language education and has collaborated on research examining the role of external funding in sustaining French programs in higher education. She has been involved in initiatives that support the development and preservation of French language curricula. Diercks' work focuses on identifying strategies to enhance the viability of French studies in academic institutions. She serves as the executive director of the American Association of Teachers of French.

Hamza Djimli is an expert in educational and linguistic cooperation. He holds an M.A. in Language Sciences and Cooperation and a B.A. in Italian Literature. His teaching career spans six countries, from military bases to international schools, including leading the Language Department at the French Institute in Jordan. He later joined France Education International, where he developed certification programs in 173 countries, and served as National Coordinator for the Alliance Française network at the Embassy of France in the United States. A published textbook author with Didier Publishing House, Djimli continues to champion innovative language education and cross-cultural collaboration.

Elcie Douce, Ed.D. is the World Language Department Chair at Nyack High School in Upper Nyack, New York. She has been recognized for her innovative teaching methods, receiving an Innovative Teaching Grant from the Rockland Community Foundation. Dr. Douce is dedicated to promoting multilingualism and cultural understanding among her students.

Rebecca Fortgang is an educator dedicated to French language education across generations. She has instituted initiatives that encourage bilingual education from early childhood to senior citizens. Her work focuses on creating inclusive, intergenerational learning environments for French speakers. She has collaborated with institutions and organizations that promote linguistic diversity and cultural exchange.

Frédérique Grim, Ph.D. is a professor of French whose research focuses on language acquisition and pedagogy. She has published extensively on the challenges and successes of learning French in the United States. Her work addresses how French can be maintained across generations, from young learners to senior citizens. She actively participates in projects that enhance French students' teaching and learning experience.

Jessamine Irwin, Ph.D. is a Clinical Assistant Professor of French Literature, Thought, and Culture at New York University, as well as a documentary filmmaker. She earned a dual M.A. in Teaching French as a Foreign Language and TESOL from NYU and a B.A. in French from the University of Maine. Her research interests include community-based pedagogy, language and identity, and the Francophone presence in North America. In addition to her academic work, she co-directed *Le Carrefour / The Intersection*, a documentary that explores the intersection of Franco-American and Franco-African identities in Maine. Through her teaching and filmmaking, Irwin is committed to amplifying the voices of French-speaking communities and fostering cross-cultural understanding.

Fabrice Jaumont, Ph.D. is a scholar-practitioner, award-winning author, non-profit leader, and education advisor based in New York. He currently serves as Education Attaché for the Embassy of France to the United States, a Research Fellow at Fondation Maison des Sciences de l'Homme in Paris, and an adjunct professor both at New York University and Baruch College. He is President of the Center for the Advancement of Languages, Education, and Communities, a nonprofit publishing organization based in New York and Paris. He has published nine books on education, language, and development.

Emmanuel Kayembe holds a Ph.D. in French Language and Literature and specializes in Francophone studies. He teaches French and Latin, focusing on historical and contemporary linguistic trends. His research includes Franco-American heritage and cultural retention among migrants. As a research associate, he contributes to documenting and preserving Franco-American traditions.

Melody Keilig is a writer and researcher exploring the intricacies of Franco-American artistry. Her work delves into the cultural expressions and artistic contributions of Franco-Americans. She has highlighted the unique blend of traditions and innovations within Franco-American communities. Keilig's research offers insights into the evolving nature of Franco-American art and its impact on broader cultural landscapes.

Sophie Kerman is an Upper School French teacher at St. Paul Academy and Summit School. She holds a B.A. in Sociology/Anthropology from Carleton College and an M.A. in French from the University of Minnesota-Twin Cities. She is committed to fostering inclusion and cultural competence in the classroom, from introductory to advanced levels. Her work presents students with multiple perspectives and encourages them to think critically about their roles as global citizens.

Patrick Lacroix, Ph.D., has served as director of the Acadian Archives in Fort Kent, Maine, since 2021. Originally from Cowansville, Quebec, he has taught at colleges in Canada and the United States and worked with Franco-American groups across New England. He is the author of *"Tout nous serait possible": Une histoire politique des Franco-Américains, 1874-1945* (Presses de l'Université Laval, 2021). He has also contributed articles to *Québec Studies*, the *Revue d'histoire de l'Amérique française*, the *American Review of Canadian Studies*, and the *Journal of History* among other peer-reviewed journals. His long-running blog, *Query the Past*, features more than 200 posts on topics relating to Acadian and French-Canadian history.

Camden Martin, from Lewiston-Auburn, Maine, studied in France and Québec, before teaching French at Saint Dominic Academy. He previously worked at Museum L-A (Maine MILL) and is dedicated to promoting Franco-American heritage. He serves as a board member of the following organizations: Franco-American Genealogical Society, the Alliance Française du Maine, the Franco-American Collection at USM and the Franco-American Education Foundation.

Jesse Martineau is a historian, attorney, and public speaker. He holds a B.A. in History and a Juris Doctor degree and has served as a State Representative in New Hampshire. He hosts the *French-Canadian Legacy Podcast*, which explores Franco-American heritage and culture. His work promotes awareness and preservation of Franco-American identity through digital media and community engagement.

Monique Martineau Cairns is an educator, entrepreneur, and advocate for Franco-American cultural heritage. She holds a B.A. in Social Science Secondary Education and a Master of Science in Special Education. She owns and operates Northern Explosion, a dance studio in Sanford, Maine, where she incorporates elements of French-Canadian heritage into the arts.

Franck Mounier, M.D. is a medical doctor and holds a master's degree in marketing and business administration. With a long history working as an executive director in the pharmaceutical industry across many cultural environments in the US, Europe, Japan, and Africa, Franck Mounier is described as an inspirational leader who enhances effective collaborations to reach collective goals. He has always enjoyed learning from different environments while showcasing the French culture when residing overseas. He has been teaching in the spirit industry since retirement and has been a member of Mensa for over two decades.

Jonathan Olivier is an author and journalist who has written extensively about French revitalization efforts in Louisiana. His work also often focuses on the region's multifaceted culture, including his book *Gumbo*, which traces the history of Louisiana's most famous dish. He holds a B.A. in journalism from Louisiana State University and a M.A. in French from the University of Louisiana at Lafayette. He currently works at CODOFIL, the Council for the Development of French in Louisiana, where he focuses on promoting economic opportunities for the state's Francophone community.

Jerry L. Parker, Ed.D., has been a French educator for 15 years. His research agenda focuses on issues of curriculum, instruction, leadership, and policy in world language education and higher education. His advocacy work aims to align the goals and resources of state legislatures with education leaders in world languages and higher education to increase educational attainment and bilingual skills for all students.

Steven J. Sacco, Ph.D. is a professor emeritus with expertise in French language education and program development. He has researched the role of external funding in building and preserving French college and university programs in the United States. His work provides insights into the challenges and opportunities French language programs face in higher education. Dr. Sacco's research contributes to language education policy and program sustainability discourse.

Jasmine Grace Saint Pierre is a future educator and advocate for French language education. She has been involved in initiatives that promote bilingualism and the transmission of French language and culture across generations. Her work focuses on developing educational programs that engage learners of all ages in French language acquisition. St. Pierre's efforts contribute to the sustainability and growth of Francophone communities.

Jennifer Schwester is a writer and educator who identifies as a Francophile from New Jersey. She has a passion for French language and culture, which she incorporates into her teaching and writing. Schwester has been involved in programs that promote French language learning and cultural exchange. Her work includes developing educational materials and organizing events that celebrate Francophone culture.

Rebecca P. Sewall, Ph.D. is a scholar with a focus on Franco-American cultural heritage. She has conducted extensive research on the architectural and cultural contributions of Franco-American communities in New England. Her work highlights the historical significance and lasting impact of these communities on the region's built environment. Dr. Sewall's research provides valuable insights into the preservation of Franco-American history and culture.

Maya Angela Smith, Ph.D. is an Associate Professor of French at the University of Washington. Her research focuses on sociolinguistics, language and identity, and Francophone African diasporas. She has published works examining the experiences of Senegalese immigrants in America, exploring how language shapes their identities and communities. Dr. Smith's interdisciplinary approach provides valuable insights into the intersections of language, migration, and culture.

Kathleen Stein-Smith, Ph.D. is a dedicated advocate for multilingualism and language education. She has authored several publications on the importance of language learning in global contexts.

As a seasoned educator and speaker, she promotes the benefits of bilingualism and cultural competence. An Officier dans l'Ordre des Palmes académiques, she also serves as Chair of the AATF Commission on Advocacy. Dr. Stein-Smith's work emphasizes the role of language in fostering global understanding and collaboration.

Marguerite Tabusse is a French economist and researcher with a strong background in economic policy and taxation. She studied at the École normale supérieure de Lyon (ENS de Lyon), where she specialized in income taxation, sustainable development, and public policy analysis. She has worked as a research assistant at ENS de Lyon and France Stratégie, analyzing topics such as income tax systems across U.S. states and the reform of natural disaster compensation in France.

Bertrand Tchoumi, Ed.D. is an educational leader with a focus on bilingual education and African-centered pedagogy. He has extensive experience in developing curricula that integrate Francophone African perspectives. His work aims to build strong Francophone identities among students in bilingual schools. Tchoumi advocates for inclusive education that reflects diverse cultural narratives. He serves as Principal at the New York French-American Charter School.

Scott Tilton is the founder of the Nous Foundation, an organization dedicated to promoting and preserving Louisiana's Francophone culture. He has been instrumental in initiatives that highlight the contributions of Francophone communities to American music and culture. Tilton's work includes organizing events and programs that celebrate and educate the public about Louisiana's rich French-speaking heritage. His efforts have been recognized for their impact on cultural preservation and community engagement.

John Tousignant is an advocate for Francophone heritage and cultural preservation. He has worked extensively to document and promote the contributions of Francophone communities in the United States. Tousignant's efforts include organizing cultural events, developing educational programs, and collaborating with organizations dedicated to preserving Francophone history and culture. His work aims to ensure that the rich heritage of Francophone Americans is recognized and celebrated.

Joëlle Vitiello, Ph.D. is a professor specializing in Francophone studies, with a focus on literature and cultural expression within Francophone communities in the Americas. She has published extensively on topics related to Francophone identity, migration, and cultural production. Dr. Vitiello's research includes examining the intersections of language, culture, and identity among Francophone populations in North America. She is actively involved in academic and community initiatives that promote understanding and appreciation of Francophone cultures.

About TBR Books

TBR Books is a program of the Center for the Advancement of Languages, Education, and Communities. We publish researchers and practitioners seeking to engage diverse communities on education, languages, cultural history, and social initiatives. We translate our books into various languages to further expand our impact.

BOOKS IN ENGLISH

Myths and Facts about Multilingualism by J. Franck, F. Faloppa, T. Marinis.
Mosaic of Tongues: Multilingual Learning for the Arabic-speaking World by C. Allaf, F. Jaumont, and S. Tahla Jebril
A Bilingual Revolution for Africa by A.C. Hager M'Boua, F. Jaumont
Bilingual Children: Families, Education, Development by Ellen Bialystok
The Heart of an Artichoke by Linda Ashour and Claire Lerognon
French All Around Us by Kathleen Stein-Smith and Fabrice Jaumont
Navigating Dual Immersion: by Valerie Sun
Conversations on Bilingualism by Fabrice Jaumont
The Hummingbird Project by Vickie Frémont
One Good Question by Rhonda Broussard
Can We Agree to Disagree? by Sabine Landolt and Agathe Laurent
Salsa Dancing in Gym Shoes by T. Oberg de la Garza and A. Lavigne
Beyond Gibraltar; The Other Shore; Mamma in her Village by M. Lorch
The Clarks of Willsborough Point by Darcey Hale
The English Patchwork by Pedro Tozzi and Giovanna de Lima
Peshtigo 1871 by Charles Mercier

The Word of the Month by Ben Lévy, Jim Sheppard, Andrew Arnon
Two Centuries of French Education in New York by Jane Flatau Ross
The Bilingual Revolution by Fabrice Jaumont

BOOKS FOR CHILDREN (available in several languages)

The Adventures of Zenzi and the Talking Bird by Fadzai Gwaradzimba
Biscotte and The New Kid by K. Cohen-Dicker and A. Angeles
Lapin is Hungry by Tania & Olivier Czajka
Uniquely You! by Bertrand Tchoumi
Franglais Soup e by Adrienne Mei
Morgan; Rainbows, Masks, and Ice Cream by Deana Sobel Lederman
Korean Super New Years with Grandma by Mary Kim, Eunjoo Feaster
Math for All by Mark Hansen
Rose Alone by Sheila Decosse
Uncle Steve's Country Home; The Blue Dress; The Good, the Ugly, and the Great by Teboho Moja
Immunity Fun!; Respiratory Fun!; Digestive Fun! By D. Stewart-McMeel
Marimba by C. Hélot, P. Velasco, A. Kojton

Our books, such as paperback and e-book, are available on our website and in all major online bookstores. Some of our books have been translated into over twenty languages. For a listing of all books published by TBR Books, information on our series, or our submission guidelines for authors, visit our website at:

www.calec.org

About CALEC

The Center for the Advancement of Languages, Education, and Communities (CALEC) is a nonprofit organization that promotes multilingualism, empowers multilingual families, and fosters cross-cultural understanding. The Center's mission aligns with the United Nations' Sustainable Development Goals. Our mission is to establish language as a critical life skill by developing and implementing bilingual education programs, promoting diversity, reducing inequality, and helping to provide quality education. Our programs seek to protect world cultural heritage and support teachers, authors, and families by providing the knowledge and resources to create vibrant multilingual communities.

The specific objectives and purpose of our organization are:

- To develop and implement education programs that promote multilingualism and cross-cultural understanding and establish an inclusive and equitable quality education, including internship and leadership training. [SDG # 4, Quality Education]
- To publish and distribute resources, including research papers, books, and case studies that seek to empower and promote the social, economic, and political inclusion of all, focusing on language education and cultural diversity, equity, and inclusion. [SDG # 10, Reduced Inequalities]
- To help build sustainable cities and communities and support teachers, authors, researchers, and families in advancing multilingualism and cross-cultural understanding through collaborative tools for linguistic communities. [SDG # 11, Sustainable Cities and Communities]

- To foster solid global partnerships and cooperation, mobilize resources across borders, participate in events and activities that promote language education through knowledge sharing and coaching, empower parents and teachers, and build multilingual societies. [SDG # 17, Partnerships for the Goals]

SOME GOOD REASONS TO SUPPORT US

Your donation helps:

- Develop our publishing and translation activities so that more languages are represented.
- Provide access to our online book platform to daycare centers, schools, and cultural centers in underserved areas.
- Support local and sustainable action in favor of education and multilingualism.
- Implement projects that advance dual-language education.
- Organize workshops for parents, conferences with large audiences, meet-the-author chats, and talks with experts in multilingualism.

DONATE ONLINE

For all your questions, contact our team by email at contact@calec.org or donate online on our website:

www.calec.org

www.ingramcontent.com/pod-product-compliance
Lightning Source LLC
Chambersburg PA
CBHW031845220426
43663CB00006B/507